does not include the g[?]
from which story his exponent, other are
really two diff. game of min's; who are
equally certain that they know the due well.

Abraham Lincoln's Religion

Abraham Lincoln's Religion

An Essay on One Man's Faith

Stephen J. Vicchio

WIPF & STOCK · Eugene, Oregon

ABRAHAM LINCOLN'S RELIGION
An Essay on One Man's Faith

Wipf & Stock
An Imprint of Wipf and Stock Publishers
199 W. 8th Ave., Suite 3
Eugene, OR 97401

www.wipfandstock.com

PAPERBACK ISBN: 978-1-5326-4161-9
HARDCOVER ISBN: 978-1-5326-4162-6
EBOOK ISBN: 978-1-5326-4163-3

Manufactured in the U.S.A.

This book is dedicated to the memory of my dear friend, Dr. Umberto Villa Santa (1927–2007), and to his lovely wife, Marguerite, about whom I said to her husband, "She is the most beautiful woman I have ever seen."

Contents

Acknowledgements

LIKE ANY CREATIVE WORK, this book could not have been possible without the aid of many family members, friends, and other scholars. Among those who have supported the making of this book are: Matt Wimer, my editor, and Nathan Rhoades, my copy-editor. These two are the best at their respective jobs, as I have seen in my publishing of two dozen books; Sheila Young; Larry Miller; Thomas Raszewski, the director of St. Mary's Seminary and University Library, and his staff, including Suzi, Patricia, and Anita; Paula Thigpen, the registrar at St. Mary's, and Brent Laytham, the dean of the Ecumenical Institute there; Rick Armiger and John Fitzpatrick; mi amiga, Dina; the Sab's monday lunch crowd: Petie, Larry, Rocco, Phil, Lisa, Lauren and Lynn; my friend "Scoop"; Mario Villa Santa; Jay Freyman; Carole Troia; mi amiga, Irene; Tom and Mary Lee Parsons, my in-laws; Tina Gioioso, Esquire; Katie and Sarah; my mother, Elmira Vicchio; and most especially my wife, Sandra, and our son, Jack, who make my life a meaningful one; I am also indebted to the Institute for Public Philosophy in Baltimore. And finally, this work is dedicated to Mrs. Marguerite Villa Santa, my dear friend, who is still "the most beautiful woman I have ever seen," and to the memory of her beloved husband and my dear friend, Dr. Umberto Villa Santa (1927–2007), studioso, insegnante, e chirurgo.

Abraham Lincoln
His hand and pen
He will be good but
God knows when.

—ABRAHAM LINCOLN, *Early Diaries*

In his early political days when asked his religious views, Lincoln
would answer, "My parents were Baptists and brought me up in the
beliefs of the Baptist Church.

—JOHN E. MARSHALL, "Lincoln and the Baptists"

The will of God prevails. In great contests each party claims God.
Both may be, and one must be, wrong.

—ABRAHAM LINCOLN, "Meditation on the Divine Will"

Introduction

IN THIS INTRODUCTION, WE will sketch out what will be discussed in the next seven chapters of this work. Abraham Lincoln grew up in a highly religious family, but he never counted himself as a member of any church. He was a skeptic about religious matters as a young man, but he frequently quoted from Holy Scripture and referred to God in his speeches, in his written works, and in many of his letters. Eventually, the sixteenth president of the United States attended Protestant church services with his wife and family; and after the death of two of his sons, Eddie in 1850 and Willie in 1862, he became "more intensely concerned with God's Plan for Human kind."[1]

The life of Abraham Lincoln exemplified two of the most important facts about life in the United States. The first is that even the poorest citizen can prosper through great ambition and attain a lofty status in American society. And the second, that this lofty status can only be achieved with a set of principles as a foundation of the effort. In Mr. Lincoln's religion we find a firm, moral commitment that you do not find in many Americans, either before or since. The purpose, in many ways, of this essay is to discover the theological, philosophical, and ethical principles at the heart of Mr. Lincoln's faith.

In the last hundred years, more than twenty thousand books have been written and published about Abraham Lincoln, our sixteenth president.[2] The vast majority of these have been written by historians or political

---

1. Foner, *Fiery Trial*, 35.

2. This figure was arrived at by looking at estimates from a story on National Public Radio, on February 20, 2012; at ranker.com; at quora.com; and by examining the "Tower of Books" at Ford's Theatre in Washington, DC.

scientists. Considerably few of those books were authored by theologians, philosophers, or biblical scholars. In that regard, we come to this task of yet another book on Mr. Lincoln having been trained as a philosopher, a theologian, and as a biblical scholar and linguist. As far as we know, this collection of specific skills has not been brought to bear before on the religious life of Abraham Lincoln.

Very much like Thomas Jefferson, in his mature years, Abraham Lincoln was accused of being an atheist, a deist, a Unitarian, and an Episcopalian/Presbyterian; and like Jefferson, Lincoln was also accused of being a "scoffer" of traditional Christian religions, or as an infidel; and like Mr. Jefferson, in point of fact, Mr. Lincoln was not any of these things.[3] Indeed, there is not sufficient evidence that Abraham Lincoln ever joined a church in his adult life. He did, however, attend services with his wife, both in Springfield, at the Episcopal church there, and in Washington, DC, as president, at the First Presbyterian Church on New York Avenue. As a child, Mr. Lincoln also attended with his parents their Separate Baptist church, but there is no indication in the record of just how devout the president was in his youth.

The purpose of this study, then, is to explore the phenomena, of President Abraham Lincoln's religious beliefs, as well as his attitudes toward the Bible, ethics, the role of religion in the Civil War, Mr. Lincoln's opinions on the problem of evil, as well as his views on organized religion. We will begin by making some general observations on the earliest relations and contacts Mr. Lincoln had with the Christian religion, particularly the Separate Baptists, the faith of his parents. This will be followed by chapters of this work on subsequent times, places, and works where Lincoln had something to say about religion, ethics, religion in war time, slavery, the Bible, and the problem of evil .

In subsequent chapters of this work, we also will explore the following topics: what some have called "President Lincoln's period of skepticism"; the role of religion in Lincoln's inaugural addresses; Lincoln's uses of the Bible; Mr. Lincoln's perspectives on ethics and morality; Lincoln's religious conversion; the role of religion in Lincoln's Civil War; and Lincoln's points of view on the classical problem of evil.

In chapter 2 of this study, we will explore the view that Mr. Lincoln went through a period of skepticism in regard to his religious views. Lincoln's third law partner, William Henry Herndon (1818–1891), thought this period began when Abraham left his father's house at age twenty-one, continued while in New Salem and Springfield and, in Mr. Herndon's view, that religious skepticism continued for the remainder of the president's life.

---

3. See chapter 1 of Stephen Vicchio's *Jefferson's Religion*.

Other interpreters closer to Mr. Lincoln at the end of his life believed that the sixteenth president went through a return to the Christian faith, in the 1850s and 1860s, as we shall see later in this study.

Chapter 3 of this work will be devoted to the religious references that Mr. Lincoln made in his two inaugural addresses, in 1861 and 1865. As we shall see, Mr. Lincoln's second inaugural is among his most theological works, perhaps his most boldly theological, where he attempts to make sense of the evil and suffering of the Civil War.

Mr. Lincoln's uses of the Bible is the subject matter of chapter 4 of this essay. In that chapter, we will describe and discuss many of the references that the sixteenth president made to Holy Writ, pointing out his favorite passages of the Bible. We also will discuss a number of specific Bibles that have played roles in the religious life of Mr. Lincoln. Among these Bibles were his family's three-volume copy of the Geneva Bible, bought by his father Thomas in 1819, and a King James Version Bible given to Mr. Lincoln by a group of Baltimore ministers, during the Civil War, in 1864.[4]

Chapter 5 of this essay explores what might be called "Mr. Lincoln's ethics." In this chapter we will examine four major theories in the history of Western philosophy about the nature of the moral good, and how the president's ethics were related to those theories. In chapter 5, we also will examine five central leadership traits exemplified in the life of the sixteenth president—traits to be imitated by any leader, and traits that Mr. Lincoln found in all good men, and that all who knew him believed were exemplified in him.

In chapter 6 of this essay, we shall take up two separate topics. First, we will examine the claim that Mr. Lincoln returned to Christianity in the 1850s and 1860s, in a religious conversion, in the eyes of many around the president at that time. In the second half of chapter 6 of this study, we will make some very general observations about the roles that religion played in the lives of Northerners and Southerners, as well as in the lives of American slaves, in Mr. Lincoln's time as president. As we shall see, each of the three perspectives understood religion in their own individual and distinct way.

The issues of theodicy and the problem of evil—and what Mr. Lincoln had to say about these issues—are the central concerns with chapter 7 of this essay. As we shall see, two principal works of Mr. Lincoln provided his most complete responses to these issues. These were his 1862 essay called "Meditation on the Divine Will" and his March 4, 1865 second inaugural

---

4. This Bible was presented to the president on September 11, 1864. More is said of this Bible in chapter 5 of this essay.

address, given in Washington, DC. Mr. Lincoln was much more theological in these two texts than in any other place in the Lincoln corpus.[5]

This work will end with a final chapter in which we will explore the major conclusions that can be made about the sixteenth president's relationships to God, Jesus, the Bible, and many other issues. After the notes to this introduction, we move first, then, to the role of religion in Lincoln's earliest life, in Kentucky, Indiana, and then Illinois.

5. Altogether, Mr. Lincoln makes seventeen direct references to the Divine in his second inaugural address.

CHAPTER 1

The Role of Religion in Lincoln's Early Life

It was a struggle with trees, logs and grubs.

—ABRAHAM LINCOLN, *Autobiography*

He was a good boy and never did anything disrespectful
or disobedient to his mother.

—SARAH BUSH LINCOLN, *Autobiography*

He was surrounded by a class of people exceedingly liberal
in matters of Religion

—WILLIAM H. HERNDON, *Abraham Lincoln*

THE CHIEF AIM OF this initial chapter of this work on Mr. Lincoln's religion is to describe and discuss his earliest religious life, in Kentucky, then Indiana, and finally in Illinois. Additionally, in chapter 1 we also will describe and discuss the central beliefs of Mr. Lincoln's family's Separate Baptist faith. This will be followed by a description of the sect's major beliefs, their scriptural support for those beliefs, as well as some remarks on the several churches to which the Lincoln family belonged and attended when the president was a boy.[1]

1. Among the secondary sources we have used on the Separate Baptist movement were the following: Lumpkin, *Baptist Foundations in the South*; Goen, *Revivalism and Separatism*; Peart, *Separate No More*; and Warren, *Religious Background of the Lincoln Family*.

1

Abraham Lincoln, the sixteenth and perhaps greatest president of the United States, was born in a log cabin in Hardin County, Kentucky, on February 12, 1809, the same day as the birth of Charles Darwin, in England. The boy Abraham was named after his paternal grandfather, and he was not given a middle name. Lincoln's grandfather had been killed by Native Americans and the killing was witnessed by Abraham's father, Thomas Lincoln.[2] Thomas Lincoln was uneducated, as was the president's mother, Nancy Hanks Lincoln, who is reported to have signed her name with an X. [3]

When the Thomas Lincoln family was still in Kentucky, they belonged to the Separate Baptist church in Hardin. In 1807, the Little Mount Separate Baptist Church split from the South Fork Baptist Church over the issue of slave ownership. This rift is recorded in the minutes of the South Fork Church. At the time, the question of slavery was dividing many congregations as they disagreed over the matter in areas where the practice of slavery was prevalent.

The log structure of the Little Mount Meeting House, to which the Lincoln family belonged, stood three miles east of the Lincoln home and now five hundred yards west of current-day Leafdale community, off route 31 East in LaRue County, Kentucky. The structure was destroyed by a windstorm in 1909. While in Kentucky, the Lincolns were members of the anti-slavery faction of the Separate Baptists.

This affiliation and upbringing may account for Abraham Lincoln's later statement that he made in a solemn letter to A. G. Hodges of Kentucky on April 4, 1864, when he wrote, "I am naturally anti-Slavery. If Slavery is not wrong, then nothing is wrong. I cannot remember when I did not so think, and feel."[4]

According to the 1811 census records of Hardin County, Kentucky, when Abraham Lincoln was two years old, and living at Knob Hill Creek, there were 1007 slaves and only 1627 White males over the age of sixteen living inside the boundaries of the county. It was against these slaves—wageless workers—that Thomas Lincoln, a carpenter, farmer, and laborer of the land, was forced to compete for a living.[5]

The *New Kentucky Composition of Hymns and Spiritual Songs*, a collection of songs and musical compositions used by the Little Mount Meeting House, when the Lincolns lived on their farm on Knob Creek, in Kentucky, was the principal source for religious music in the early Separate Baptist

2. Donald, *Lincoln*, 22.

3. Ibid., 19–20.

4. Lincoln, letter to Albert G. Hodges, April 4, 1864.

5. See http://www.linkpendium.com/hardin-il-genealogy/.

churches. This hymnal was used by the anti-slavery group of the church. It was produced by the Gerard and Berry Printers of Frankfurt, Kentucky. The hymnal was published in 1816.

The minister of the Little Mount Separate Baptist Church was the Rev. William Downs. The clergyman, who was born in 1782, was the minister, teacher, Bible scholar, and musical composer for the congregation. The Rev. Downs baptized Thomas Lincoln when he joined the flock at Little Mount Separate Baptist Church.

As a young child, Abraham Lincoln must have heard readings from the "Neufchatel Bible," printed in 1799, in England. The Neufchatel Bible was a version of the Geneva Bible. It was also the version of Scriptures purchased by Thomas Lincoln in 1819, when Abraham was ten years old. The Neufchatel Bible was named after Charles de Naufchatel, a French prelate who lived in the latter portion of the fifteenth century. At any rate, both the Little Mount Separate Baptist Congregation and the Thomas Lincoln family used a version of the Geneva Bible, while still in Kentucky.

After a land dispute over the title to his farm's land in Kentucky, Thomas Lincoln moved his clan to Knob Creek Farm, eight miles to the north. In 1816, Thomas and Nancy Lincoln, their nine-year-old daughter, Sarah, and their seven-year-old son, Abraham, moved to Indiana, where they settled in Hurricane township, in Perry County. Their land was part of what was to become Spencer County, Indiana.

Abraham Lincoln then spent his formative years, from the age of seven until twenty-one, on this family farm in Indiana. As was common at the time in Midwest America, Mr. Lincoln received a meager education, an aggregate of which was a little more than a full year altogether.

At the age of nine, Lincoln was instructed by Mr. Zachariah Riney for two months in the fall of 1815, when Mr. Lincoln was six years old. The following Autumn, another circuit teacher, Caleb Hazel, taught Abe and his sister for another three months. In 1822, when Lincoln was then thirteen years old, a third itinerate teacher named James Swaney instructed the Lincoln children for ninety days; and two years later, for a period of three months, Lincoln was taught by Azel W. Dorsey, another travelling teacher. These eleven months are the sum total of Abraham Lincoln's formal education, with the exception of tutelag under William Mentor Graham for six months in the New Salem period of the sixteenth president's life. [6]More will be said about Mr. Graham, and his frontier school, subsequently in this essay.

6. Donald, *Lincoln*, 41–42.

In one of his autobiographical essays, Mr. Lincoln writes about these early years on the frontier and his education. He says:

> It was a wild region, with many bears and other wild animals in the woods. There I grew up. There were some schools, so-called, but nothing was ever required of a teacher beyond 'readin, writin, and ciphering. If a straggler supposed to understand. Latin happened by the neighborhood, he was looked upon as a wizard. [7]

When Mr. Lincoln later in life discussed his youth, he was fond of quoting a line from Thomas Gray's "Elegy Written in a Country Churchyard." The line is, "The short and simple annals of the poor."[8]

The area in Illinois where the Lincoln family settled was sparsely populated, an average of three people per square mile in 1800. The land was terribly overgrown and very difficult to farm. Mr. Lincoln later described his early life in Illinois in Little Pigeon Creek as a struggle with "trees, logs and grubs."[9] Thomas Lincoln mostly relied on hunting for food. The log cabin he built had no flooring and little furniture.

Many scholars report that Thomas Lincoln sometimes was hard on his son Abe. He was known to have knocked him around in anger at times. Today, he might be viewed as "abusive," but he clearly was a "man of his times." In one of his autobiographies, just before his candidacy for the Senate in 1858, which he gave to his friend Jesse Fell, an Illinois attorney and businessman, Mr. Lincoln described himself this way: "If any personal description of me is thought desirable, it may be said that I am six feet four inches nearly; lean in flesh, weighing on an average one hundred and eighty pounds; dark complexion, with coarse black hair, and grey eyes—no other marks or brands recollected."[10]

It is of some interests that this form that Mr. Lincoln chose to describe himself is very much like the advertisements taken out by the owners of runaway slaves, in local and state newspapers for the recovery of runaway slaves, from the late eighteenth to the mid-nineteenth century, up until the Civil War period. Before the 1858 debates with Stephen Douglas, Jesse Fell reported that Mr. Lincoln one day had remarked, "I used to be a slave."[11] What he most likely meant by that remark was a reference to the fact that his father rented out Abraham's labor to surrounding farmers. He split logs,

7. Lincoln, *Autobiography*, 3–4.
8. "Says Record Shows Lincoln a Baptist."
9. Ibid.
10. Lincoln, *Autobiography*, 31–39.
11. Ibid., 33.

did minor carpentry, and labored in other physical tasks; and then he gave the money he had earned to his father.

Having been beaten by his father and his supposed "slave labor" for his father may well be two of the reasons that Abraham Lincoln ultimately did not get along well with his father. In fact, he did not attend his father's funeral in 1851. Mr. Lincoln's stepmother said this about her stepson's early attitudes toward religion: "Abe had no particular religion. He didn't think of these questions at the time."[12]

David Donald, in his classic work, *Lincoln*, suggests the rift between Abraham Lincoln and his father was more than a teen age rebellion. He says that the young Abe began to reassess his father's prospects in life, and "he kept his judgments to himself." Mr. Donald continues:

> But years later, it crept into his scornful statements that his fa-
> ther "grew up literally without education . . . and that he chose
> to settle in a region where there was absolutely nothing to excite
> ambition for education.'"[13]

Mr. Donald concludes this section of his biography this way: "To Abraham Lincoln that was a damning verdict. In all of his published writings, and indeed, even in reports of hundreds of stories and conversations, he had not one favorable word to say about his father."[14]

Later in Mr. Lincoln's life, when he was twenty-four years old, in 1833, he lived for six months with New Salem, Illinois teacher William Mentor Graham, beginning in February of that year, as indicated earlier in this essay. More will be said about Mr. Graham and his classroom later in this essay.

Lincoln's father was a farm owner and skilled carpenter, and he appears to have been outspoken about his beliefs against the practice of slavery, as we have indicated earlier. In Abraham's early life, his entire formal schooling amounted to a little more than a year, by itinerate teachers who would travel the West and teach for a few months and then move on. Lincoln, neverthe-less, had a thirst for knowledge.

Mr. Lincoln was an avid reader and borrowed books from neighbors. Thomas Lincoln believed his son may have done all this reading to avoid farm work, even though the boy was said to be quite skillful with an axe.[15]

---

12. Donald, *Lincoln*, 33.

13. Ibid.

14. Ibid.

15. Ibid., 21.

Perhaps this contributed to the poor relationship between Lincoln and his father, Thomas Lincoln, as well.

Thomas Lincoln was a religious Baptist and was outspoken in his stance against slavery. Although this anti-slavery attitude was shared by his son, Abraham, he did not share in his father's religious beliefs, apparently even in early adulthood. In fact, he seems to have been turned off by the ecstatic and sweaty elements of his father's faith and did not consider himself a church member in this time of his life, or any other time, for that matter.

The combination of Thomas Lincoln's refusal to accept slavery and the increasing debt stemming from disputed land grants led to the family leaving Kentucky to what is now known as Spencer County, Indiana. At the age of seven, Thomas Lincoln moved his family—his wife, son, and daughter, Sarah, usually called Sally—to Spencer County, Indiana. By the time the boy had his tenth birthday, Abraham had lost two of his family members: Lincoln's younger brother Thomas, who died early in life, just shy of his fourth birthday, and his mother, who died by what was known as "milk sickness."[16] Milk sickness was a disease contracted by drinking the milk of a cow that had grazed on the poisonous white snakeroot, or *Ageratina altissima*.

Milk sickness was also known as "tremetol vomiting," or in animals as "trembles." It was characterized by trembling, vomiting, and severe intestinal pain that affected an individual who drank milk, consumed other dairy products, or ate meat from a cow that had fed on the white snakeroot plant that contains the poison tremetol. In the nineteenth century, particularly in the Midwest region of America, milk sickness took the lives of thousands of people on the frontier. Nursing calves and lambs also died from their mother's milk contaminated with the white snakeroot, even if the adult cow or sheep showed no symptoms.

Nancy Lincoln succumbed to the disease. She took to her bed for a week, during which time she knew she was failing. Her nephew, Dennis Hanks, reports that Nancy called her children to her death bed, and asked them to be good and kind to their father, to each other, and to the world. She passed away on October 5, 1818, at the age of thirty-four. Nancy Lincoln's grave is located in the Lincoln Boyhood National Memorial, in Lincoln City, Indiana.

Frontier physician Anna Pierce Hobbs Bixby (1812–1873) is credited with the discovery of the disease and its cause. Bixby was a midwife, herbologist, and frontier physician in Southern Illinois. She is said to have learned the properties of the deadly plant from some Shawnee she had befriended.[17]

16. Ibid., 26–27.

17. For more on Dr. Bixby, see Bailey, "Dr. Anna and the Fight for the Milksick,"

When Thomas Lincoln's wife Nancy died, her husband returned to Kentucky the following year, where he met and married widow Sarah Bush Johnson. In 1819, Abraham's new stepmother and her three children—Elizabeth, Matilda, and John—joined the Lincoln family in Indiana. A cousin, Dennis Hanks, kin to Nancy, also joined the group, to make a family of eight. Sarah Lincoln became very fond of the young Abraham. In fact, when she moved to Indiana she brought a number of books with her to be read by her stepson. Among those books were *The Life and Memorable Actions of George Washington, Robinson Crusoe, Pilgrim's Progress,* and *Aesop's Fables.* All comments that Sarah Lincoln later made about her relationship to the president relate that he was a good boy and never did a thing that was disrespectful or disobedient to his "mother." She meant, of course, his stepmother.

The Separate Baptists were an eighteenth-century religious movement that formed during the Great Awakening in New England, which began in 1734 under the leadership of Jonathan Edwards, Gilbert Tennent, and George Whitfield. The Separate Baptists split from the General Baptists in that year. The first identifiable congregation of Separate Baptists was formed in Boston in 1740, under the direction of the Rev. Whitfield.[18] Congregations of Separate Baptists also formed in Philadelphia, Virginia, and Kentucky.

George Whitfield came to America from England on two tours, in 1740 and 1745. He first landed on American soil in Newport, Rhode Island in September of 1740. Huge crowds gathered to hear him preach. The effect was electrifying. Whitfield recorded in his journal at the time: "Many wept exceedingly, and cried under the Word, like persons that were hungering and thirsting for righteousness."[19]

Wherever the Rev. Whitfield preached, thousands attended. A heartfelt religion spontaneously burst forth, in great contrast to the more stern and stoic form of religion practiced by the Calvinist Puritan Congregationalists of the established church. New converts in the established church soon became uneasy by the coldness and hostility of the members who were not awakened nor "born again."

The Rev. Whitfield returned to America for his second tour in 1745. His return was not welcomed by many of the established churches. The Separate Baptist churches, however, greeted him enthusiastically. Because of their fervent support and attendance, the Separate Baptists received most

---

quoting Kelly A. Cichy, *Women Meet the Challenge in Southern Illinois History.* Also see Dearinger, "Dr. Anna and the Milksick."

18. Dallimore, *George Whitefield's Enlightenment,* 33–41.

19. Whitfield, *Journals,* 131.

of the benefit from the Rev. Whitfield's second tour. Three men of note were Isaac Backus, Daniel Marshall, and Shubal Stearns.

Dr. James H. Sightler gives this account of the origins of the Separate Baptists:

> The Separate Baptists took their origin in Connecticut. Valentine Wightman was a grandson of Edward Wightman, the last man burned at the stake in England in 1612. Valentine Wightman was born in 1681 and raised in Rhode Island. He was saved and became a member of the North Kingstown Baptist Church. In 1705, he moved to Groton, Connecticut and founded the first Baptist Church in the state. He pastored there for 42 years and was succeeded by his son, Timothy Wightman. In 1743, Valentine Wightman and his church began a mission church at North Stonington, Connecticut. Waitt Palmer was the first Pastor. It was just at this time that the Great Awakening had come to prominence.[20]

Dr. Sightler speaks here of the founding of the Separate Baptists by Valentine Wightman, his establishment of the church in Groton, Connecticut, his being followed as minister by his son, Timothy Wightman, and their establishment of a mission church in North Stonington, Connecticut.

Dr. Sightler continues his analysis of the history of the Separate Baptists:

> In Tolland, Connecticut in 1745 a Congregationalist named Shubal Stearns, under the influence of the Great Awakening, withdrew from his church and organized a Separate Congregationalist Church. By 1751, he became convinced, by contact with Waitt Palmer, that infant baptism was not Scriptural and he became a Baptist. Palmer baptized Stearns in the middle of the night in the Willamantic River because of great opposition to his views. He then organized a Baptist Church in Tolland.[21]

Mr. Sightler speaks of the early relationship between Waitt Palmer and Shubal Stearns. Indeed, the former baptized the latter into the Separate Baptist church. He also speaks of conversations between the two ministers about whether the baptism of infants is supported by the Scriptures. Thus, both Palmer and Stearns turned to total immersion, mostly on the authority of Jesus' baptism by John the Baptist.

---

20. Sightler, "Separate Baptist Revival and Its Influences in the South," 1–5.
21. Ibid., 1–2.

In the fall of 1754, Mr. Stearns and his family, along with five couples related by blood or marriage, left Tolland and joined Daniel Marshall and his wife at Cacapon Creek, thirty miles west of Westchester, in Virginia. They built shelters and began to preach. Eventually, the church spread to the Carolinas, as well. The most important Separate Baptist church in North Carolina was at Sandy Creek, near Liberty, in Randolph County.

Sandy Creek Baptist Church was organized there on November 22, 1755. By 1755, the Separate Baptists had established four churches in South Carolina and the Charleston Association, six churches in Virginia, and twelve churches in North Carolina, but none in Georgia. By 1775, that would change.

In 1771, the first session of the Virginia Separate Baptist Association was held. The new association consisted of fourteen churches. Very quickly, the association grew to more than fifty churches. It eventually divided into thirteen associations in Virginia. The Separate Baptists also organized their first churches in Tennessee, on Boone's Creek, in Washington County. The spread of Tennessee churches was halted, however, by Lord Dunmore's War of 1774.

By 1779, the Separate Baptists had expanded into Kentucky. Squire Boone, the brother of Daniel Boone, moved with his family from North Carolina, down the Kentucky and Ohio Rivers, to Louisville. Mr. Boone had been ordained as a Separate Baptist minister in 1776, and Boone began a congregation there. By 1791, the Separate Baptists had grown to Mississippi, where Joseph Murphy was baptized and ordained as the first minister.

By 1800, then, Separate Baptist churches had developed from Western Virginia into areas such as Kentucky, Indiana, Tennessee, Mississippi, and Illinois. The Separate Baptists were an eighteenth-century group of Protestants in the United States, primarily in the South, that grew out of the Great Awakening. The Great Awakening was a religious revival and revitalization of piety among Protestant churches. It existed in English-speaking congregations and swept through the American Protestant churches. Many denominations divided into Old Lights—holding a low view of revivalism and conversion—and New Lights, who enthusiastically embraced them.

The movement of the Separate Baptist church westward was mostly at the efforts of Shubal Stearns. Robert B. Semple described Stearns efforts in the West:

> Mr. Stearns and most of the Separates had strong faith in the immediate teachings of the Spirit. They believed that those who sought him earnestly, God gave evident tokens of the will. Mr. Stearns listened to his instructions from Heaven, conceived

himself called forth by the Almighty to move far to the westward, to execute a great and extensive work.[22]

Stearns took one New Testament passage and one from the Old Testament
as his foundations. He understood by Acts 26:19 that he should yield to a
heavenly vision, and from Proverbs 24:27 that the work should be completed for the church, so that things could be made ready for the field.

When Mr. Stearns died in 1771, his Separate Baptist church had over
six hundred members. A monument to Stearns was erected at Sandy Creek
at that time. It mostly speaks of Stearns's organization of Separate Baptist
churches in Virginia and in North and South Carolina. The monument to
Stearns says nothing, however, of his personal history, including his family
or his fine preaching style.[23]

The Separate Baptists were dedicated to the same old-time religion
that had characterized the Greer Baptist Camp Meeting and the Pelham and
Tabernacle Baptist churches. They preached the gospel with strong gestures,
with tears, and with altar calls, during which the preacher frequently left the
platform and went into the congregation, exhorting sinners to come forward and express a desire to be "born again" in the Spirit. Baptist minister
and historian Morgan Edwards, of the Philadelphia Association, said the
Separate Baptists grew rapidly from the mid-eigtheenth century to the early
nineteenth century.

One of the reasons that Separate Baptists stayed clear of Regular Baptists and the Particular Baptist church was that these other groups held more
orderly and "dignified" services. But a few of the Regular Baptist churches,
like that at Chappawomsick in Virginia, which was pastored by Davis
Thomas and Daniel Fristoe, also participated in what was called the "New
Lights." Indeed, they held services much like those of the Separate Baptists.

A second reason that the Separate Baptists kept that name until after
the American Revolution was their strict obedience to 2 Corinthians 6:17,
which says in the King James Version, "Come out from among them, and
be ye separate, saith the Lord, and touch not the unclean thing; and I will
receive you."

Morgan Edwards said of the Separate Baptists, " I believe that a preter-
natural and invisible hand works in the assemblies of the Separate Baptists,
bearing down the human mind, as was the case in the Primitive Churches."[24]
This is an obvious reference to economist Adam Smith's *Wealth of Nations*,

22. Semple, "Separate Baptists."

23. Shubal Stearns (1706–1771) was a Great Awakening preacher, mostly in North
Carolina. See Sparks, *Roots of Appalachian Christianity.*

24. Edwards, *Materials Towards a History of the Baptists*, 174.

where he refers to God acting in the economy as an "Invisible Hand." The "Invisible Hand" also was a term used by eigtheenth- and nineteenth-century Deists to stand for the Divine. In fact, George Washington regularly used that name for God.

The Separate Baptists grew out of the Arminian movement, a theological group based on the beliefs of Dutch Reform theologian Jacobus Arminius (1560–1609.) The Arminians held to five basic principles that later were adopted by the Separate Baptists. These were related to salvation, atonement, what they called "saving grace," the actions of the Holy Spirit, and resistance to sin.

Morgan Edwards, in his *Materials Towards a History of the Baptists*, tells us about the Separate Baptists, "They are called Separates, not because they withdrew from the Regular Baptists but because they have hitherto declined any union with them."[25]

The early Separate Baptists often chose as their favorite biblical text, 2 Corinthians 6:17, that advises us, "Come out from among them, and be ye separate," in the King James Version of the Bible. This led the group to be called the Separate Baptists, as indicated earlier. By the 1780s, Separate Baptists groups had spread to Virginia, North and South Carolina, and then to Kentucky, where Thomas Lincoln was exposed to the sect. Morgan Edwards recorded that in "Seventeen years Separate Baptists had spread their branches as far as the great river of the Mississippi, southward as far as Georgia, eastward to the sea of the Chesopeck [sic] Bay, and grandmother to 42 churches, from which sprang 125 ministers."[26]

The Separate Baptists in Christ today have twelve *Articles of Doctrine* for all associations of Separate Baptists. These are related to the following theological beliefs:

- Article 1: Sola Scriptura.
- Article 2: The Trinity.
- Article 3: Humans are in a fallen state.
- Article 4: Salvation by grace.
- Article 5: Endurance to the end.
- Article 6: Resurrection of the vody.
- Article 7: Double predestination.
- Article 8: Three ordinances.

25. Ibid., 173.
26. Ibid., 175–76.

- Article 9: The Sabbath.

- Article 10: Tenderness and affection toward all others.

- Article 11: Role of Jesus in salvation.

- Article 12: Christ coming in the clouds.[27]

Each of these twelve articles is accompanied by biblical proof texts for the idea. These are:

- Article 1: Rom 15:4; 1 Cor 10:11; 2 Tim 3:16–17; Gen 1:1; and Rev 22:21.

- Article 2: Matt 28:19; 1 Cor 12:3; 1 Tim 2:5; Heb 1; and 1 John 5:7.

- Article 3: Isa 63:1–5; John 6:44; John 14:6; Rom 8:1–20; and 1 Cor 15:22.

- Article 4: John 17:13–17; Heb 4:1–3; Eph 4:1–8; Titus 3:3–7; and Rev 1:18.

- Article 5: Matt 10:22; 24:13; Heb 3:12; 10:38–39; Rev 2:10.

- Article 6: Dan 12:2; Matt 25:46; and Rom 5:21.

- Article 7: Dan 12:2; Matt 25:46; and Rom 5:21.

- Article 8: Matt 28:19–20; Luke 22:17–20; John 13:14; Acts 2:41; Rom 6:4; and Col 2:12.

- Article 9: Luke 23:56; John 20:26; Acts 20:7; 1 Cor 16:2; Rev 1:10.

- Article 10: Isa 53:1–10; Rom 12:10; Gal 6:1–2; 2 Cor 9:14.

- Article 11: Matt 9:13; Luke 18:15–18; John 3:15–17; Acts 4:12; Rom 5:15; 1 Tim 2:5–6.

- Article 12: Matt 24:29–31; Rev 10:6; 1 Thess 4:15–18; and 2 Pet 3:10.[28]

From these twelve articles of faith, and their proof texts, in more practical terms the Separate Baptists had twelve major beliefs. The first of these was assent to the Calvinist idea of "Sola Scriptura," the idea that one may be saved by the use of Scripture alone. The Separate Baptists believed that the Holy Scriptures are the infallible word of God. They used the 1611 King James Version of the Bible, and believed that the KJV was the "only safe rule of faith and practice."[29] Thus, the Separate Baptists were firm believers in the inerrancy of the biblical text, as well.

27. Separate Baptists in Christ, "Articles of Doctrine for All Associations."
28. Ibid.
29. Ibid.

The second belief of the Separate Baptists had to do with the phenomenon of religious conversion. Separate Baptist Preacher Robert Semple made the claim that adherence to their faith is "more than the practice of outward rules and duties. He said, "A Christian should be able to ascertain the time and place of one's religious conviction and conversion."[30] Thus, ecstatic religious experiences of conversion were a central part of the faith of the Separate Baptists, as was being "born again." Being "born again" in the Spirit, of course, is a reference to what Jesus says to Nicodemus when the latter asks how he can be saved, in John 3.

In this regard, the Separate Baptists saw themselves as the "New Lights," as opposed to the "Old Lights," the more traditional Baptist church. The Old Lights found revivalism and religious experience to be distasteful and unproductive spiritually. The New Lights, on the other hand, believed that revivalism should be at the center of a Christian church.[31]

Thirdly, the Separate Baptists believed that the second coming of Jesus Christ was to be a physical return of the Savior. Indeed, in article 12 of their *Articles of Doctrine*, the Separatists tell us about Jesus: "All Christians will be gathered with Him in the clouds and at that time, time shall be no more. We do not believe in a thousand-year reign, as is common in many other Churches."[32]

The Separate Baptist *Articles of Doctrine* are referring here to Revelation 20:4–6, whereby the devil will be released and Jesus will reign for a thousand years on Earth. As verse 4 tells us in the King James Version, ". . . and they lived and reigned with Christ a thousand years."

The fourth belief of the Separate Baptists has to do with the "day of rest." They held that "The first day of every week is a day to be spent in public or private worship."[33] In only rare cases did the Separate Baptists allow for "worldly activities" on that day. article 4 says about these cases, "They are special and necessary cases of showing mercy."[34] The Separate Baptists also held to the Calvinist view of the "priesthood of all believers." Under this ordinance, the new church held that ministers and congregational leaders should not be chosen because they possess special gifts. Rather, under the priesthood of all believers God is equally accessible to all believers.[35] They

---

30. Ibid.
31. Ibid.
32. Ibid.
33. Ibid.
34. Ibid.
35. Ibid.

also did not require their ministers to be seminary trained, nor do they now require it.

A fifth proposition of the Separate Baptists is related to the "providence of God." Later in life, Lincoln called this the "principle of necessity." By this idea, the Separate Baptists assented to John Calvin's view of double predestination, whereby everything happens solely by the provisions of the will of God. All that happens in the heavens and on the Earth occurs solely by the will of God.[36] Much more will be said about this principle later in this essay.

In a sixth religious beliefs of the Separate Baptists, they held contrary beliefs to the General Baptists in regard to slavery, dancing, and alcohol. They were strictly against the idea of holding slaves, and against the General Baptists' views, they allowed the consumption of alcohol, as well as the practice of dancing in public places, like barn dances and church socials. Other than these differences, the Separate Baptists held to a fairly orthodox Christianity common to other Baptist groups and Protestant congregations.

Seventh, the Separate Baptists of the American South and Midwest of the nineteenth century also were firm believers in the Calvinist idea of predestination. They believed that God had preordained some to salvation, as well as some to damnation. In this regard, like Calvin the Separate Baptists were believers in double predestination. Throughout much of his adult life, Abraham Lincoln referred to this religious idea as the "law of necessity," as we shall see later in this work.

Eighth, ninth, and tenth, the Separate Baptists were against the idea of seminary-trained clergy, as well as paid clergy; they discouraged the idea of creating Missions; and they found a much more prominent role for women than many other Protestant denominations in the eigtheenth and nineteenth centuries. The best-known Separate Baptist woman was Martha Stearns Marshall. Along with her husband, Daniel, Martha converted to the Separate Baptists during the First Great Awakening. The couple eventually migrated from New England to Virginia, where they introduced Separate Baptist beliefs and started several churches.

After being baptized, Daniel and Martha joined a Separate Baptist church, and Daniel became licensed to preach, though both Marshalls were preachers, and Martha's zeal in the pulpit was no less than that of her husband's. In a publication that celebrates four hundred years of the Separate Baptists, it says of Martha Marshall, "She was without the shadow of a usurped authority over the other sex, Mrs. Marshall being a lady of good

---

36. Lotz, *Celebrating 400 Years of the Baptist Life.*

sense, singular piety, and surprising elocution."[37] Thus, Martha Marshall was responsible for women having a more central role in ministry in the early Separate Baptist churches.

Eleventh, in the place of sacraments, the Separate Baptists ascribed to what they call "ordinances." These include baptism, the Lord's Supper, and the washing of feet. The latter practice usually occurred in Friday-evening meetings of a congregation. The Separate Baptists believed that a "saved" person can choose to turn away from God and engage in a life of sin. These people were known as "backsliders." The Separate Baptists believed a backslider must ask God for the forgiveness of his sins in order to be saved.

This view of three "ordinances was distinct from the rites observed by the Regular Baptists, at the same time. In fact, the Old Lights had nine ordinances: baptism, the Lord's Supper, love feasts, the laying on of hands, feet washing, the anointing of the sick, the right hand of fellowship, the kiss of charity, and devotion to children. And a final belief of the Separate Baptists is that they were against the practice of infant baptism, and in favor of the practice of total immersion, when it came to the ordinance of baptism.

While still in Kentucky, and after the Lincolns had joined the Separate Baptists, the minutes of a fall meeting of the sect tell us this about a couple in the church:

> A young man, who had been absorbed in prayer, began leaping, dancing, and shouting, while to his left a young woman, as though inspired by the example she had witnessed, sprang forward, her hat falling to the ground, her hair tumbling down in graceful braids, her eyes fixed heavenward, her lips vocal with strange, unearthly song, her rapture overflowing until, grasping the hand of the young man, they both began singing at the top of their voices.[38]

More will be said about the couple in this passage later in this chapter. It is enough now, however, to say the pair described are Thomas Lincoln and Nancy Hanks, the sixteenth president's mother and father, just prior to their marriage.

David Donald suggests in his work *Lincoln* that there were two principal causes for Thomas Lincoln to move his family across the Ohio River to Indiana. The first was his staunch stance against slavery. The other reason, Donald suggests, was disputes over land grants and the borders of farm

---

37. *Minutes of the Nolynn Association of Separate Baptists* (1819–1884).

38. Ibid.

properties. Donald relates, "Small farmers like Thomas Lincoln worried about the titles to their land."[39] Later, Donald adds:

> He had trouble gaining a clear title to any of the three farms that he purchased in Kentucky. The details were exceedingly complicated, and not particularly important: one had been improperly surveyed, so that it proved to be 38 acres smaller than what he thought he had purchased; another had a lien on it because of a small debt by a previous owner. In the case of the Knob Creek Farm, non-Kentucky residents brought suit against Thomas Lincoln and other occupants of the rich Valley, claiming prior title.[40]

The minutes mentioned above, as we have indicated, identify the couple mentioned above as Thomas Lincoln and Nancy Hanks, who were married the following week in a ceremony performed by the Rev. Jesse Head. It is clear that the Lincolns, even before they left Kentucky, were caught up in the ecstatic elements of the Separate Baptists. The young Abraham certainly attended services and prayer meetings filled with a most intense form of religious experiences, experiences of regeneration and conversion.

In the winter of 1816, the Lincoln family took their meager possessions, ferried across the Ohio River, and settled near Pigeon Creek, close to what is now Gentryville, Indiana. Because it was winter, Thomas Lincoln immediately went to work on a crude, three-sided shelter that served as the family's home until Thomas could later build a log cabin. Southern Indiana at the time was forested wilderness. Mr. Lincoln described it as a "wild region, with many black bears and other wild animals in the woods."[41] Later, some of Nancy Hanks's family followed the Lincolns to the area.

When the Lincoln family moved to Indiana, the forests were filled with wild animals. Lincoln summed up that time in this childhood verse: "When first my father settled here, 'Twas then the frontier line. The panther's scream filled night with fear, And bears preyed on the swine."[42]

When Thomas Lincoln moved his family to Indiana, they joined the Little Pigeon Baptist Church, near Little Pigeon Creek, in what was then Warwick County, Indiana. The church was founded in June of 1816—the year that the Lincolns moved from Kentucky. The site of the meeting house was about a mile west of Thomas Lincoln's home. When Nancy Lincoln died, she was buried in land between their home and the new church. The graveyard at the church had not yet been built. When Lincoln's sister, Sarah

39. Donald, *Lincoln*, 158.

40. Lincoln, *Autobiography.*, 7.

41. Ibid., 11.

42. Nowlin, *Kentucky Baptist History*, 188.

Grigsby, died in 1828, she was interred in the church's burial grounds. Sarah was married in 1826 and she died in childbirth in 1828. Thus, by the time that Abraham Lincoln was twenty-one years old, he had lost his brother, Thomas, his mother, Nancy, and his sister, Sarah, also called Sally.

The Separate Baptists worshipped in a more evangelical style than Regular Baptists. They were far more engaged with the biblical text and placed far more emphasis on experience and conversion than traditional Baptists. They first broke from the Regular Baptists in the 1740s under the direction of Shubal Stearns, who had been inspired by the preaching of George Whitefield. By 1758, the Separate Baptists had formed the Sandy Creek Baptist Association. The Association soon dispatched preachers to spread the faith in North Carolina, and beyond.

We turn now to the immediate antecedents to the Baptist community of Little Pigeon Creek, Kentucky, not far from where Thomas Lincoln lived in his early life. The Little Mount Church from which Thomas Lincoln brought his letter of introduction to the Little Pigeon congregation in 1823 was part of the Salem Association. Elder William Downs, who preached the funeral of the young Tommy Lincoln, just before the family migrated to Indiana, was the brother of Elder Thomas Downs, one of the two men who organized the church at Pigeon Creek in 1816.

William D. Nowlin, in chapter 16 of his *Kentucky Baptist History: The Mystery of Lincoln's Religion Cleared Up*, describes the Pigeon Creek church this way:

> Pigeon Creek Church was founded on June 8, 1816, the year that Thomas Lincoln and his family moved from Kentucky and settled on Little Pigeon Creek, in what was then Warwick County, Indiana Territory. It was then, as now, the chief church in the vicinity. When the meeting-house was built, its site was selected about a mile West of Thomas Lincoln's home. The church building today occupies practically the same place. When Lincoln's mother died, she was buried between their home and the church—the graveyard of the church had not yet been established. But when Lincoln's sister, Sarah Grigsby died in 1828, she was interred in the church Burying grounds, where her grave is now marked by a rough stone.[43]

Mr. Nowlin continues his analysis:

> This Church, with its continuance existence since 1816, has only two books containing its records and minutes, the first covering the period from 1816 to 1840. It is in this book that we find

43. Ibid., 109.

Abraham Lincoln's father, stepmother, and sister as active members of the hardshell Baptist Church of Pigeon *Creek*, and this
book, with its deerskin cover, the hair still remaining, not only
reveals in its crude, historic way the true religion of Lincoln's
parents, but gives us the best insight yet found to his own religious views.[44]

It is not entirely clear that Mr. Nowlin is correct about Abraham Lincoln's
earliest religious beliefs. We do know that the young Abe attended church
with his parents, and that he was most likely introduced to the twelve beliefs
of the Separate Baptists mentioned in the above analysis. What we can be
certain of is that of these theological ideas the most important of these for
our purposes are their views on slavery and on predestination.

The Separate Baptists of the early nineteenth century in the Midwest
region of America were sometimes called "Hardshell Baptists," as Mr. Nowlin calls them. Originally, they were called "Hard-Shall Baptists" because of
all the "shalls" in texts like Matthew 1:21 and Romans 10:14–17. Hardshell
Baptists are also sometimes called "primitive Baptists" in the same region.
Early leaders of the movement included John Leland, Samuel Trott, John
Taylor, Gilbert Beebe, and Joel Hume.

The Hardshell Baptists were distinct in that they believed that in order
to be saved one must experience both regeneration and conversion, or being
"born again." Even today, in the state of Kentucky, there remain a number
of Separate Baptist or Hardshell Baptist churches. Among these are Aarons
Chapel's and Beckham Ridge, in Glenn Forks, Kentucky, as well as Beech
Grove and Bethlehem, in Russell Springs, Kentucky.

Abraham Lincoln, then, was raised among the Separate or Hardshell
Baptists. One of the reasons that he never joined a church as an adult may
well have been because of his experiences watching the infighting and
church splits among those Baptists when he was a child and an early adult.
These experiences may have soured him on any kind of Christianity that
required regeneration and conversion. Lincoln appears to have been turned
off by his parent's religion full of altar calls and ecstatic religious experiences.

Indeed, at his father's home, as well as meetings of the family's churches in Lincoln's youth, the future president was raised to see the practice of
slavery to be an abomination. This was a central tenet of the Separate Baptists faith. Indeed, it was one of the major reasons that the sect split from the
General Baptist tradition to begin with. This belief grew out of the Lincoln
family's understanding of article 10 of the Separate Baptist's *Articles of Faith*,
which points out a moral requirement or ethical duty to treat others with

---

44. Benedict, *General History of the Baptist Denomination in America*, 119.

tenderness and affection, including the least advantageous people of the American community—that is, particularly the slaves and the poor.

We do know that two of the most crucial sessions of the Indiana Associations of Separate Baptists were held at the Little Pigeon church in 1823 and 1829. Secondly, we know that Lincoln's childhood church was very much involved with the question of whether to send missionaries from the church. It is likely that Thomas Lincoln agreed with his pastor and took a stand against the practice. Indeed, for the most part, the Separate Baptist churches were against the idea of supporting mission churches, mostly on economic grounds. Indeed, they even were against the idea of paying ministers for their services rendered in the church, as well for monetary reasons.

With the exception of the Separate Baptists in Christ, the denominational name Separate Baptist disappeared in many locales of the country, with formal and informal agreements of union between the Regular Baptists and the Separate Baptists. These agreements began in Virginia in 1787, then in the Carolinas in 1789, followed by Kentucky in 1797 and then again in 1801.[45] David Benedict, in his *General History of the Baptist Denomination in America*, tells us: "In terms of the union in Virginia, we are united and desire hereafter, that the names Regular and Separate be buried in oblivion; and that from henceforth, we shall be known by the name of the United Baptist Churches of Virginia."[46]

Allen C. Guelzo, in an essay entitled, "Abraham Lincoln and the Doctrine of Necessity," sketches out Lincoln's beliefs about predestination and related issues of the Separate Baptists. Guelzo begins his essay this way:

> Abraham Lincoln was a Fatalist. That is, at least, what he told many people over the course of his life. Lincoln informed his Illinois Congressional ally, Isaac Arnold. "Mr. Lincoln was a fatalist," remembered Henry Clay Whitney, one of his Springfield Law clerks. "He believed . . . that the universe is governed by one uniform, unbroken primordial law.[47]

Mr. Lincoln's belief in fatalism, or the law of necessity, is specifically mentioned in articles 4 and 7 of the Separate Baptist's *Articles of Faith*. Indeed, article 7 expressed a belief in what John Calvin called "double predestination," in his *Institutes of the Christian Religion*.

Henry Clay Whitney was one of Mr. Lincoln's companions on the Eighth Circuit Court in the 1840s and 1850s. Allen Guelzo also points out that Lincoln's Springfield law partner, William Henry Herndon, likewise

45. Guelzo, "Abraham Lincoln and the Doctrine of Necessity."

46. Ibid.

47. Ibid.

affirmed that Lincoln "believed in predestination, foreordination, and that all things were fixed, doomed one way or the other, from which there was no appeal."[48] Even Mary Todd Lincoln, Abraham's wife, believed that her husband had been guided by a conviction that "What is to be, will be, and no cares of ours can arrest nor reverse those decrees."[49] Indeed, at times Mr. Lincoln described himself as a "leaf floating on the ocean," with no will to change its course.

In an 1864 letter, while Mr. Lincoln was president, he wrote, "I claim not to have any control over events, but confess plainly that events have controlled me . . . God alone can claim responsibility for a nation's conditions."[50] Describing this belief of Mr. Lincoln's, William Herndon wrote:

> Things were to be, and they came, irresistibly came, doomed to come; men were made as they are made by superior conditions over which they had no control; the fates settled things as by the doom of the powers, and laws, universal, absolute, and eternal, ruled the universe of matter and mind . . . Man is simply a simple tool, a mere cog in the wheel, a part, a small part, of this vast iron machine, that strikes and cuts, grinds and mashes, all things, including man, that try to resist it.[51]

Thus, Mr. Herndon described Mr. Lincoln's belief in the law of necessity in purely mechanistic terms, something akin to the laws of nature, or to a scientific worldview; and Herndon believed Lincoln held that view for the remainder of his adult life, while others, as we will see later, staunchly disagreed that Lincoln held that position until his death.

Not only did Lincoln hold this views when he was younger, he also professed it during his presidential years. He described himself in those years as "but an accidental instrument, temporary, and to serve but a limited time."[52] He compared himself over the years to a "piece of floating driftwood." Even at the height of the American Civil War, Mr. Lincoln told Canadian journalist Josiah Blackburn that he had "drifted into the very apex of this great event."[53]

William Herndon points out that some of the repercussions of this belief about fatalism, or the law of necessity, are that "There is no freedom

---

48. Ibid.

49. Lincoln, letter to Albert Hodges, April 4, 1864.

50. Herndon, *Life of Lincoln*, 336.

51. Ibid., 199.

52. Josiah Blackburn, quoted in Guelzo, "Abraham Lincoln," 57. Blackburn (1823–1890) was a London-born journalist who emigrated to Canada in 1850.

53. Ibid.

of the will" and that "Men had no free choice."[54] Herndon even tells us in his biography of Lincoln that the law partner sometimes disagreed with the future president about his fatalism. Herndon writes:

> We often argued the question, I often taking the opposite view
> ... I once contended that man was free and could act without a
> motive. He smiled at my philosophy, and answered that it was
> impossible, because the motive was born long before the man
> ... He defied me to act without motive and unselfishly; and
> when I did the act and told him of it, he analyzed and sifted it
> to the last grain. After he had concluded, I could not avoid the
> conclusion that he had demonstrated the absolute selfishness of
> the entire act.[55]

In the course of this work, we will say much more about these two early beliefs of Abraham Lincoln. Besides not believing in human free will, Lincoln appears to have rejected a number of other traditional religious beliefs of American Protestantism. We will close this opening chapter of this essay on Lincoln's religion by saying that in his late teens and early adulthood, Abraham Lincoln never claimed to be a Baptist, a Separatist, or any other affiliation of the Christian church; but he did hold fast to his doctrine of necessity, as well as an abhorrence to the practice of slavery, both of which he inherited from his parents and their Separate Baptist church.

By the age of twenty-one, Abraham Lincoln set out on his own by making his living in the frontier village of New Salem, in Menard County, Illinois. Lincoln lived there from 1831 until 1837. In successive jobs, Lincoln worked as a boatman, a soldier in the Black Hawk War, a general store owner, as a postmaster, surveyor, and rail splitter. He also was elected to the Illinois General Assembly in 1832.

The town of New Salem had been established in 1828 when James Rutledge and John Camron built a mill on the Sangamon River. In 1831, when Thomas Lincoln relocated his family to a new home in Coles County, Illinois, the young Abraham had struck out on his own. He arrived in New Salem by way of a flatboat he was piloting. When Lincoln lived in New Salem, the village had a cooper, a blacksmith, a mill, four general stores, a tavern owned by James Rutledge, a grocery store, two physicians, a shoemaker, a carpenter, a schoolhouse, and a church, but there is no evidence that the sixteenth president was a member of that congregation.

The New Salem community had a Separate Baptist or "Primitive Baptist" church, which was organized in 1829. Mr. Lincoln's name appears

54. Herndon, *Life of Lincoln*, 331.
55. Ibid.

among the "receipts" of the June 1835 edition of *Signs of the Times*, an old-school Baptist newspaper. The receipt shows that Mr. Lincoln paid three dollars for church subscriptions, but we do not know if this was for himself or for remitting the subscriptions of three local residents, for we do know that the subscription rate was a dollar a year.

There is no evidence, however, that Mr. Lincoln attended services at the New Salem church, nor is there any agreement about where the church was located. The available evidence simply says the church was "on a ridge the other side of Green's Rocky Branch," a Creek South of New Salem. Careful study by both historians and archeologists, however, has not determined with absolute certainty the exact location of the New Salem Separate Baptist church.

We do know, however, that the church was a member of the Sangamon Separate Baptist Association, from 1829 until 1860. We also know that Mentor Graham, Lincoln's schoolmaster, and Joshua Miller, the village blacksmith, were members of the church. The loss of the church's records is a great misfortune for scholars who study the life and times of Abraham Lincoln, the sixteenth president of the United States.

In the New Salem period, Mr. Lincoln also appears to have had a romantic relationship with the blue-eyed daughter of James Rutledge, Ann Rutledge, who died a few years later of typhoid fever. This event had a deep effect on Mr. Lincoln. Biographer Ida Tarbell, after Ann Rutledge's death, said of Mr. Lincoln:

> He seemed to his friends to be in the shadow of madness. They kept a close watch over him; and at last, Bowling Green, one of the most devoted friends of Lincoln, took him home to his log cabin, a half a mile North of New Salem, under the brow of a big bluff. Here under the loving care of Green, and his good wife, Nancy, Lincoln remained until he was once more the master of himself.[56]

Throughout the remainder of President Abraham Lincoln's adult life, he appears to have suffered from a clinical form of depression, brought on and exacerbated by the deaths of his brother, mother, and sister, early in life, followed by Ann Rutledge and his two sons, later in life. Although he was never diagnosed, it now is quite clear that the sixteenth president of the United States suffered from a major form of mental disease.

Joshua Wolf Shenk, in his recent book, *Lincoln's Melancholy: How Depression Challenged a President and Fueled His Greatness*, suggests that Mr.

56. Tarbell, "Progressive Look at Lincoln," 58–59.

Lincoln at times suffered from a serious form of depression, to which he may have been genetically predisposed from both sides of his family.[57]

In this work, Dr. Shenk concentrates on the genetic precedents in the Lincoln family toward depression. He tells us, "Three elements of Lincoln's history—the deep, pervasive sadness of his mother, the strange spells of his father, and the striking presence of mental illness in the family of his uncles and cousins—suggest the likelihood of a biological predisposition toward Depression."[58]

In the second chapter of this work, we will speak of some of these other beliefs that Mr. Lincoln held during his period of skepticism. We will turn, then, to a chapter we have labeled "Lincoln's Period of Skepticism." Before that chapter, however, we will address one final aspect of the Lincoln family's version of baptism. Madison C. Peters, in 1909, published a biography of Lincoln he called *Abraham Lincoln's Religion*.[59]

When the book was reprinted a few years later, it had a subtitle, to wit, "His Parents Were Free-Will Baptists in Kentucky."[60] Mr. Peters did not justify this claim. All Peters said on page 17 was, "Lincoln's mother and father were Free-Will Baptists in Kentucky."[61] There is absolutely no evidence that Thomas Lincoln and his two wives ever believed in the classic Christian view of free will.

This observation about the Lincoln family was incorrect. Lincoln's parents, as we have argued in this chapter, attended Separate Baptist churches, and the Separate Baptists were firm believers in predestination. Indeed, nearly all Baptist churches west of the mountains adhered to the propositions of the Calvinistic *Philadelphia Confession* promulgated in 1765, including a belief in predestination. Free Will Baptists were those who did not adhere to predestination and rather put their emphasis on human free will; so Mr. Lincoln's family were decidedly not Free Will Baptists.

Allen Guelzo, in an interview with Brian Lamb on C-Span's *Booknotes* from April of 2000, sums up the Lincoln's form of Baptism this way:

> Well, he was born into a Baptist family—in fact, a Baptist group who were very sectarian, very come-outerish. They were radical predestinarians. In other words, they believed that God ordained every event, whatever comes to pass. For that reason,

57. Shenk, *Lincoln's Melancholy*, 11–12.

58. Ibid., 4–5.

59. Peters, *Abraham Lincoln's Religion*, 17.

60. Ibid.

61. Guelzo, "Abraham Lincoln," 59.

this particular Baptist group, sometimes known as the Separate
Baptists, would not sponsor missionaries.[62]

A little later on , in the same interview, Professor Guelzo again speaks of the
Lincoln family's notion of predestination. He observed, "But he does carry
with him the stamp of that belief in predestination. He secularized it into a
belief in necessity or determinism."[63]Guelzo continues, "But like those folks
he grew up with, he does not believe that human beings have free will. He
does not believe that human choices come from within ourselves. And he
often described himself throughout his life as a fatalist and would say to
people, 'I do not believe that human beings make their own choices."[64]

There is some evidence that Abraham Lincoln began to reject his father's Calvinism, very early in adolescence or early adulthood. Apparently,
Lincoln did not care for the ecstatic religious services of the Separate Baptists. We shall now move on to the second chapter, which we have called
"Lincoln's Period of Skepticism."

CHAPTER 2

Lincoln's Period of Skepticism

As to Mr. Lincoln's religious views, he was, in short, an infidel
. . . Mr. Lincoln told me a thousand times that he did not believe
the Bible was the revelation of God as the Christian world
contends.

—WILLIAM HERNDON, *Abraham Lincoln*

When he went to Church, he went to mock
and came away to mimic.

—CHARLES MINOR, *The Real Lincoln*

As wrong as we think slavery is, we cannot afford
to change it now wherever it may be.

—ABRAHAM LINCOLN, *Letters*

IN THIS SECOND CHAPTER of this study on Lincoln's religion, we will explore
the claim that the sixteenth president of the United States went through
a period of religious skepticism that allegedly began in his early twenties
when he left his father's home, and continued until some time in his forties,
or even into his fifties, late in his political life. It is our view that late in life, as
we shall see in a subsequent chapter of this essay, Mr. Lincoln went through
what amounted to a conversion experience, after the deaths of his two sons,
Eddie and Willie, in 1850 and 1862.

In a review of Steven Spielberg's film *Lincoln*, critic Edward McNulty begins the review this way:

> There has long been controversy over whether Abraham Lincoln was a believing Christian, an issue that Steven Spielberg's film largely ignores, as does its source book. Lincoln was unorthodox in that he was more of a Universalist than most Christians: He just could not see how a God of infinite love could send persons Into everlasting torment.[1]

Mr. McNulty argues that Lincoln was a universalist, that is, one who believes in universal salvation, a movement also called "universal reconciliation" that was popular in various periods of the history of the Christian church. Indeed, beginning with the figure of Origen (185–254), and continuing on in the thought of Gregory of Nyssa (335–395), various thinkers in the history of the Christian church have been firm believers in universal salvation, or universal reconciliation. Among those thinkers were: Saint Isaac the Syrian, bishop of Ninevah, Reformation thinker Michael Servetus, German Anabaptist Hans Denck, and George Whitefield, who in a letter to John Wesley privately confessed that he believed that all the damned "would hereafter be brought out of Hell."[2] More recently, the Unitarian Universalists also have held the doctrine of universal salvation.

Mr. McNulty also suggests that the sixteenth president was against the idea of eternal damnation, mostly because he thought an omnibenevolent, all-loving God would not allow it. Mr. McNulty continued his review of Spielberg's film with this paragraph:

> As a young man, Lincoln was a skeptic, very much like his law partner, William H. Herndon; their keen, analytic minds turned off by the fundamentalist frontier preachers who appealed to emotions and scorned reason. A "freethinker," Lincoln did not join a church, which has bolstered the belief of some that he believed in fate rather than God. However, the latter view ignores a great amount of evidence from Lincoln's life and writings.[3]

The reference to "fate," of course, is nothing more than what Mr. Lincoln referred to as the "law of necessity," which we have already introduced in the first chapter of this work. In Lincoln's mind, it is the belief that all that

---

1. McNulty, "Abraham Lincoln: Complex Man of Faith." Mr. McNulty chose Romans 8:28 to explicate the film. "We know that all things work together for the good, for those who love God, who are called according to God's purposes."

2. Bauckham, "Universalism."

3. Ibid.

occurs in the heavens and on the Earth happens solely by the will of God. Mr. McNulty also points out that the Spielberg film only covers the period of the final four months of Lincoln's life, January 1 to April 19 of 1865—not much of a sampling of the president's adult life.

Mr. McNulty praises the performances of Daniel-Day Lewis and Sally Fields as the Lincolns. He also singles out the performances of David Strathern and Tommy Lee Jones, who played Secretary of State William Seward and Republican Thaddeus Stevens, respectively. McNulty also provides a few questions for discussion in the case of churches who may wish to discuss the film in their programs. Mr. McNulty is certain, however, that Mr. Lincoln believed in universal salvation at the end of his life.

William J. Wolf, in his work *The Almost Chosen People*, published by Doubleday in 1959, agrees that Mr. Lincoln believed in universal salvation, and was contrary to the doctrine of "endless punishment."[4] Wolf claims that Lincoln's mentor and teacher, William Mentor Graham, also thought that the sixteenth president was in favor of these two theological beliefs.[5]

In the previous chapter of this work, we also have suggested that Abraham Lincoln was turned off by Separate, or Hardshell, Baptist theology. In fact, there was some evidence that as a child, after attending church on Sunday and hearing a sermon that preached Separatist doctrine, the young Abe is said to have stood atop tree stumps and repeated the homily he had heard on Sunday. Even later, in early adulthood, many Lincoln friends say that the sixteenth president went through a period of religious skepticism. Chief among these friends was Lincoln's third law office partner in Springfield, William Henry Herndon.

There is little doubt that Abraham Lincoln, as a young man, went through a period of skepticism towards Christianity. This period of the president's life, then, appears to have begun in late adolescence and continued well into his time in his law practice in Springfield, after 1837. As indicated above, some reports tell us that when Lincoln was a young man he would attend church on Sunday with his family, and then repeat the sermons he had heard there throughout the remainder of the week, sometimes, as was indicated earlier, on the perch of a tree stump. Thus, even early on, it may have been the case that Mr. Lincoln began to reject his parents' conservative Separate Baptist faith.

Mr. Guelzo also reports that Mr. Lincoln was "enthusiastic in his infidelity," and even wrote a tract debunking orthodox Christianity, which

4. Wolf, *Almost Chosen People*, 8–9.
5. Ibid.

some of his friends, fearing the impact on his political career, persuaded him to destroy the essay, as we shall see later.

In his biography of Lincoln, Mr. Herndon describes the episode in question this way:

> He read his manuscript to Samuel Hill, his employer (who) said to Lincoln, "Lincoln, let me see your manuscript." Lincoln handed it to him. Hill ran it in a tin-plate stove, and so the book went up in flames. Lincoln in that production attempted to show that the Bible was false: first on the grounds of reason, and, second, because it was self-contradictory; that Jesus was not the Son of God any more than any other man.[6]

Mr. Herndon believed, then, that Mr. Lincoln thought that Jesus was not the Son of God, any more than any other man is. Herndon also indicates that Lincoln had firm doubts that Holy Scripture always yields metaphysical truths, purely against the test of reason alone. Additionally, Herndon suggests that Lincoln thought that the Bible was filled with contradictions.

Samuel Hill was the owner of a general store in New Salem, at which Mr. Lincoln worked as a clerk during his period of skepticism. Although Mr. Herndon introduces this tale in his biography of Lincoln, a number of other scholars point out that there was no pot-bellied stove in Samuel Hill's general store, and thus the story is apocryphal.

Other Lincoln scholars, like Gore Vidal, for example, repeat the Herndon telling and suggest the authenticity of the tale.[7] After repeating the version from Mr. Herndon, complete with burning the manuscript in the pot-bellied stove in Samuel Hill's Store, then Mr. Vidal adds: "Lincoln in that writing attempted to show that the Bible was false, first, on the grounds of reason, and secondly, it was contradictory, that Jesus was not the Son of God."[8]

Other critics, however, point out that there was no pot-bellied stove in Mr. Hill's store. At this point in the discussion, the jury remains out on this question about Lincoln's essay on infidelity, and its possible destruction. The issue, at this point, cannot be settled one way or the other about its authenticity.

Samuel Hill (1800–1857) was born in New Jersey and came to New Salem in 1829, where he partnered in a general store with a man named John McNamar. The partnership dissolved in 1832, and Mr. Hill erected a mill in

6. Herndon, *Life of Lincoln*, 334.

7. Vidal, *Lincoln*. The novel sparked a controversy between Vidal and historian Richard N. Current in the *New York Times Review of Books*.

8. Vidal, "First Notes on Abraham Lincoln."

1835. Abraham Lincoln's period in New Salem went from 1830, when he was twenty-one years old until 1837, when he moved to Springfield. Lincoln briefly worked as a clerk for Mr. Hill in that period.

At any rate, in the same essay by Mr. Guelzo mentioned above, he points out that these "Calvinist origins and overtones, however, do not go very far in explaining the specific shape of Lincoln's fatalism."[9] As early as the 1830s, Lincoln appears to have gone through a profound period of skepticism, accompanied by a reading list that included Thomas Paine's *Age of Reason*, Francois Volney's *Ruins, or a Survey of Empires*, and Robert Chambers's proto-Darwinist work, *Vestiges of the Natural History of Creation*.

For Lincoln, all of these books confirmed a basic skepticism toward Christian dogma. In fact, William Herndon suggests the young Lincoln may have written an essay of his own in the mid-1830s on "infidelity" that denied the miraculous conception of Christ, ridiculed the Trinity, and denied that the Bible was the divine special revelation of God. Lincoln may well have acquired some of these ideas from Thomas Paine who ridiculed predestination as a "senseless doctrine."[10]

Mr. Lincoln also read David Hume, perhaps the greatest eigtheenth-century critic of religion and metaphysics, as well as other Enlightenment thinkers from whom he might also have borrowed some of his skeptical views, in regard to metaphysics in general and religion, in particular. Figures like Thomas Paine, Francois Volney, Immanuel Kant, and John Locke, among other thinkers could have been sources for Abraham Lincoln's skepticism.

One of the earliest mentions of religion in Lincoln's written and spoken words came in July of 1846 when he wrote, "That I am *not* a member of any Christian Church is true; but I have never denied the truth of Scripture, and I have never spoken with intentional disrespect of religion in general, or any denomination of Christians in particular . . . I do not think myself that I could be brought to support a man for office whom I knew to be an open enemy of, or Scoffer at, Religion."[11]

Ever mindful of his pragmatic interests in his budding political career, Mr. Lincoln makes three important points here. First, he was not a member of any Christian church, nor is there any evidence that he ever joined a church; second, he had never been disrespectful of any Christian denomination; and finally, he would not vote, nor would he expect anyone else to vote, for a man who was against religion, Christian or otherwise.

9. Guelzo, "Abraham Lincoln," 61.

10. Paine, *Age of Reason*, 53.

11. Lincoln, handbill replying to charges of infidelity, July 31, 1846.

At around the same time, still in 1846, Mr. Lincoln speaks of the conditions that would have to be present for him to join a Christian church. Mr. Lincoln wrote:

> When a Church will inscribe over its altar, as its sole qualification for membership the Savior's condensed statement of both the Law and the Gospel, 'Thou shalt love the Lord with all thy heart and with all thy soul and thy neighbor as thyself,' that Church I will join with all my heart and soul.[12]

This passage confirms that Mr. Lincoln believed that the core Christian belief was love. Later, we shall argue, as we shall see later in this essay, that compassion and humility, at least for Mr. Lincoln, would have to be appended to that core principle. Indeed, Mr. Lincoln held to an ethic that was based on the core principles of the life of Jesus Christ, as exemplified in the Gospels, as well as the Ten Commandments and the Golden Rule. At any rate, we say much more about Mr. Lincoln's views on ethics and moral theory in a later chapter of this essay, chapter 5.

It is true that Mr. Lincoln never did join a church, though he did attend regular services while he was in Springfield, at the First Presbyterian Church of the Rev. James A. Smith, and as president, in Washington, at the Rev. Phineas Gurley's First Presbyterian Church on New York Avenue. The reason Mr. Lincoln reportedly gave for not joining a church was that he could "never be satisfied" with all the dogma and creeds that the denominational churches of his day seemed to require.

It is likely, that Abraham Lincoln became disillusioned with the dogma and creed of the Separate Baptist church he attended during his childhood. Certainly, in the periods of his life in Springfield, as well as in New Salem, Lincoln most likely had serious doubts about Christian doctrine in general, and the Separate Baptists in particular.

Indeed, this turn toward religious skepticism may have been one of the principal reasons that Abraham Lincoln had an enormous falling out with his father, Thomas Lincoln. This rift was of such a serious character that the son did not attend the father's funeral in January of 1851.

One of the earliest of the Lincoln biographies was Ward Hill Lamon's *Life of Lincoln*, published in 1872. Mr. Lamon claimed that when Lincoln came to New Salem in the 1830s, he consorted with what were called "freethinkers" in matters of religion. Lincoln is said to have joined with them in deriding the Gospel story of Jesus, he read Volney and Paine, and then wrote a deliberate and labored essay, wherein he reached similar conclusions to

12. Ibid.

those of the freethinkers, as we have indicated earlier in this chapter.[13] This has come to be known as Lincoln's "essay on infidelity," mentioned earlier.

Mr. Herndon dates the essay on infidelity to the year 1835. He says of the book, as indicated earlier, which was not published, and may have been destroyed, "It was an attack on the whole grounds of Christianity and especially upon the idea that Jesus was the Christ, the true and only begotten Son of God . . . .I think Mr. Lincoln was a Skeptic at the time and his friend Samuel Hill, after reading the manuscript, suggested it be destroyed, but Lincoln refused." Herndon sums up Lincoln's period of skepticism this way:

> He was surrounded by a class of people exceedingly liberal in matters of religion. Volney's "Ruins" and Paine's "Age of Reason," passed from hand to hand . . . Soon He began openly attacking Christianity. Friends recall that he openly criticized the Bible, that he called Christ a bastard, and that his closest friends doubted his Atheism.[14]

By the time Lincoln moved to Springfield in 1837, he became acquainted with various men of his own way of thinking. At the time they called themselves "freethinkers," or "free-thinking men." Herndon comments, "I remember these things distinctly, for I was with them, heard them, and was one of them."[15] Herndon goes on to indicate further readings of the future president that included David Hume's *Dialogues Concerning Natural Religion* and the works of Edward Gibbon, British historian, writer, and politician. Herndon concludes about this period of Abraham Lincoln's life, "He drank them in. He made no secret of his views, no concealment of his religion. He boldly avowed himself an Infidel!"[16]

David Hume, in his *Dialogues*, explores whether religious beliefs can be rational. Because Hume was an empiricist, someone who thought that knowledge came from sense experiences alone; he thought that a belief is only rational if it is sufficiently supported by experimental evidence. So the question is, really, is there enough evidence in the world to allow us to infer an infinitely wise, powerful, and perfectly wise God? In Hume's mind, belief in God is allowed by reason, but not required by reason.

Hume does not ask whether we can rationally prove that God exists, but rather whether we can rationally come to any conclusions about God's nature. He asserts that the first question is beyond doubt; the latter is initially undecided. It is likely that Mr. Lincoln, along with the other Enlightenment

13. Lamon, *Life of Abraham Lincoln*, 474.
14. Herndon, *Life of Lincoln*, 336–37.
15. Ibid., 337.
16. Ibid.

books he read in this skeptical period of his life, approached the *Dialogues* with some admiration and confidence that not all of traditional Christianity is true. Thus, many of his critics after Lincoln's time suggest he was an infidel, a skeptic, or even an atheist, in his period of skepticism.

In an 1892 editorial, the *Chicago Herald* summarized Mr. Lincoln's religion in his skeptical period. It said:

> He was without faith in the Bible or its teachings. On this point the testimony is so overwhelming that there is no basis for doubt. In his early life, Lincoln exhibited a powerful tendency to aggressive infidelity. But when he grew to be a politician, he became secretive and non-committal in his religious beliefs . . . It must be accepted as final by every reasonable mind that in Religion Mr. Lincoln was a Skeptic.[17]

There can be little doubt, then, that in his youth Mr. Lincoln had an intoxication with Thomas Paine's deism. His youthful Baptism was strict, determinist, and providential, but the god of philosophy and science made a wonderful, and coherent, world for him. Lincoln's law partner, William Herndon speaks of lending Lincoln a number of other books in the sixteenth president's time in Springfield. Mr. Herndon writes:

> I had an excellent private library, probably the best in the city for admired books. To this library, Mr. Lincoln had, as a matter of course, full and free access at all times. I purchased such books as Locke, Kant, Fichte, Lewes, Sir William Hamilton's *Discussions on Philosophy*; Spencer's *First Principles, Social Statics*, etc.; Buckle's *History of Civilization*, and Lecky's *History of Rationalism*. I also possessed the works of Paine, Parker, Emerson, and Strauss; Gregg's *Creed of Christendom*, McNaught *On Inspiration*; Volney's *Ruins*, Feuerbach's *Essence of Christianity*; and other works on infidelity. Mr. Lincoln read some of these works. About the year 1843, he borrowed *The Vestiges of Creation* of Mr. James W. Keyes, of this city, and he read it carefully.[18]

Included in Mr. Herndon's list are works of philosophy, theology, the natural sciences, political thought, the social sciences, economics, and one work, that of Feuerbach's, a critical, and direct attack on monotheism. Indeed, Ludwig Andreas Feuerbach (1804–1872), was a German philosopher and anthropologist who also expressed his atheism publically, much like Sigmund Freud and Karl Marx in the same time. In the *Essence of Christianity*,

17. "Lincoln's Faith."
18. Herndon, *Life of Lincoln*, 338.

Feuerbach wrote his famous line, "The essence of theology is anthropology."[19] By this, he meant that humans, in speaking of God, simply project their best characteristics onto the image of the Divine, to get all-good, all-knowing, all-powerful, etc. Freud developed a similar thesis in his book *Moses and Monotheism*, published in 1939 and in English translation that same year.[20]

Sigmund Freud called religion an "infantile neurosis," for he believed that human beings project the characteristics that a child has for his father onto a imaginary figure called "God." Indeed, Freud wrote a number of books on religion. In addition to *Moses and Monotheism*, he also wrote *Totem and Taboo*, published in 1913; *The Future of an Illusion*, published in 1927; and *Civilization and Its Discontents*, published in 1930. Feuerbach's view of religion was very much like Freud's view of the issue, and this is likely a view about which Abraham Lincoln was aware.

Mr. Herndon continues his analysis to the passage above:

> He [Lincoln] subsequently read the sixth edition of this work, which I loaned to him. Mr. Lincoln had always denied special creation, but from his want of education, he did not know just what to believe. He adopted the progressive and development theory as taught more directly in that work. He despised speculation, especially in the metaphysical world. He was a purely practical man. He adopted Locke's notions as to his notions of mental Philosophy, with some modifications to suit his own views.[21]

The reference to "special creation" is the view, from the medieval church, that God created the universe "out of nothing," as outlined in the first two chapters of Genesis. The theory of James Keyes mentioned earlier was nothing less that Charles Darwin's evolutionary theory, and John Locke's theory of the mind is the English philosopher's version of British empiricism.

What all these works listed have in common is that they were believed to be the products of what then were called "religious skeptics," or "infidels," as Mr. Herndon suggests in the above analysis. Lincoln's law partner in the time at Springfield also claimed that the sixteenth president was an infidel at that time, as well as the remainder of his life, in Mr. Herndon's view.

Lincoln's close friend Jesse Fell, a Republican leader, said that "Mr. Lincoln did not believe in the innate depravity of man . . . the Atonement, the infallibility of the written revelation, the performance of miracles [or] . . . future

19. Ibid.
20. Lincoln, *Autobiography*, 39.
21. Ibid.

rewards and punishments."[22] Presumably, by "innate depravity of man" Mr. Fell meant original sin. A number of other sources suggest that Lincoln did not believe in the divinity of Christ in this period of skepticism, as well.

In fact, Mr. Lincoln rarely mentioned the name Jesus in his public words, but he did employ the term "Savior" to refer to Jesus Christ. Some of these sources say the young Lincoln also was critical of the idea that God forgives sins because that would make moral laws absolute and Lincoln could not believe that. More will be said about Mr. Lincoln's understandings of ethics, moral theory, and the nature of the moral good in a later chapter of this essay, that is, chapter 5.

Jesse W. Fell (1808–1887) had been secretary of the Illinois Republican State Central Committee, and was also instrumental in bringing Mr. Lincoln forward as a candidate for president in 1860. Mr. Fell later wrote of Mr. Lincoln's religious views during the latter's period of skepticism:

> He fully believed in a superintending and overruling Providence that guides and controls the operations of the world, but maintained that law and order, not their violation or suspension, are the appointed means by which this Providence is exercised.[23]

Mr. Fell mentions here Mr. Lincoln's assent to divine providence, to the law of necessity, and to the belief that the universe runs according to the laws of nature and scientific principles. Indeed, most who were close to Lincoln in his Period of skepticism replaced that view with these scientific precepts, as we said, a kind of scientific worldview.

The New York City newspaper, the New York World, in an 1875 edition, commented on Mr. Lincoln's period of skepticism. The newspaper wrote, "He declared frequently that he would do anything to save the Union and among the many things he did was the partial concealment of his individual religious opinions."[24] Thus, the anonymous New York writer suggests that Mr. Lincoln was cautious about revealing his personal thoughts on religion and metaphysical matters, because they may have smacked of infidelity, or religious skepticism, and be at odds with the norm of the day.

Famous American orator and essayist Robert Ingersoll corroborated these facts of Mr. Lincoln's skepticism. Ingersoll was acquainted with Lincoln because he served as the Illinois attorney general in the 1860s. After suggesting that Mrs. Lincoln had told Ingersoll that her husband was not a Christian, Ingersoll added:

22. "Mr. Lincoln's Skepticism."
23. Ingersoll, "Lecture on Lincoln," 91.
24. Wilson, David Davis, 112–13.

> Hundreds of his acquaintances have said the same thing. Not only so, but many of them have testified that he was a Freethinker that he denied the inspiration of Scripture, and that he always insisted that Jesus Christ was not the son of God . . . [25]

Mr. Ingersoll makes three claims in this quotation. First, Mr. Lincoln was a "freethinker." Second, he did not assent to the divine inspiration of Holy Scripture. And finally, he was not a believer in the divinity of Jesus Christ.

David Davis (1815–1886), who later would become Mr. Lincoln's campaign manager and then a supreme court justice, under him, said, "At the time, Mr. Lincoln had no faith in the Christian sense of the term."[26] He adds, "But he did have faith in laws, principles, causes, and effects. He adhered firmly to what he called the "law of necessity.""[27]

Lincoln's teacher, William Mentor Graham, also suggests that his student was accused of being a deist and an infidel, but he "essentially was a Universalist." By this term Graham means the Lincoln believed in "universal salvation," that is, that all shall go to heaven.[28] Mr. Graham also indicates that Mr. Lincoln was against the idea of eternal damnation because Lincoln did not believe an all-good God could prescribe eternal punishment. Lincoln's first law partner, John T. Stuart, also confirmed that "He went further against Christian principles . . . than any man I ever heard."[29] We cannot be sure, however, what Christian principles Mr. Stuart had in mind in this comment.

William Mentor Graham (1800–1886) instructed Mr. Lincoln in grammar and arithmetic, when Graham ran the only schoolhouse in New Salem, Illinois. Graham also may have instructed the sixteenth president in the practice of surveying in that same six-month period in 1833. Lincoln at the time was twenty-two years old, and had recently set out on his own. Anne Rutledge, Abraham Lincoln's first love, also was a student in Mr. Graham's prairie schoolhouse. In fact, Ms. Rutledge was the only girl who attended the school.

In 1865, Mentor Graham described Ann Rutledge this way:

> I know that Miss Ann Rutledge took sick while going to my school. Lincoln and she were studying at my house. Miss Rutledge died in 1834. She was about twenty years old, blue eyes, a large and expressive face, fair complexion—sandy or light

25. Ibid.
26. Graham, quoted in Duncan and Nikols, *Mentor Graham*, 292.
27. Stuart, quoted in Herndon, *Life of Lincoln*, 349.
28. Graham, letters to William Herndon, May 29 and July 15, 1865.
29. Ibid.

auburn hair not flaxen. About five feet four, 120 pounds . . . ingenious, amiable, kind, and an exceptionally good scholar, in all common branches, including Grammar.[30]

Two letters about Mr. Lincoln's education under Mr. Graham are extant. Both written to William Herndon when he was researching his biography on Mr. Lincoln. The first of those letters is dated July 15, 1865, where Graham mentions that he first encountered Thomas and Abraham Lincoln while working in their Kentucky fields.[31]

In the other letter, dated May 29, 1865, Mr. Graham speaks of his relationship with Abraham Lincoln. He wrote to William Herndon, "I think that I may say that he was my scholar and I was his teacher."[32] Mr. Graham opened the schoolhouse in his mid-thirties. He was twelve years Mr. Lincoln's senior. Graham was a tall, muscular, and straight man, with the courage sufficient to conduct a proper classroom, a place where, on the frontier, it took both brains and brawn to do the job.

One incident about Mr. Graham gives us the character of his classroom. One day a strapping and burly young man approached Graham and remarked, "When I was a boy I always said when I got older, I would thrash you, and I am going to do it now."[33] Thereupon the teacher ministered a punishment that taught the young man a lesson, thrashing the former student.

In this second letter from Graham to Herndon, the former describes the mind of the young Lincoln as "rich and virgin soil in which to sow the seeds of knowledge."[34] Mr. Graham indicates that at Mr. Lincoln's core was the heart of a scholar, and not that of a politician.

Another Lincoln biographer, Charles Minor, points out that in this period of skepticism the president rarely attended church, "but when he went to church, he went to mock and came away to mimic."[35] Scholar Gordon Leidner, in his essay "Lincoln's Faith in God," agrees about Lincoln's disenchantment with the Christian religion in his early adulthood in New Salem and in Springfield. Leidner writes, "There is little doubt that Lincoln, as a young man, went through a period of Skepticism towards Christianity."[36]

William Herndon also doubts Mr. Lincoln's belief in immortality in this period of skepticism. in a letter to Francis E. Abbott, in 1870, the law

30. "Ann Rutledge."
31. Duncan and Nikols, *Mentor Graham*, 299.
32. Ibid.
33. Minor, *Real Abraham Lincoln*, 53.
34. Leidner, "Lincoln's Faith in God."
35. Herndon, letter to Francis E. Abbot, February 18, 1870.
36. Ibid.

partner speaks of looking through Lincoln's speeches and letters, and finding no reference to immortality, but once! He tells us:

> I diligently searched through Lincoln's letters, speeches, and
> state papers, etc., to find the word immortality and I could not
> find it anywhere except in a letter to his father. The word im-
> mortality appears but once in his writings.[37]

Mr. Herndon adds, "If he had been asked the plain question, 'Do you know
that a God exists?' he would have said, 'I do not know that a God exists.'"[38]
Herndon continues:

> At one moment of his life, I know that he was an Atheist. I was
> preparing a speech on Kansas, and in it, like nearly all reformers,
> I invoked God. He made me wipe out that word and substitute
> the word Maker, affirming that his Maker was a principle of the
> universe. When he went to Washington, he did the same to a
> friend there.[39]

Like many Enlightenment thinkers, such as George Washington and Thomas Jefferson, Mr. Lincoln preferred to employ other terms besides the simple
"God." Jefferson used thirty-six different terms to designate God. George
Washington employed more than a hundred. In this case, Lincoln employed
the term "Maker" to stand for the Divine. Mr. Herndon indicated that in
Springfield Mr. Lincoln was not simply a skeptic, but he may have been an
outright atheist.

Mr. Herndon also points out how sensitive the sixteenth president appears to have been in invoking the name of God, and he rarely invoked
the name of Jesus. Mr. Lincoln appears to have been ever mindful of what
effects any religious comments may have had on his political career.

More recently, in another review of the 2013 Steven Spielberg film
Lincoln, historian Stephen Mansfield goes so far to suggest that Mr. Lincoln
was an atheist in his period of skepticism. After cataloguing several of the
president's well-known words about the Divine, like "The Almighty has his
own purposes," Mansfield goes on to state in the review:

> Yet this God was not always Abraham Lincoln's God. In his early
> years, Lincoln hated this being. It was a natural response. He
> was thoroughly convinced that God, in turn, hated Abraham
> Lincoln. It is one of the most surprising facts of Lincoln's life, a

37. Ibid.

38. Mansfield, "Abraham Lincoln's Atheist Period." Also see Mansfield's *Lincoln's
Battle with God*, 189–200.

39. Ibid.

fact that makes his religious journey among the most unique in our history.[40]

As far as we know, this observation of Mr. Mansfield that Lincoln "in his early years hated God" was not held by any other scholar in this essay, or in contemporary scholarship on the sixteenth president, for that matter. Certainly, it was a possible point of view, but at this point there is little confirming evidence that it was true.

Like Mr. Herndon, then, Mr. Mansfield also was convinced that in Springfield Mr. Lincoln was not just a religious skeptic, but rather an atheist. He also maintained that the sixteenth president hated God, presumably for the many hardships that were dealt to him in his early life, including the deaths of his mother, brother, and sister, and his first love, Anne Rutledge, who died at twenty-one when Mr. Lincoln was twenty-two years old.

In his review, Mr. Mansfield also comments on Lincoln's rejection of the Separate Baptists. Commenting on Thomas and Nancy Lincoln's son, he writes:

> Their intelligent, sensitive son found it all too much. Young Abraham rejected his parents loud, sweaty brand of faith and in part because he could not reconcile the weepy, religious version of his father with the man who beat him, worked him 'like a slave,' and resented his dreams of having a more meaningful life.[41]

In his review, Mr. Mansfield points to a tension in the life of Thomas Lincoln, one of which his son was apparently very conscious. That is, on the one hand, his father seemed to be devoted to his conservative Separate Baptist faith, while, on the other hand, he disciplined his son with the rod.

Stephen Mansfield, in the review, goes on to quote historian Allen Guelzo to support his claim about Mr. Lincoln's early views of religion: "On no other point did Abraham Lincoln come closer to an outright repudiation of his father than on his religion, and appears to have been a major contributor in Lincoln's not having a good relationship with his father."[42] The ecstatic religion of his father and mother appears to have been too much for him.

Mr. Mansfield believes that Lincoln was repulsed by the religious fervor that swept across the American frontier when he was an adolescent and young man. Mansfield contends he "openly criticized the Bible and Christianity and believed that God had it out for him." Ultimately, however, as we shall see later in this study, the death of his two sons and the most extensive

40. Ibid.

41. Herndon, *Life of Lincoln*, 399.

42. Herndon, letter to Francis E. Abbot, February 18, 1870.

carnage of the Civil War may have caused him to reflect on the purposes of God, and to reevaluate his earlier skepticism.

Among Mansfield and other historians like him, Abraham Lincoln is remembered as a religious skeptic, as a young man one who scoffed openly at Christianity, as well as many of its central beliefs. In his skeptical period, Lincoln also wrote an essay examining all the falsehoods that he thought were contained in the Bible, as indicated earlier in his "essay on Infidelity."

Mr. Herndon said that there is no evidence that the sixteenth president ever changed his religious ideas from those of his skeptical period, particularly after he became president of the United States. Mr. Herndon wrote in his biography of Lincoln, published in the 1890s, "Now let it be written in History, as well as on Mr. Lincoln's tomb; He died an Unbeliever."[43]

Mr. Herndon appears to have believed that Mr. Lincoln remained a skeptic for the remainder of his life. In a lengthy letter to Francis E. Abbot in 1870, five years after Lincoln's death, Herndon, the sixteenth president's final law partner, wrote:

> He did not believe in the efficacy of prayer, although he used that conventional language. He said in Washington, 'God has his own purposes. If God has his own purposes, then prayer will not change those purposes.[44]

The law partner points here to one of the inherent problems with Lincoln's form of fatalism, or determinism: it raises the question of whether, if everything is already decided, God would answer prayers or not. If that were true, then why pray? Mr. Herndon then goes on to sum up Lincoln's skeptical period this way:

> I have often said to you, and now I repeat it, that Lincoln was a Scientific Materialist, i.e., that this was his tendency as opposed to Spiritualist ideas. Always did—do now—and ever will. He was an agnostic generally, sometimes an atheist.[45]

Indeed, there is some evidence that Mr. Lincoln may have attended a séance at the White House conducted by a medium. During the years of the Civil War, spiritualism was experiencing its golden age. Every Victorian parlor was host to mediums, both famous and infamous. Among those enraptured by these spiritualists was the First Lady, Mary Todd Lincoln, and perhaps, even the president himself.

---

43. Ibid.
44. Miers, *Lincoln Day by Day*, vol. 3, April 23, 1863.
45. War Department, *War of the Rebellion*, August 5, 1862.

In fact, some report there were as many as eight séances conducted at the Lincoln White House. Lincoln scholar Earl Schenck Miers, who edited *Lincoln Day by Day*, for example, says that the sixteenth president "attended a spiritualist séance in the White House" on April 23, 1863.[46] Mary Todd, however, was the true devotee to the supernatural in the Lincoln family. She attempted to contact her two dead sons, Eddie and Willie, as well as four of her brothers, who had died for the Confederacy.

The most significant of these was Lt. Alexander H. Todd (1839–1862), who had been slain fighting for the Confederates at Baton Rouge. According to the official records of the war, the lieutenant was wounded in a friendly-fire skirmish before dawn on August 5, 1862, and he died two weeks later.[47]

After her White House years, the former first lady continued to associate with her spiritualistic friends. She believed they had not abandoned her, as so many others had done after her husband's assassination. In a letter to her half-sister, Emile Todd Helm, Mrs. Lincoln wrote of one of those experiences:

> Willie lives. He comes to me every night and stands at the foot of the bed with the same sweet, adorable smile he always has had. He does not come alone. Little Eddie is sometimes with him, and twice he has come with our brother, Alex.[48]

In the 1870 letter to Mr. Abbott, Mr. Herndon says that Lincoln held to his skeptical view throughout the remainder of his life. He observes about his former law partner:

> That Mr. Lincoln was an Infidel from 1834 to 1861, I know, and that he remained one until the day of his death, I honestly believe. I always understood that he was an Infidel, sometimes bordering on Atheism. I never saw any change in the man, and the change could not have escaped my observation had it happened.[49]

One must keep in mind, however, the fact that William Herndon had little contact with Lincoln after he left Springfield in 1861, and did not see the president but one time from 1861 until his death in 1865. This leaves open the possibility that Mr. Lincoln did, in fact, experience a religious conversion at the end of his life, even if it might have been unbeknownst to his third and final Springfield law partner.

Nevertheless, in the letter to Francis Abbott, Herndon does conclude by saying, "I do not think that anyone who knew Mr. Lincoln—his history—his

---

46. Mary Todd Lincoln, letter to Emile Todd Helm, December 12, 1863.

47. Herndon, letter to Francis E. Abbot, February 29, 1870.

48. Abbot, letter to William Herndon, March 27, 1870.

49. Carpenter, "On Describing Lincoln," *New York Tribune*, February 6, 1864.

philosophy—his opinions—and still asserts that he was a Christian, is an unbounded falsifier. I hate to speak plainly, but I cannot respect an untruthful man.[50]

On the other hand, over and against these observations of William Herndon, a number of friends and companions of Mr. Lincoln's argue against the view that he was a skeptic or infidel late in life. A newspaperman, friend, and biographer of Lincoln wrote this about the alleged skepticism:

> Mr. Lincoln was at heart a Christian man, believed in the Savior, and was seriously considering the step which would formally connect him with the visible church on Earth. Certainly, any suggestion as to Mr. Lincoln's Skepticism or Infidelity, to me who knew him intimately, from 1862 until the time of his death, is a monstrous fiction, a shocking perversion.[51]

This friend of Mr. Lincoln, Francis Bicknell Carpenter (1830–1900), also believed him to be a "sincere Christian."[52] The Rev. Madison Clinton Peters (1859–1918), who wrote a 1909 biography of Abraham Lincoln, referred to his subject as a "true and sincere Christian."[53] Lincoln's own wife, Mary Todd Lincoln, describes her husband as "A religious man always, I think, but was not a technical Christian."[54] Presumably, by this she meant that he was skeptical of many of the traditional core beliefs of Christianity mentioned in the above analysis.

From the analysis above, it appears that in President Lincoln's period of religious skepticism, which took up much of his early adulthood, he had doubts or reservations about the following Christian beliefs: the Trinity; Miracles, divine inspiration of scripture, original sin, the atonement, the divinity of Jesus, and thus the dual natures of Jesus, the forgiveness of sins, an objective standard for morality, and eternal damnation.

This period of skepticism, if it existed, continued up until Lincoln began his law practice in Springfield in 1837. Like most lawyers outside urban areas at that time, Lincoln acquired his legal education on the job as a junior partner in an already established law practice, headed by John T. Stuart. His legal education began with the reading of basic legal texts, particularly English jurist Sir William Blackstone and the legal commentaries of Supreme Court Justice Joseph Story.[55]

50. Ibid.
51. Peters, *Abraham Lincoln's Religion*, 61.
52. Ingersoll, *Lecture on Lincoln*, 99.
53. David, *Lincoln*, 70–74.
54. Lincoln, handbill replying to charges of infidelity, July 31, 1846.
55. Ibid.

Mr. Lincoln went on to have two other law partners in Springfield: Stephen Logan and, of course, Mr. Herndon. Lincoln's reading of these fundamental law texts contributed to the future president's skepticism, when he saw how arbitrary and subjective points of view about issues in the law tended to be in the early nineteenth century, for example, the nature and origins of the concept of law. In 1846, when Lincoln was a candidate for U.S. Congress against the Rev. Peter Cartwright (1785–1872), the future president was accused of being an infidel and a deist, if not an outright atheist. Mr. Cartwright, a noted evangelist, tried to make Mr. Lincoln's skepticism a major issue of the campaign.

Responding to these accusations, Lincoln defended himself, publishing a handbill to "directly contradict the charges made against him." This handbill, addressed to "The Voters of the Seventh Congressional District," said the following:

> Fellow Citizens: A charge having got into circulation in some of the neighborhoods of the District, in substance that I am an open scoffer at Christianity. I have by the advice of some friends concluded to notice the subject of this form. That I am not a member of any Christian Church is true; but I have never denied the truth of the Scriptures; and I have never spoken with intentional disrespect of religion in general, or of any denomination of Christians in particular.[56]

In the same document, Lincoln goes on to confess his belief in the "doctrine of necessity." He says,

> It is true that in early life I was inclined to believe in what I understand is called the "Doctrine of Necessity"—that is, that the human mind is impelled to action, or held in rest by some power, over which the mind itself has no control; and I have sometimes tried to maintain this opinion in argument. The habit of arguing thus, however, I have entirely left off for more than five years. And I add here, I have always understood this same opinion to be held by several of the Christian denominations. The foregoing is the whole truth, briefly stated, in relation to myself, upon this subject.[57]

Surely, Mr. Lincoln had in mind here the Lutherans, the Presbyterians, the General Baptists, and the Separate Baptists, among other Protestant denominations.

56. Ibid.
57. Sandburg, *Abraham Lincoln: The Prairie Years*, 100.

If these facts reported by Mr. Lincoln were correct, then he rejected the doctrine of necessity while still in Springfield. Mr. Lincoln ends this handbill to the citizens of his district this way:

> I do not think I could myself be brought to support a man for office, whom I knew to be an open enemy of, or a scoffer at, religion. Leaving the higher matters of eternal consequences, between him and his Maker, I still do not think that any man has the right thus to insult the feelings, and injure the morals, of the community in which he might live. If then, I was guilty of such conduct, I should blame no man who should condemn me for it; but I do blame those, whoever they may be, who falsely put such a charge in circulation against me.[58]

Lincoln dates the document to 31 July, 1846, at the end of the handbill.

The Rev. Peter Cartwright (1785–1872), who served as a chaplain in the War of 1812, met Abraham Lincoln just prior to the Black Hawk War, in which Lincoln served as a captain in 1830. Lincoln had been working for Reuben Brown, a prairie developer in the 1830s and 40s.

Carl Sandburg, in his book *Abraham Lincoln: The Prairie Years*, relates an incident in which the future president attended one of the Rev. Cartwright's services, which was full of fire and brimstone. At one point Cartwright asked the crowd, who among them expected to go to heaven? Naturally, the response was robust. Next, he asked, "Who of you wishes to go to hell?" Not surprisingly, there were not many takers. Cartwright noticed that Lincoln did not respond to either question. The minister then asked, "May I inquire as to where you believe you are going?" Lincoln is reported to have replied, "I did not come here with the idea of being singled out, but since you asked, I will answer with equal candor. I intend to go to Congress."[59]

James W. Keyes in a letter to William Herndon about Lincoln's views on central Christian concepts, said the president "Believed in a Creator of all things, who had neither beginning nor end . . . but as to the belief that Christ was God, this must be taken for granted and against the test of reason."[60] Mr. Keyes, then, believed that Lincoln did not believe in the proposition that Jesus Christ was God because that belief went against Mr. Lincoln's new scientific worldview.

In regard to this period of skepticism, a number of other Lincoln scholars assent to the view that Lincoln in his early adult life did not profess

---

58. Keyes, "Statement for Mr. Herndon" (1865–1866), document 464 in *Prairie Fire: The Illinois Country before 1818.*

59. Herndon, *Life of Lincoln*, 366.

60. Hsavlik, "Abraham Lincoln and the Rev. James A. Smith."

in many of the central Christian tenets, including views about ᵤ.ture of Jesus, the Trinity, the atonement, original sin, the validity of ᵤcripture, and many other central beliefs.

The point of view regarding religion in this period of skepticism for Mr. Lincoln appears to have been a combination of scientific naturalism and the law of necessity, or determinism. In William Herndon's biography of Lincoln, he sums up this view by quoting the sixteenth president. Herndon says Lincoln reveals that "There are no accidents. Every effect must have its cause. The past is the cause of the present, and the present will be the cause of the future. All these are links in the endless chain stretching from the finite to the infinite."[61]

Here Mr. Lincoln assents to his belief in the law of necessity, the denial of free will, and his dedication to what may loosely be called the "laws of nature," on which all that happens operates, and thus a purely scientific, and natural, worldview—a form of determinism or fatalism, at the time.

One final note about William Herndon and President Lincoln. The former did not accompany, nor was he entertained in Washington by the latter, except on one occasion. If Mr. Lincoln did undergo a religious conversion of sorts, it could have been unconnected or unknown by Mr. Herndon. Later, in this study, in chapter 6, we will, in fact, argue that Mr. Lincoln did experience a religious conversion, one that was most likely known to almost no one other than himself and his wife, Mary Todd Lincoln.

In summary, then, among the Christian beliefs about which President Abraham Lincoln appears to have had some skepticism in the 1830s to the 1850s were the following: the divinity of Jesus, the miraculous conception of Jesus, the Trinity, miracles, the divine inspiration of Holy Scripture, creation out of nothing, original sin, free will, eternal damnation, the forgiveness of sins, and an objective standard of morality.

It also appears that what Mr. Lincoln replaced these beliefs with was a form of scientific naturalism, a set of beliefs that rely most fundamentally on the laws of nature. Nevertheless, in this period of skepticism, then, Mr. Lincoln appears to have relied on the views of the deists, the naturalists, and the determinists. He rarely spoke or wrote of religion, for he seems to have rejected his parents' form of conservative, and ecstatic, Christianity, the Separate Baptist Faith, and he rarely mentioned Jesus in his public words and pronouncements, and when he did he called him "the Savior" or "our Savior." It also appears that Lincoln avoided using the word "God" in this period of skepticism, substituting the deist-sounding "Maker" in its stead.

61. Smith, *Christian's Defence.*

Another way to see Mr. Lincoln's period of skepticism in regard to religion, which lasted from early adulthood until the mid-1850s, is to look at 1850, when Lincoln's son Eddie died. The Rev. Dr. James A. Smith, the pastor of First Presbyterian Church in Springfield, preached so effectively at the boy's funeral that Mary Todd Lincoln joined the church after that time. Although her husband did not join, he did attend Sunday services with her, and purportedly even gave a lecture on the Bible to Dr. Smith's congregation.[62]

Dr. Smith was born and raised in Calvinist Glasgow, Scotland, and he became a spiritual minister and mentor to Mr. Lincoln. The sixteenth president admired Dr. Smith's book *The Christian's Defence*, a work that was based on reason as well as revelation, thus appealing to the mind of a young attorney like Lincoln.[63] The Rev. Dr. Smith and Lincoln became friends. Smith had himself come to a "reasonable faith," the only kind that would appeal to Lincoln, after coming through a period of intense doubt. In fact, late in his administration Mr. Lincoln appointed Smith to a diplomatic post in Scotland, but it appears that early on the Rev. Smith contributed to the sixteenth president's penchant for looking at the world through skeptical, or scientific, eyes.

Although several writers, like William E. Barton and the Rev. James Smith, report that Mr. Lincoln delivered this lecture on the Bible in the Presbyterian church, other than these two there are no other independent reports that say it ever occurred. Neither of the two Illinois daily newspapers, the *Illinois State Register* and the *Illinois State Journal*, report about the alleged lecture. Robert Bray, in his article "What Lincoln Read," deems the giving of the lecture on the Bible "to be unlikely."[64]

Thomas Lewis, another man who alleged that the lecture in question was genuine, and who was quoted by Mr. Barton, made his remarks about it on December 10, 1898, forty-six years later. It is of some interest, however, that William Herndon did not interview Mr. Lewis when the former was preparing his biography of the sixteenth president. Hence, Mr. Herndon did not think Mr. Lewis was all that important in gathering materials about Mr. Lincoln. The best bet about the alleged lecture on the Bible seems to be that the event never took place.

Finally, another element that went into the making of Mr. Lincoln's period of skepticism and his turn toward naturalism and rationalism was his study of the law. For nearly a quarter century, Mr. Lincoln made his living as an attorney. In that time, he was a country lawyer, serving the Eighth Judicial District. Altogether, Mr. Lincoln had three law partners—John T.

62. *Lewis v. Lewis*, 1849; see Deckle, *Prairie Defender*, 94–98.

63. Donald, *Lincoln*, 73.

64. Bray, "What Lincoln Read," 75.

Stuart, Stephen T. Logan, and William H. Herndon. All three of these partnerships were in the city of Springfield.

Mr. Lincoln's greatest asset as a lawyer was his ability to simplify cases into their most fundamental elements. He had a gift for brevity and clarity, not unlike the skills of the Enlightenment philosophers he so greatly admired. Surely, one of the elements that went into the making of Mr. Lincoln's period of religious skepticism was the logical and orderly skills he employed in his legal practice. And this role of Lincoln's legal practice on his mature religious views should not be underestimated. The fact that Lincoln was a jack of all trades when it came to his law practice also contributed to the development of his legal skills, and, perhaps, to his ongoing religious skepticism.

Lincoln took cases from farmers, small businesses, and larger firms, like the railroad companies. All of this went into the making of a skepticism about the nature and validity of the law, as well as a skepticism concerning organized religion, Calvinist Christian or otherwise.

The papers of the Abraham Lincoln Project suggest that the sixteenth president was involved in 5,173 cases, either solely or with his partners. His practice included cases involving contracts, debts, bankruptcies, divorces, and deeds. Lincoln argued several hundred cases before the Illinois Supreme Court, and one case before the U.S. Supreme Court, the 1849 *Lewis v. Lewis*.[65] Mr. Lincoln's legal fees generally were in the five-to-twenty-dollar range, but in one railroad tax case his fee was five thousand dollars.[66]

Thirty-four of Mr. Lincoln's legal cases dealt with slavery or issues related to race. In one case Lincoln defended a free Black woman accused of failing to repay a loan, and in another he helped to eventuate the freedom of a runaway slave. In 1847, he defended a slave owner whose captives had sued him for their freedom on the grounds that they were brought to Illinois, a free state, from Kentucky, a slave state.[67] In another case, Lincoln argued that a Black woman and her child should be delivered to a client of his as repayment of a debt.[68]

Mr. Lincoln's excellent logical skills and his ability to be brief and cogent, as we have indicated earlier, went into the making of the sixteenth president's period of skepticism. The real subsequent question is just how long this period of skepticism lasted in the life of Mr. Lincoln. More will be said about this question in a subsequent chapter of this essay.

65. Ibid.

66. Ibid.

67. Herndon, *Life of Lincoln*, 377.

68. Ibid.

In sum, as we have shown in this chapter of this essay, William Herndon Jesse Fell, David Davis, and a number of other thinkers who knew Mr. Lincoln support this view that the sixteenth president of the United States, Abraham Lincoln, went through a period of religious skepticism in the 1830s to the 1850s. Mr. Herndon believed that Lincoln remained that way for the rest of his life.

Other thinkers, however, maintain that near the end of his life Abraham Lincoln went through a religious conversion, of sorts, after the deaths of his sons Eddie and Willie, in 1850 and 1862, and accompanied by the carnage of the Civil War. We will explore this possibility in a subsequent chapter of this essay, chapter 6.

Clearly, the most significant question about Mr. Lincoln's skepticism is just how long it lasted. Mr. Herndon points out that, "While Lincoln frequently, in a conventional way, appeals to God, he never appeals to Christ nor mentions him. I know that he at first maintained that Jesus was a bastard, and later that he was the son of Joseph, and not of God."[69]

Mr. Herndon continued:

> Lincoln was not a Christian in any sense other than that he lived a good life and was a noble man. If a good life constitutes one as a Christian, then Mill and a million other men who repudiated and denied Christianity were Christians, for they lived good and noble lives.[70]

The reference above is to John Stuart Mill (1806–1873), English philosopher, political economist, and civil servant. Mill was also one of the founders of the moral theory called utilitarianism, as outlined in the chapter of this essay on Mr. Lincoln's ethics, chapter 5. As we have said earlier, this view of Mr. Herndon has been countered by many people close to Mr. Lincoln. More will be said about this issue in a subsequent chapter of this essay entitled "Mr. Lincoln's Conversion," chapter 6.

In the summer of 1864, President Lincoln invited his Kentucky friend Joshua Speed to spend an evening at the White House, along with Mr. Herndon. When Speed arrived in Washington, he found Lincoln reading the Bible. Speed said to Lincoln, "I am glad to see you profitably engaged."[71] "Yes," replied the sixteenth president, "I am profitably engaged."[72] "Well," Speed continued, "If you have recovered from your Skepticism, I am sorry

---

69. This exchange reportedly took place in the White House during the presidential campaign of 1864.

70. Herndon, *Life of Lincoln*, 377.

71. Ibid.

72. Ibid.

to say that I have not."[73] Then Lincoln arose, placed his hands on Speed's shoulders, and is reported to have said, "You are wrong, Speed. Take all of this book upon reason that you can and the balance upon faith, and you will live and die a happier and a better man."[74]

This is the only time in the extant record when Mr. Herndon was in the physical presence of President Abraham Lincoln from the time the latter left Springfield in 1861 until his death in 1865; but it sounds as though by the summer of 1864 Lincoln had begun to give up his dedication to skepticism and now was in favor of a new enlightened theism, and a God who is all-good, all-knowing, and all-powerful. Joshua Speed, on the other hand, still appears to have be devoted to the skeptical religious point of view, as had Mr. Herndon as well, as late as July of 1864.

Lincoln's second inaugural address in March of 1865 is also further evidence that the sixteenth president had moved to a belief in a more traditional monotheism. More will be said about this supposed religious conversion of Mr. Lincoln in a subsequent chapter of this essay on Abraham Lincoln's religion, chapter 6. It is enough to say now, however, that we believe the sixteenth president went through a profound religious conversion at the end of his life. At any rate, a third time and place where we may look to discover Abraham Lincoln's Religious Faith are his two inaugural addresses, to which we turn in the third chapter of this essay.

73. Ibid.
74. Ibid.

CHAPTER 3

God and Religion in Lincoln's Inaugural Addresses

I am loath to close. We are not enemies but friends.

—ABRAHAM LINCOLN, First Inaugural Address

The Almighty has his own purposes.

—ABRAHAM LINCOLN, Second Inaugural Address

The Address sounded more like a sermon than a state paper.

—FREDERICK DOUGLASS, *The Life and Times of Frederick Douglass*

IN THIS THIRD CHAPTER of this work on Abraham Lincoln's religion, our central aim is to explore what role religion played in the sixteenth president of the United States' two inaugural addresses, delivered in March of 1861 and March of 1865, in New York City and Washington, DC.

As indicated, Abraham Lincoln delivered two inaugural addresses as President of the United States. The first of these was on Monday, March 4, 1861, and was mostly taken up with the national crisis of the Civil War. Lincoln delivered his first inaugural address immediately after the oath of office, which was administered by Chief Justice Roger Taney (1777–1864).

The Maryland-born Taney was the fifth chief justice of the U.S. Supreme Court. He was appointed to the court by Andrew Jackson, and served the court from 1836 until his death in 1864. Ironically, it was Justice Taney who four years before had written the controversial Dred Scott decision, to which President Lincoln was bitterly opposed.

Dred Scott v. Sanford, also known as the Dred Scott decision, was a landmark decision by the U.S. Supreme Court that involved U.S. labor and constitutional law. It essentially said that "A Negro, whose ancestors were imported into the United States and sold as slaves, "whether enslaved or free," are not now American citizens. Therefore, they have no standing in American courts. In essence, it also says that the federal government had no power to regulate slavery, in the war or afterwards.

One of the most interesting aspects of U.S. presidential inaugural addresses in general is that the word "God" did not appear in any of them until 1821, when James Monroe, in his second inaugural, pledged to carry out his presidential duties "with a firm reliance on the protection of the Almighty God."[1] In 1881, after Chester Arthur assumed power after the murder of James Garfield, Arthur added the phrase "so help me God" to the end of his presidential oath. Every American president since then has included the phrase as well.

In the Revolutionary War era, American presidents, perhaps influenced by their deism, preferred Washington's "Almighty Being," Adams's 'His Providence," or Jefferson's "Being in Whose hands we are" to the employment of the actual word "God." With the coming of Chester Arthur, however, the word "God" became a permanent fixture to presidential oaths of office.

By Mr. Lincoln's time, perhaps influenced by the Great Awakening, as discussed in the opening chapter of this essay, or his childhood Separate Baptists, he employed the word "God" more often than any president before him or since, in his inaugural addresses. President Lincoln also used a number of other terms or synonyms to indicate the Divine in his major speeches and addresses, particularly in his two inaugural addresses. In chapter 2, for example, we indicated Mr. Lincoln's employment of the word "Maker" to represent the Divine, a word among the many substitutes that Lincoln employed for the word "God." Mr. Lincoln was not, however, the president who employed the most synonyms for the Divine. That figure, as indicated earlier, was George Washington, who used more than one hundred different terms to stand for "God." Thomas Jefferson, on the other hand, also employed three dozen different names to stand for "God."[2]

---

1. Monroe, second inaugural address, March 5, 1821.
2. See Michael and Jana Novak's book, *Washington's God*, 243–45.

Mr. Lincoln carefully sketches out his two principal goals in his first inaugural address. First, to avoid war. Indeed, he explicitly stated that he would not interfere with slavery where it now existed. Secondly, the sixteenth president makes the claim that the U.S. Constitution had no provisions for a state's right to secede. He points out that it does give the president the job to make it such that the laws of the Union be faithfully executed, and those laws apply to the South as well as to the North, and many were not being followed, at the time, in the South, by the Secessionists.[3]

Mr. Lincoln supplied some context for his first inaugural address by telling his audience this:

> Fellow Citizens of the United States: In compliance with a custom as old as the Government itself, I appear before you to address you briefly and take in your presence the Oath prescribed by the Constitution of the United States to be taken by the President before he enters the execution of his office.[4]

In this opening, Mr. Lincoln begins by pointing out that we were all in this together, and thus his use of "fellow citizens." Next, he points out that the oath of office is as old as the Union itself. Thirdly, the sixteenth president mentions his reliance on the founding documents of America, particularly the Constitution. In fact, Mr. Lincoln repeatedly appealed to these founding documents throughout his first inaugural, and his presidency as well.

Nevertheless, Lincoln's first inaugural struck an overtly religious tone. During the address, the president did make four comments in regard to religion. He said in one of these: "Intelligence, patriotism, Christianity, and a firm reliance on Him who has never yet forsaken this favored land are still competent to adjust in the best way in our present difficulty."[5]

Mr. Lincoln seems to make the following points in this remark. First, he gives the essential attributes of good citizenship, intelligence, patriotism, and Christianity as characteristics of the American republic. Second, he makes the claim that God has not forsaken America, and sees its land as a new "Promised land." And finally, Lincoln believes that God will provide a way out of America's "present difficulty," that is, out of the Civil War.

In a second religious passage from the same inaugural, Mr. Lincoln said, "If the Almighty Ruler of nations, with his eternal truth and justice be on the side of the North, or on yours of the South, that truth and that

3. Lincoln, first inaugural address, March 4, 1861.

4. Ibid.

5. Ibid.

justice, will surely prevail by the judgment of this great tribunal, the American people."[6]

Mr. Lincoln seems to indicate that God does not pick sides, and that it is possible that justice will prevail on either side of the conflict. He also suggests that the people of America will be the final judge about the slavery question, and that the victory will not be accompanied without the hand of God.

Mr. Lincoln makes a third theological reference in his first inaugural address. It comes at the very end of the speech. The president speaks of "mystic chords of memory stretching from every battlefield and patriot grave to every living heart and hearthstone all over this broad land."[7] In this metaphor, the core principles of America are seen as "mystic chords" that reside in the hearts of Americans, both alive and dead.

He closed his first inaugural address with these words, the final religious reference in the first inaugural: "These will yet swell the Chorus of the Union, when again touched, as surely they will be by the better angels of our nature."[8]

In these remarks, Mr. Lincoln appears to express a belief that the Union will again exist in harmony and be governed by justice and equality. He also appears to have thought that the better nature of human beings, or Americans—that is, the nature that we are born basically good—will one day prevail in the Union. Donald J. Trump, in his presidential inauguration, quoted Lincoln's line of "better angels of our nature" on January 21, 2017.[9]

The line "better angels of our nature" had four possible sources, one biblical, the other three literary. The biblical source is Hebrews 1:4, which mentions, "Being made so much better than the angels" (KJV), a reference to Jesus being better than the created *ton aggelon*, or "the angels." The author of Hebrews seems to be responding to the first-century belief that angels are more appropriate mediators between God and humans.

This becomes clear in the NIV translation, which has it, "He is more superior to the angels," or the NAB translation, which says, "He is superior to the angels." The Greek of Hebrews 1:4 also suggests these latter interpretations. The Greek verb is not *poieo*, the normal term for "to make" or "to create." Rather, the verb is *ginomai*, which means "to become," and this meaning is conveyed by most modern translations. In the Septuagint this Greek verb is only predicated of God. Jesus Christ has always existed, but he

6. Ibid.

7. Ibid.

8. Ibid.

9. Trump, inaugural address, January 21, 2017.

became "better than the angels" in his exaltation, a statement that is better understood when we learn that in his incarnation on Earth he was "made for a little while lower than the angels . . . , that by the grace of God he might taste death for everyone," a direct reference to Psalm 8:5 and Hebrews 2:7–9.

Two of the possible literary sources of "better angels" are to be found in William Shakespeare's works. "Better Angels" are mentioned in Sonnet 144 of the Bard, and in *Othello*, where the Venetian Gratiano, after the death of Desdemona, must have his "better angel" keep him from exacting bloody revenge against Othello.[10] Gratiano is the brother of Brabantio. He is one of the Venetians who arrived on Cyprus after Othello's victory. Walking home with Lodovico, Gratiano comes across the wounded Cassio and is convinced by Iago of Bianca's likely guilt in the matter.

Shakespeare's Sonnet 144 was published in 1599 in a volume entitled *The Passionate Pilgrim*. The standard text of the sonnet is now the 1609 Quarto. It tells us this:

> Two loves I have of comfort and despair,
> Which like to spirits do suggest me still;
> The better angel is a man right fair,
> The worser spirit a woman colour'd ill.
> To win me soon to hell, my female evil
> Tempeth my better angel from my side
> And would corrupt my saint to be a devil,
> Wooing his purity with her foul pride.
> And whether that my angel be turn'd fiend
> Suspect I may, but not directly tell
> But being both from me, both to each friend,
> I guess one angel in another's hell:
> Yet this shall I ne'er know, but live in doubt
> Till my bad angel fire my good one out.[11]

In this sonnet, Shakespeare describes two different angels, one good and the other evil, that war against each other in human hearts and souls. The good angel is referred to as the writer's "better angel" twice in the poem. Shakespeare seems to suggest something much like the ancient Jewish belief that God placed into every human heart two *yetzerim*, or imaginations or inclinations. The *yetzer ha-ra* was the inclination toward evil, and the *yetzer*

10. Shakespeare, Sonnet 144, lines 3 and 6; *Othello*, act 5, scene 2.

11. Shakespeare, *Passionate Pilgrim*.

ha-tov the inclination toward the moral good. It was the human will that ultimately decided which of these two "imaginations" will be put to use.[12]

In the Islamic faith, there is a belief that there are two *Mala'kayn*, or "angels," one good and one evil, that sit on the shoulders of all human beings—a good angel on the right, and an evil one on the left. These two angels have the job of writing down the good and bad deeds of the human being to whom they had been assigned. At the end of time, these angels are to read out loud—before Allah and the other angels—the sins they have recorded, before Allah decides if they will be given Paradise or damnation, or so the *Qur'an*, the Muslim holy book, tells us.

One other possible literary source for Lincoln's use of "better angels" is Charles Dickens's novel *Barnaby Rudge*. In the novel, Dickens writes:

> It is curious to imagine these people of the world, busy in thought, turning their eyes towards the countless spheres that since above us, and making them reflect the only images their minds contain . . . so do the shadows of our own desires stand between us and our better angels, and thus their brightness is eclipsed.[13]

It is not clear whether Mr. Lincoln read the Dickens novel. What is clear is that the meaning of the phrase for both Dickens and Mr. Lincoln appears to be the same. "Better angels," for both, appears to mean something like "the better parts of ourselves." For the ancient Jews, this was the *yetzer ha-tov*. For early Muslims, it was the good angel that rests on the right shoulder. The same view also appears to be that of Shakespeare in his use of the expression in *Othello*, and these views are consistent with the two-*yetzerim* theory of the Hebrew Bible. But there is no evidence that Mr. Lincoln was aware of this ancient Jewish moral theory.

Nevertheless, when Mr. Lincoln arrived in Washington on February 23 of 1861 for his first inaugural address, he invited William Seward—his chief rival for the Republican Party's nomination, but by then also Lincoln's secretary of state—to read a draft of Lincoln's Speech. To the president's surprise, Seward responded with seven pages of comments on the address, which contained fifty suggestions for how to improve it. Mr. Seward was one of several of Mr. Lincoln's former political rivals. Indeed, the sixteenth president filled his first cabinet with a collection of those political rivals.[14]

---

12. Viviano, "Eschatology and the Quest for the Historical Jesus," 44.

13. Dickens, *Barnaby Rudge*, 153.

14. Lincoln's secretary of state, William Henry Seward; secretary of the treasury, Salmon P. Chase; secretaries of war, Simon Cameron and Edwin M. Stanton; as well as his attorney general, Edward Bates, all sought the 1860 Republican Party nomination for president.

One of Seward's suggestions was to forget the final paragraph and to choose one of two new paragraphs that the secretary of state provided as substitutes. One of these substitutions was, "The guardian angel of the nation," but Mr. Lincoln immediately changed it to, "The better angels of our nature." Seward's suggestion was personal; Lincoln's final choice was deeply personal, and profound.

In his first inaugural address, the largest portion of the speech is directly addressed to the people of the South. Indeed, he speaks of eight separate themes in the talk, themes he would return to many times over the next four or five years. These themes are the following:

1. Slavery
2. The legal status of the South
3. The use of force
4. Secession
5. The protection of slavery where it existed
6. Slavery in the territories
7. The continuation of the postal service
8. Federal offices in the South[15]

Mr. Lincoln concluded his first inaugural address with an eloquent plea for calm and a cool deliberation in the face of mounting tension and destruction. He assured the rebellious states that the federal government would not initiate any conflict with those states. Lincoln waxed that his own conviction that, once "touched" once more "by the better angels of our nature," the "mystic chords of memory, North and South, would yet swell the chorus of our Union."[16]

In Lincoln's view, these "mystic chords" are connected to the eternal principles embodied in the founding documents of this nation, and first among these founding principles are justice and equality for all people, as well as the right of a man to benefit from his own labor.

In his first inaugural address, the sixteenth president also outline the moral sources of the American republic. He points out:

> The Union is much older than the Constitution. It was formed,
> in fact, by the Articles of Association in 1774. It was matured
> and continued in the Declaration of Independence in 1776. It
> was furthered matured, and the faith of all of the then Thirteen

15. Lincoln, first inaugural address, March 4, 1860.
16. Ibid.

States expressly plighted and engaged that it should be perpetual, by the Articles of Confederation in 1778. And finally, in 1787,
one of the declared objects for ordaining and establishing the
Constitution was "to form a more perfect Union."[17]

The foundations of this "more perfect Union," of course, were the eternal
truths outlined earlier in the founding documents of the nation; and among
these truths were equality, justice, the right to profit from one's own labor,
and many others found in the Declaration of Independence, the Constitution, and the Bill of Rights, among other documents.

The emphasis, then, in Lincoln's first inaugural was primarily to address the people of the South, and succinctly to state Lincoln's intentions,
policies, and desires toward that section of the country, where seven states
already had seceded from the Union and formed the Confederate States of
America. These states were Alabama, Florida, Georgia, Louisiana, Mississippi, South Carolina, and Texas. After the beginning of the war, they were
joined by Arkansas, North Carolina, Tennessee, and the Commonwealth of
Virginia.

But along the way, the president took great care to mention the providence of Almighty God, his continual blessings on America, his view that
America is chosen nation, as well as the fact that Lincoln reminded Americans of their better nature—that humans were made "very good" in the
Genesis account of creation (Genesis 1:27–31).

In the second inaugural address of Abraham Lincoln, however, the
president made far more theological and religious remarks, as well as direct
references to God, as we shall see next.

Abraham Lincoln's second inaugural address was a mere 703, the second shortest inaugural in American history. George Washington's inaugural
address in 1793 was the shortest. 505 of the 703 words of Lincoln's second
inaugural were one syllable. Lincoln mentions the Divine fourteen times in
his second inaugural address, he quotes directly from Scripture five times,
and invokes prayer another four times. Lincoln's second inaugural address
was delivered on March 4, 1865, four years to the day after his first inaugural.

Lincoln's second inaugural is in character with other American presidential speeches that began second-term administrations. All presidents
but Teddy Roosevelt and Rutherford B. Hayes mentioned God in their
inaugurals. The fourteen references to God in Lincoln's second inaugural
address are a record. President Obama mentioned God five times in both
of his inaugurals; George W. Bush mentioned the Divine three times in
both of his inaururals; Richard Nixon mentioned God six times in his first

17. Ibid.

inaugural in 1969; and Ronald Reagan's second inaugural is in second place behind Lincoln's second. Reagan referred to God eight times in that address.

Few public leaders in the history of America have employed the name of the Divine with greater sincerity and authority than Abraham Lincoln did in his second inaugural address. One of the most important speeches in American history, it addressed the entire nation. You find no effort to demonize the South as the enemy. Rather, Lincoln invokes the name of God, not in justification of his policies, but as the transcendent whose judgments alone are "true and true and righteous altogether."[18] Indeed, Mr. Lincoln's second inaugural address is the most overtly theological speech ever by an American president, before or since.

Indeed, in a few short paragraphs, Mr. Lincoln strung together four direct quotations of the biblical text. As we will see below, he juxtaposed Genesis 3:19 with Matthew 7:1, "Lets us judge not . . ." He reiterates his previous condemnation of slavery that it is the theft of "another's self," because it kept Black men from the profits of their own labor. His claim not to judge is a theme that runs throughout the second inaugural and Mr. Lincoln's later life. The words come directly from the Gospel of Matthew 7:1.

Abraham Lincoln's second inaugural address had been preceded by several weeks of rain and snow in Washington. This had caused Pennsylvania Avenue to become a sea of mud and standing water. Thousands of spectators stood in thick mud at the capitol grounds to hear the president. As he stood on the east portico to take his executive office, the capitol dome was still under construction.

Unlike his first inaugural, which was administered by Judge Taney, the second inaugural was administered by Chief Justice Salmon Chase. Mr. Chase (1808–1873) was the sixth chief justice of the U.S. Supreme Court. He was also governor of Ohio and a U.S. senator in that state. Chase was also a chief rival of Mr. Lincoln in securing the Republican nomination to the presidency in 1860. Lincoln also appointed Salmon Chase to be his secretary of the treasury, as indicated earlier.

When Mr. Lincoln was introduced to the audience, the enormous crowd exploded in expectation, except for those at work on an assassination plot that was already in the works. Lincoln rose from his chair and stepped underneath a temporary shelter to keep him from the rain. The shelter had been erected past the magnificent Corinthian columns so he would remain dry.

By now, the sixteenth president was fifty-six years old, but he looked considerably older than that. Later, the abolitionist and orator Frederick

18. Lincoln, second inaugural address, March 4, 1865.

Douglass would call the speech "a sacred effort," at a reception after the inauguration. Lincoln had met Douglass on two previous occasions, and for the most part he had fiercely opposed many of the sixteenth president's policies, particularly in regard to African-Americans and free slaves.

Lincoln's second address is different in at least five important ways from his first inaugural speech, as well as from the second inaugural addresses of other U.S. presidents. First, unlike those of other presidents—like Jefferson, Madison, Monroe, Grant, Reagan, Clinton, and George Bush Jr.—Lincoln's second inaugural was shorter than his first. Mr. Lincoln understood that less is more, and he employed that literary technique in many of his public, and important, speeches and written works.

Secondly, previous inaugurals had been filled with the words, "I," "my," and "mine." In his second inaugural, Mr. Lincoln employed one personal pronoun, the word "I," one time, as well as five other pronouns altogether in the speech. Each of the other five—two "he," two "him," and one "his"—all referred to God. Several places in the second address speak of the collective guilt of the war, of both North and South, and that of slavery, as well.

Thirdly, most second inaugural addresses before Mr. Lincoln's sketched out the goals in their second-term administration. Lincoln's did not. His speech was unpredictable in ways that other presidents' had not been before, and have not been since, for that matter.

Fourthly, Mr. Lincoln's second inaugural contained a good bit of scolding, of both the North and the South. He said, "Woe unto the world because of offences."[19] Later, he added, "If we shall suppose that American Slavery is one of those offences,"[20] suggesting there is a moral responsibility for slavery is to be found in both the North and the South. Finally, Lincoln's second inaugural address is full of memorable words, language that has become part of the national framework, and often repeated by Americans since they first were uttered on March 4, 1865, from a podium in Washington, DC.

By the time of Lincoln's second inaugural, he knew well that every corner of the nation had been impacted by the war. The casualties were now unimaginable, with hundreds of thousands dead, nearly 700,000 by the end of the war. Postwar reconciliation and reconstruction would be an incredibly arduous and complex an undertaking that would involve the economy, the rebuilding of cities and towns, the promotion of racial harmony, the caring for the maimed and widowed, as well as legal and constitutional changes. Lincoln, of course, would not live to lead the reconciliation and

19. Ibid.
20. Ibid.

reconstruction. He was murdered forty-one days after his second inaugural address.

Nevertheless, Mr. Lincoln was optimistic and hopeful, as March 4, 1865, Inauguration Day, grew near. The Confederacy was splintered if not shattered. The president who had been besieged by critics for much of the war was finally beginning to receive some recognition for his leadership. But beneath his outward optimism lay a different set of emotions, the chief of which was frustration with the incompetent military men on the Union side of the war.

Mr. Lincoln was very disappointed in the performances of many of his top generals during the Civil War, General McClellen among them. Indeed, in total, during the Civil War period, Mr. Lincoln fired Generals Burnside, McClellen (twice), McDowell, Pope, and "Fighting Joe" Hooker; and he forced General Winfred Scott, who was old, fat, and possibly senile, to retire.

General Scott, who commanded troops in the Mexican War, as well as in the War of 1812, may have been the only person who knew both Thomas Jefferson and Abraham Lincoln personally. Ironically, it was General Scott's strategy to capture the Mississippi River, from end to end, so that the Confederacy was split. The beginning of the end of the Civil War was when General U.S. Grant took Vicksburg, and then exactly followed General Scott's "Anaconda Plan."

The Anaconda Plan was the Union army's strategy to defeat the Confederacy at the beginning of the Civil War. The goal was to defeat the rebellion by blockading southern ports and controlling the Mississippi River. This would cut off the South from the outside world. This plan was developed by General Winfield Scott at the beginning of the war, following the attack on Fort Sumter, on April 12, 1861.

If the plan had been implemented when General Scott wished, and if he had received more support from fellow Union generals, many lives in the war might have been saved early on. At least theoretically, if the plan had been put in place early on, many of the giant battles of the war may not have occurred.

Mr. Lincoln also had a number of other disputes with many of his top generals, including Generals George Meade, Joseph Hooker, Henry Halleck, and Don Carlos Buell. Mr. Lincoln was so perturbed with Buell and Halleck, who together commanded the Western Theatre, that the president wrote them a letter that said, "I state my general idea of this War to be, that we have the greater number. That we must fail unless we can find some way of making our advantage an overmatch for his; and this can only be done by menacing him with superior forces at different points, at the same time."[21]

The references to "him" and "his" in this letter are to General Robert E. Lee (1807–1870), the commander of the Confederate army of Northern Virginia from 1862 until 1865. General Lee was the son of a Revolutionary War hero. He was also a graduate of the U.S. Military Academy, in West Point, as was Ulysses S. Grant.

One of the little-known facts of the Civil War is just how many generals, on both sides of the war, were graduates of West Point Academy. 220 of Lincoln's 560 generals matriculated at West Point; and 140 of the Confederate's 400 generals also attended West Point.

Mr. Lincoln's second inaugural address was delivered on March 4, 1865. As the president prepared the speech, the Civil War was drawing to a close. Newspapers were filled with reports of Sherman's and Grant's armies. As late as August of 1864, neither Lincoln nor his Republican Party thought he would win reelection. In fact, Lincoln was the first president in thirty-two years to win a second term.

The crowd for Lincoln's second inaugural was enormous. The address was delivered in the rain, and many onlookers stood in the mud. Snipers were placed on rooftops. Rumors abounded that Confederates might abduct or assassinate the president. In fact, John Wilkes Booth was in the audience of Mr. Lincoln's second inaugural, as were several of his co-conspirators, as we will discuss later in this chapter of this essay.

Writing for the journal *The American Catholic*, scholar Donald R. Mc-Clarey wrote that, "Hands down, Lincoln's Second Inaugural is the most moving inaugural in American history."[22] He adds, "It is also the most important theological document written by an American President."[23] Lincoln biographer, Ronald White Jr., called Lincoln's second inaugural address "Lincoln's Sermon on the Mount."[24] Best-selling author Stephen Mansfield refers to Lincoln's second inaugural address as "The greatest of American political sermons."[25]

An anonymous correspondent writing for the *London Spectator* agreed with this assessment. He also pointed out that "At least half the multitude of those who attended were Colored People."[26] Frederick Douglass, in an epi-

21. This letter is quoted in McPherson, "Lincoln as Commander in Chief."
22. McClarey, "March 4th, 1865: The Greatest Inaugural Address."
23. Ibid.
24. White, *Lincoln's Greatest Speech*, 8.
25. Mansfield, *Lincoln's Battle with God*, 8.
26. Anonymous, in the *London Spectator*, March 5, 1865.

graph used for this chapter of this essay, suggests that the second inaugural was "more like a Sermon than a Speech."[27] Indeed, most scholars who have addressed the question of Lincoln's faith concur in regard to the importance of this speech. It was a masterpiece.

In some ways, this is peculiar, for Lincoln's second inaugural is a mere 703 words long, more than 500 of them only a single syllable. It took the president six minutes to deliver the address to a crowd present at the inaugural estimated to have been between 25,000 and 30,000 onlookers, 6,000 of whose hands he personally shook that day, including that of Frederick Douglass.

The second inaugural is important for our purposes because Mr. Lincoln mentions God fourteen times, quotes the Bible directly five times, and invokes prayer another four times. During the course of the second inaugural, the audience broke into applause on only four occasions. Many present were not sure of how to respond to much of what he had to say.

One of the peculiarities concerning Lincoln's second inaugural address is that it apparently was only finished the same day it was delivered. Mrs. Lincoln reports about this phenomenon:

> Mr. Lincoln wrote the conclusion to his Inaugural Address the morning it was delivered. The family being present, he read it to them. He then said he wished to be left alone for a short time. The family retired to an adjoining room, but not so far distant but that his voice of prayer could be heard. There, closeted with God alone, surrounded by the enemies who were ready to take his life, he commended his country's cause and all dear to him to God's care and with a mind calm by communion with his Father in Heaven, and courage equal to the danger, "He came forth from that retirement ready for duty."[28]

In addition to these references to God, Lincoln also makes mention of "war" throughout the second inaugural address, as well as the practice of "slavery" in many places in the speech. Hidden beneath many of these comments is a certain moral theory that appears in most of his major speeches—a moral theory made up of fundamental American moral principles to be found in the founding documents of this nation. Justice and equality, and the right to gain from one's own labor, of course, are the most important of these, in Mr.

---

27. Douglass, *Life and Times of Frederick Douglass*, 321. Later, Douglass also sent a letter to Mary Todd Lincoln on her husband's second inaugural address, on August 17, 1865.

28. Burt, "Collective Guilt in Lincoln's Second Inaugural Address."

Lincoln's mind. More will be said about Mr. Lincoln's views on ethics and morality in a later chapter of this work, chapter 5.

These places in the second inaugural where Mr. Lincoln mentions God are significant, for his overall theological views on the issue of suffering and what has been called the issues of theodicy and the problem of evil are most forcefully revealed. Over and over in the short address, Mr. Lincolns refers to the continuation of the war and "God's plan" for it, or "The Almighty God has His own purposes."[29] Indeed, in his second inaugural address President Lincoln clearly alludes to two of the most prominent responses in the Christian tradition to the issues of theodicy and the problem of evil and suffering.

The first of these views is sometimes called the "divine plan theory." It says that evil and suffering might appear to be wrong in the short run, but in the long run they are enveloped into what Mr. Lincoln refers to as "The Almighty God has His own purposes."[30] More also will be said about Mr. Lincoln's views on the problem of evil in a subsequent chapter of this essay, chapter 7.

More specifically in the second inaugural address, Mr. Lincoln wrote and delivered these words in regard to the war between the states:

> Both read the same Bible and pray to the same God, and each invokes His aid against the other. It may seem strange that any men should dare to ask a just God's assistance in wringing their bread from the sweat of the other men's faces, but let us judge not, that we be not judged. The prayers of both could not be answered. That of neither have been answered fully. The Almighty has His own purposes.[31]

Mr. Lincoln observes that it may seem "strange" that a morally good and just God would play any role in the war. Obviously, he is referring to the traditional Christian view, where God is said to be omnibenevolent. Nevertheless, this theme of President Lincoln as a believer in the divine plan theory in regard to the theological problem of evil is one that we find throughout many of his speeches and addresses, particularly late in his life, from 1862 until 1865.

In his "Meditations on the Divine Will," for example, an unpublished manuscript that Lincoln's secretary found in his desk after the president's death, the sixteenth president wrote:

29. Lincoln, second inaugural address, March 4, 1865.

30. Ibid.

31. Ibid.

> The will of God prevails—in great contests each party claims to act in accordance with the will of God. Both may be, and one must be wrong. God cannot be for and against the same thing at the same time. In the present Civil War, it is quite possible that God's purposes are somewhat different from the purposes of either party—and yet the human instrumentalities, working just as they do, are the best adaptation to effect this.[32]

Clearly, this language about "God's will" and "God's purposes" refer to the divine plan theory in regard to the problem of evil. In September of 1864, Lincoln also placed the Civil War squarely within the divine providence. In this letter to a member of the Society of Friends, the Quakers, the president wrote:

> The purposes of the Almighty are perfect, and must prevail, though we erring mortals may fail accurately to perceive them in advance. We hope for a happy termination of this terrible war long before this; but God knows best, and has ruled otherwise . . . we must work earnestly in the best light He gives us, trusting that so working still conduces to the great ends He ordains . . . Surely, he intends some great good to follow this mighty convulsion, which no mortal could make, and no mortal could stay.[33]

The reference to "erring mortals," of course, is a reference to the fact that humans are frequently ignorant of the ways of God, while God has omniscience, or perfect knowledge of all things. This is also consistent with belief in the divine plan theory, with respect to the issues of theodicy and the problem of evil. The mention of "great ends," and "great goods to follow," of course, is an appropriation and use of Lincoln's dedication to the divine plan theory.

Lincoln's second theory of theodicy in his second inaugural address comes in a passage where he implies that the Civil War has been a form of retribution for all Americans, both North and South. In the passage in discussion, Mr. Lincoln wrote:

> If we shall suppose that American Slavery is one of these offences which, in the Providence of God, must need come, but which, having continued through His appointed time, He now wills to remove; and that He gives to both North and South this terrible war as the woe due to those by whom the offences came, shall

32. Lincoln, "Meditation on the Divine Will," September, 1862.
33. Lincoln to Mrs. Eliza Gurney, September 4, 1864.

we discern therein any departure from these divine attributes which the believers in a living God always ascribe to Him?[34]

The "woe due," of course, in the above quotation refers to Mr. Lincoln's belief in a collective form of retributive justice in regard to punishment for the sins of slavery. Indeed, Mr. Lincoln saw the Civil War as God's punishment to both North and South for slavery, and the sins of the war, on both sides. We will say more about this view in chapter 7 of this essay.

Imagine the reaction of the American public today if, after American troops were engaged in a terrible war, an American president were to say that the war was God's punishment, and the Americans are just as guilty as their adversaries.

At the end of the American Civil War, citizens on both sides were sick of the conflict and desperately yearned for victory and peace, and yet, in another passage of the second inaugural, President Lincoln makes the claim that the war will continue until there is additional suffering for which an additional penance must be paid for the evils of slavery—that the judgment of God will be true and righteous, for both sides of the war. In the passage in question, Mr. Lincoln wrote:

> Fondly do we hope, fervently do we pray, that this mighty scourge of war may speedily pass away. Yet, if God wills that it continue until all the wealth piled by the bondsman's two hundred and fifty years of unrequited toil shall be sunk, and until every drop of blood drawn with the lash shall be paid by another drawn with the sword, as we said three thousand years ago, so still it must be said, "The Judgments of the Lord are true and righteous altogether."[35]

The reference to 250 years is the number of years before the Civil War that slavery was practiced in America. The 3,000 refers to Moses and the exile out of Egypt.In this sense Lincoln was seen by abolitionists and by slaves to be a "new Moses," and America a "new Promised Land." The above passage ends with a mention of the final reckoning when God's "judgments" will be brought to bear, to both the North and the South.

Again, more will be said about Mr. Lincoln's views on theodicy and the problem of evil in a later chapter of this essay, chapter 7. Three other elements of Lincoln's second inaugural address are significant for our purposes. One of these is ironic; the other two are explanatory. The ironic element is that John Wilkes Booth, mentioned earlier, as well as other co-conspirators

---

34. Lincoln, second inaugural address, March 4, 1865.
35. Ibid.

involved in the president's assassination, such as David Herod, Lewis Paine, John Surratt, and Edmond Spangler, all were present in the crowd at the second inauguration.

In fact, in one photograph from Ronald C. White's *The Eloquent President*, Mr. Booth is visible in the photo. He stands in the top row of the crowd, slightly to the right of center.[36] A second image in White's book highlights both Lincoln and the man identified by White as Mr. Booth.[37] Needless to say, if Mr. White is correct and Mr. Booth was present at the second inaugural of Abraham Lincoln, then the president may have escaped assassination that day, forty-one days before his actually being shot, on the evening of Good Friday at Ford's Theatre in Washington, DC.

The three remaining significant elements of Lincoln's use of religion in his second inaugural address are his quotations from the Bible and the president's use of literary and narrative techniques throughout the address, delivered at Washington on the morning of March 4, 1865. In regard to Mr. Lincoln's use of the biblical text in the second inaugural speech, he quotes directly from Scripture five times in the address. The first of these comes in connection to Lincoln quoting Matthew 7:1, which the King James Version renders as, "Judge not, that ye not be judged!" Mr. Lincoln is clearly revealing one of the major elements of his overall moral point of view that is often expressed in his major speeches. To wit, "Don't judge others unless you realize you too would be judged."

Lincoln's ethics included the ideas of following universal moral rules, as well as a reverence for the value of all human life, like the Ten Commandments and the Golden Rule, for examples. Much more will be said of Mr. Lincoln's understanding of ethics, moral theory, and the nature of the moral good in a subsequent chapter of this essay, as well, chapter 5.

A little further on in the address, Lincoln again quotes from the sayings of Jesus: "Woe unto the world because of offenses; for it must needs be that offenses come, but woe to the man by whom the offenses cometh!"[38] The president appears to have relied on Matthew 18:7 for this quotation, though a similar discourse can be found at Luke 17:1, where the King James Version tells us, "Then said he unto the disciples, 'It is impossible but that offences will come; but woe unto him, through whom they come!'"

This line that opens chapter 17 of Luke's Gospel is the beginning of a ten-verse discourse in which Jesus freely remarks about ethical principles such as offense (v. 2), faith (v. 6), and forgiveness and repentance (vv. 3–4).

36. White, *Eloquent President*.

37. Ibid.

38. Lincoln, second inaugural address, March 4, 1865.

Mr. Lincoln thereby identifies his moral principles with those of Jesus Christ. For Mr. Lincoln, of course, the "offenses" in question are related to the terrible actions of the American Civil War, of which, at least in Lincoln's understanding, both sides will be held accountable for those offenses by Almighty God.

The sixteenth president also refers directly to prayer in his second inaugural address, three separate times. In the first, he points out that both sides of the Civil War pray to the same God. Later on in the speech, he says, "The prayers of both could not be answered," and "neither side has been answered fully."[39] Lincoln seems to be pointing out just how little either side of the war really can say about God and prayer.

In the closing paragraph of his second inaugural address, President Lincoln again turns to two additional glosses from Holy Scripture, one from the Psalms and the other from the Epistle of James. In the former, Lincoln remarks, "Let us strive on it to . . . bind up the nation's wounds."[40] This appears to be a reworking of Psalm 147:3, which informs us in the King James Version, "He healeth the broken in heart, and bindeth up their wounds."

Here Mr. Lincoln clearly calls to mind the many broken hearts and accompanying wounds and sorrows that came along with them, during the Civil War period. Lincoln also hints that reconciliation and reconstruction are going to be a difficult process for all concerned, and the president seems to hint at the possibilities of healing and reconciliation, to follow the war.

The "with malice towards none" passage in Lincoln's second inaugural address seems to be borrowed from 1 Peter 2:1, which tells us in the King James Version, "Therefore, rid yourself of all malice and deceit, hypocrisy, envy, and slander of every kind." Finally, Mr. Lincoln appears to rely on a passage in the Epistle of James that comes at 1:27. The King James Bible gives us this for the line: "Pure religion and undefiled before God and the Father is this, to visit the fatherless and widows in their affliction, and to keep himself unspotted from the world." The president, again thinking of reconciliation and reconstruction, says, "To care for whom who shall have borne the battle and for his widow and his orphans," a clear reference to James 1:27.

The Epistle of James, of course, is one of the many places in the New Testament where the issues of evil and suffering are discussed at some length. The chapter in which James 1:27 is found mentions the virtues of patience and endurance in the face of temptations in verses 3, 4, 13, and 14. Chapter 5 of the same epistle speaks of the Old Testament figure of Job

39. Ibid.
40. Ibid.

and his legendary patience in the face of adversities. More will be said about Lincoln's views on the problem of evil, as well as the book of Job and the rest of the Bible, in a later chapter of this work, chapter 4.

One final aspect of why the second inaugural address is so compelling is the realization that the president uses a variety of traditional narrative techniques in the address. Among those techniques are: alliteration, repetition, comparing and contrasting, memorable phrases, familiarity, and the use of the passive voice.

The second paragraph of the second inaugural gives us a fine example of the technique of alliteration. In that paragraph, Mr. Lincoln uses the alliterative sound of the letter "d" eight times, binding concepts together and to concentrate his readers'/listeners' thoughts.[41] In the speech's second paragraph, Lincoln also employs the technique of repetition, using the word "war" in every sentence of the paragraph.[42]

Mr. Lincoln's overarching approach in his second inaugural was to emphasize common actions and emotions shared by the two sides of the Civil War. Thus, he used "all" and "both" to show the inclusion of both the North and the South, in the guilt and responsibility for slavery.

Later in the second inaugural, Mr. Lincoln employs comparison and contrast when he writes, "Both read the same Bible, and pray to the same God; and each invokes His aid against the other."[43] He goes on to say, "The prayers of both could not be answered; that neither had been answered fully," followed by, "The Almighty has His own purposes."[44]

In his second inaugural address, Abraham Lincoln also utters some of his most memorable phrases. Consider, for example, "With malice toward none, with charity for all, with firmness in the right, as God gives us to see the right, let us strive on to finish the work we are in."[45] At the very end of his second inaugural address, Mr. Lincoln penned the words, "To do all which may achieve and cherish a just and lasting peace, among ourselves and with all nations."[46]

Indeed, Mr. Lincoln's speeches, addresses, and written works frequently contain memorable words and expressions: the "house divided" analogy from his 1858 Republican Party nomination speech for the senate; his reference in his first inaugural to a "firm reliance on Him who has never yet

41. Ibid.
42. Ibid.
43. Ibid.
44. Ibid.
45. Ibid.
46. Ibid.

forsaken this favored land"; his invocation to congress in his first inaugural address that, "With a reliance on Providence all the more firm and earnest, let us proceed in the great task which events have devolved upon us."[47] All of these words uttered by the sixteenth president have been repeated by many Americans in the years since his time.

Other memorable words and phrases uttered or written by Mr. Lincoln include: his reference in his Gettysburg address that, "This nation shall under God have a new birth of freedom"; and the sixteenth president's quotation in his second inaugural address that, "Judgments of the Lord are true and righteous altogether."[48] Interestingly enough, the entire second inaugural address of Abraham Lincoln was written in the passive voice. Passages like "Public progress of our arms . . . is as well known to the public as to myself" and "No prediction in regard to it is ventured" are all written in the passive voice. A Witness reported Lincoln's voice was strong but low in tone that day. Mr. Lincoln often employed the technique of lowering his voice in his major speeches, as a way of concentrating the listener's attention.

For Mr. Lincoln, neither the appeal to the "better angels of our nature" in the final paragraph of the first inaugural, nor his restless search for military commanders who could give him victory, nor his repeated efforts to both loyal and rebel slave states of compensated emancipation, lessened or stanched the flow of the war. Lincoln, the reasoner, was finally driven to the explanation offered in the third paragraph of his second inaugural—that God willed these horrors to punish the national sin of slavery, both North and South, or collective retributive justice.

Mr. Lincoln tried in his second inaugural to explain the devastation that already had occurred; but what does an explanation that outrages common sense and morality explain? "The Almighty has His own purposes," explained Mr. Lincoln. Some say he might have better left it at that. Thankfully, Lincoln gave us the fourth paragraph of the second inaugural, in which he sketches out a new task, embodied in a list of what Americans must now do to heal the wounds of the nation. God figures in Lincoln's new, manly vision as a guide, "as God gives us to see the Right," but the work is up to us.[49]

Lincoln's religion, and his views on God, in both inaugural addresses seems deep, dark, frightening, and distant but, at the same time, somewhat hopeful. More will be said about the two inaugural addresses of Mr. Lincoln in a subsequent chapter of this essay, chapter 7, on the problem of evil.

47. Lincoln, first inaugural address, March 4, 1860.
48. Lincoln, second inaugural address, March 4, 1865.
49. Shakespeare, *Hamlet*, act 3, scene 3.

Lincoln's second inaugural address, including its many biblical references, reminds us of the sixteenth president's opinion that "nothing equals Macbeth," and Claudius's lament that displays a kind of almost stoic moral determinism, in which Shakespeare says:

> Though inclination be as sharp as will,
>
> My stronger guilt defeats my strong intent,
>
> And, like a man to double business bound,
>
> I stand in pause where I shall first begin,
>
> And both neglect.[50]

Other poets admired by President Lincoln include Robert Burns, Oliver Wendell Holmes, Thomas Gray, Lord Byron, William Cullen Bryant, Edgar Allan Poe, and many others. In his early adulthood, the sixteenth president often composed crude and sometimes satirical poems, like this one:

> Abraham Lincoln is my name.
>
> And with my pen I wrote the same.
>
> I wrote in both hast and speed
>
> And left it here for fools to read.[51]

Lincoln rejected his father's Calvinism, and yet determinism, or the law of necessity, remained a default position in his life. It was like an incubus he could no longer shake off. In his second inaugural address, Lincoln asks the American people to recognize the disposing hand of God to be at work in human history, a hand with a darker, more compelling purpose than any human being could articulate or foresee.

The second inaugural was delivered on March 4, 1865, in a driving rain, and its major theme of providence already was anticipated in a Lincoln letter from April 4, 1864, to Kentucky newspaper editor Albert G. Hodges. In that correspondence, Mr. Lincoln wrote:

> I claim not to have controlled events, but confess plainly that events have controlled me. Now, at the end of a three year struggle the nation's condition is not what either party, or any man devised, or expected. God alone cannot claim it. Whither it is tending seems plain. If God now wills the removal of the great wrong, and wills also that we of the North as well as you of the South, shall pay fairly for our complicity in that wrong,

---

50. Armenti, "Lincoln as Poet."

51. Lincoln, letter to Albert G. Hodges, April 4, 1864.

impartial history will find therein new cause to attest and reverse the justice and goodness of God.[52]

In this letter, we find the emphasis on the ignorance of humans and the omniscience of God that is also found in the second inaugural address of President Abraham Lincoln; but we also see in the second inaugural a shift in the purposes of the war: from the preservation of the Union to an end of slavery, or what William Lloyd Garrison, in his essay "The Great Crisis," called, "The Bloody and Heaven-daring arrangement."[53] In the letter to Mr. Hodges, the president also briefly mentioned his belief in the "law of necessity," the view that all that occurs, happens by the Will of God.

These same themes of the providence of God and the divine plan theory in the second inaugural address of Mr. Lincoln can also be seen in a number of other places from 1862 to 1865. For example, at a crucial cabinet meeting after the Battle of Antietam, in September of 1862, Lincoln astounded his colleagues by making a vow to himself, and to his "Maker," that if the Divine allowed the North to repel Lee's Confederate invasion, it would be Lincoln's duty to abolish slavery.[54]

In another speech from September of 1862, Mr. Lincoln lamented, "Whatever shall appear to be God's will, I will do."[55] In another address delivered on October 24, 1863, Mr. Lincoln said:

> Amid the greatest difficulties of my administration, when I could not see any other resort, I would place my whole reliance in God, knowing that all will go well, and that He would decide for the right.[56]

It is clear that in these years from 1862 to 1865, Mr. Lincoln regularly saw the ways the War was going chiefly to be understood in terms of the providence of God and divine plan theory, with regard to the problem of evil and the issue of theodicy. We will say more about these views in a subsequent chapter of this essay on Lincoln's views on the issues of theodicy and the problem of evil, chapter 7. It is enough now, however, to conclude that

---

52. Garrison, "Great Crisis," originally delivered before the Lyceum at Roxbury. Later, it was published in the *Liberator* on December 29, 1832.

53. This meeting took place on July 22, 1862, with most of Lincoln's cabinet present. In addition to his thoughts about Antietam, he also told the cabinet members of his plans to announce the "Emancipation Proclamation" (Presidential Proclamation 95), which he did the following January 1, 1863.

54. Lincoln, Presidential Proclamation 93 (preliminary to the "Emancipation Proclamation"), September 22, 1862.

55. Lincoln, Presidential Proclamation 118, October 20, 1864.

56. Miller, *Lincoln's Virtues*, 363–66.

the law of necessity and divine plan theory were never very far from the thoughts of the sixteenth president.

At any rate, the words of Lincoln's second inaugural address are etched into the marble walls of the Lincoln Memorial in Washington, and thus they are viewed as being among his most memorable words. We have tried to show in this chapter of this essay that both of Mr. Lincoln's inaugural addresses contain a number of central ideas in regard to the sixteenth president's views on God and religion. Before Lincoln's inaugural addresses, only one president, John Quincy Adams, had quoted directly from Holy Scripture. Mr. Lincoln, of course, quoted chapter and verse a number of times, in his view to his great benefit.

The meaning and ultimate value of President Abraham Lincoln's second inaugural address is debated by a number of contemporary Lincoln scholars and thinkers. William Lee Miller, in his book *Lincoln's Virtues*, suggests that Lincoln's "practical wisdom" led to a "moral realism" that the president was "developing on the run." He argues that the speech shows an "ethic of prudent realism" that ultimately he labels an "ethic of responsibility."[57] For Miller, the most important elements in the second inaugural address are moral ones. Miller sees Lincoln's prudence as the moral virtue that led to his intellectual virtues.[58]

Ronald White, on the other hand, in his *Lincoln's Greatest Speech*, sees Lincoln's second inaugural as the result of the president's growing respect for the life of faith, especially in the light of the horrors of the war. For White, the "Meditation on the Divine Will" represents a profound shift in Lincoln's approach to God and to the war.[59]

White believe Lincoln's first inaugural shows the possibility of a providential God acting in the affairs of the nation; in the second inaugural, however, given thirty months later, Miller suggests that the sixteenth president expressed the view that God had willed the war as a just punishment for the sins of slavery, on both North and South.

Like Ronald White, James M. McPherson, in his essay "How Lincoln Won the War with Metaphors," suggests that Lincoln's second inaugural address was the height of Lincoln's rhetorical powers. McPherson says that Lincoln's power with metaphor, as well as particular kinds of metaphor, reflected his formative experiences in rural Indiana and Illinois. His skill with concrete images was nurtured, McPherson believes, with conversation with

---

57. Ibid.
58. White, "Lincoln's Greatest Speech," 10.
59. McPherson, "How Lincoln Won the War with Metaphors."

neighbors that would later become valuable in his communications with his political constituents.[60]

Ann Douglas, in the context of discussing the Calvinist background of Melville's *Billy Budd*, suggests that Captain Vere's unwillingness to spare Budd from execution is like Mr. Lincoln's reference to Luke 1:17 in the second inaugural address. She concludes that in Budd's tale, "History, presented in its uncompromised detail, merges, no matter how inscrutably and partially, and ambiguously, with Providence."[61]

Finally, in James Tackach's *Lincoln's Moral Vision*, he examines the meaning of Lincoln's second inaugural address in terms of what he sees as another example of Lincoln's White supremacy. Ultimately, Mr. Tackach understands the second inaugural as an exercise in Lincoln's "humiliation" on the question of race. As a result of that humiliation, Tackach maintains, Lincoln "reached back to find the Puritan God of his youth" in his second inaugural address. Very few subsequent scholars have shared Mr. Tackach's negative and critical views on Mr. Lincoln.

There is most likely some truth in each of these many approaches, but all agree that the second inaugural was one of Mr. Lincoln's most important speeches. It is quite possible, for example that Lincoln believed in divine plan theory, while simultaneously thinking that the use of metaphor is the best avenue to show that approach, or that Mr. Lincoln's divine plan theory was a new way of expressing his belief in the law of necessity, or determinism. At any rate, however, this brings us to the fourth chapter of this essay, in which we will discuss the uses of the Bible in Lincoln's many speeches and writings.

60. Tackach, *Lincoln's Moral Vision*.

61. Douglas, "Father and Son in 'Billy Budd.'"

CHAPTER 4

The Uses of the Bible in Lincoln's Speeches and Writings

There was one book . . . which left its mark on much of what he
wrote . That was the Bible. Upon a familiarity which extended back
to his youth he could always depend.

—PAUL ANGLE, *Lincoln's Power with Words*

My friend has said to me, I am a poor man to quote Scripture. I
will try again, however, but poor hand or not,
Lincoln was persistent.

—EARL SCHWARTZ, "A Poor Hand to Quote Scripture"

In regard to the great book, I have only to say it is the best gift
which God has ever given man. All the good from the Savior of the
world is communicated to us through this book.

—ABRAHAM LINCOLN[1]

OUR PRINCIPAL AIM IN this fourth chapter of this work on Abraham
Lincoln's religion is to describe and discuss the major views that the sixteenth president of the United States had of Holy Scripture. We will begin
the chapter with an analysis of four central conclusions we will make about

---

1. Quoted in "Presentation of a Bible to the President."

Lincoln's views on the Bible. This will be followed by some observations about how Mr. Lincoln used Holy Scripture, followed by a discussion of his favorite biblical passages. Finally, we will examine several versions of the biblical text that played roles both in childhood and in the adult life of Abraham Lincoln.

One of Abraham Lincoln biographers, William E. Barton, observed about the president, "He read the Bible, honored it, quoted it freely, and it became so much a part of him as visibly and more than any other First Executive before or since, regularly quoted from both the Old and the New Testaments."[2] In his many autobiographies, Mr. Lincoln himself frequently referred to his stepmother, Sarah Bush Lincoln, reminding him of the provisos "Thou shall not kill" and "Honor your father and mother."

We may make four major conclusions about Abraham Lincoln's uses of the Bible, in both his childhood and his adult life. First, the sixteenth president knew the Holy Scriptures intimately and thoroughly, and often quoted directly from them. In fact, Dennis Hanks, Lincoln's stepcousin, tells us that the president frequently read from the family Bible when they were children. Secondly, Lincoln used the 1611 King James Version of the Bible, as well as the 1557–1560 Geneva Bible, which was used by Shakespeare, Oliver Cromwell, John Knox, British poet John Donne, and John Bunyan, the author of *Pilgrim's Progress*, published in 1678. Indeed, the 1560 edition of the Geneva Bible was brought to the New World on the *Mayflower*, as Dr. Jiang has shown.[3] This is also the three-volume version of Holy Writ that Thomas Lincoln purchased in 1819, when Abraham was ten years old, which functioned as the Lincoln family Bible.

The Geneva Bible is also important for two other reasons. First, it was the first mass-produced, mechanical Bible to be made for the common people. And secondly, Oliver Cromwell gave a "pocketbook" edition of the Geneva Bible to all his soldiers during the English Revolution. This was the first time in Western history where soldiers carried the biblical text with them into battle.

The New Testament version of the Geneva Bible was published first in 1557. A few years later, in 1560, the Old Testament was produced. It was known as the Geneva Bible because it was published in Geneva, Switzerland. The text also contained significant translation notes. This new English Bible was dedicated to Queen Elizabeth I, who had been crowned Queen of England in 1558, following the death of Queen Mary I. Under Queen

---

2. Barton, *Soul of Abraham Lincoln*, 177.

3. The Pilgrim Hall Museum of Plymouth, Massachusetts, has a collection of Bibles from the Mayflower. Dr. Jiang is the curator of that exhibit.

Elizabeth, the persecution of Protestants was halted and she led believers back to the Anglican Church.

This led to later editions of the Geneva Bible being produced in England, beginning in 1576. All told, more than 150 editions of the Geneva Bible were published, with the 1644 version being the final and standard version of the Geneva Bible text. The first American edition of the Geneva Bible was published in Boston in 1599. A number of versions and editions of the Geneva Bible have been published in America since then.

The Geneva Bible predated the King James Bible by fifty-one years. It was the primary English Bible used by sixteenth-century Protestant Reformers, as well as Holy Writ for the likes of William Shakespeare, John Milton, John Knox, John Donne, and John Bunyan, as mentioned earlier. The annotations and notes of the Geneva Bible were Calvinistic in nature and Puritan in character. Indeed, it was one of the reasons that King James called for a new English translation, which appeared in 1611, for the king appears to have been dissatisfied with the Geneva Bible.

Needless to say, the King James Version replaced the Geneva Bible; but Protestant thinkers in America, like Abraham Lincoln's family, continued to quote from the Calvinist Geneva Bible. In Lincoln's adult life, many of his quotations from the Bible came from the Geneva Bible and not from the King James Version. In fact, the family Bible that Lincoln's father purchased in 1819 was a Geneva Bible, as indicated earlier. The notes to this chapter indicate when Mr. Lincoln was quoting from the Geneva Bible, as opposed to the King James Version.

Mr. Lincoln referred to the King James Version as the "Saxon Bible," a reference to its terse directness, something that Mr. Lincoln admired. In fact, more than two thirds of his two inaugural addresses, as well as his Gettysburg address, are words of one syllable. This made the language particularly supple in the hands of a skillful orator; but the plain words also served as a background in which Mr. Lincoln's most fundamental concepts, like "liberty" and "equality," could stand out starkly. Speeches like these are wonderful to the ear and provided the environment or a platform for the president's most fundamental beliefs.

By and large, the Geneva Bible is less terse and disjointed than the King James Version of the Bible. When Mr. Lincoln read the Bible in his early life, for the most part, it was the family's Geneva Bible, purchased by Thomas Lincoln in 1819.

A third major conclusion about Lincoln's uses of the Bible is that most of his allusions from and quotations of Holy Writ came from eight of his most important works. These are: his Peoria address (1854) his "House Divided Speech" (1858), his Chicago address (1858), in which he describes his views of the principle that all men are created equal; his Lewiston address (1858), in which the president entreats the nation to return, or "come back," to the "eternal principles" of the Declaration; in his "Word Fitly Spoken Speech" (1861), where Lincoln consciously identifies the Declaration with the Bible; his Gettysburg address (1863), in which he associates the founders of America with the patriarchs of the Old Testament; his second inaugural address (1865), where Mr. Lincoln puts forward a complex mural of divine providence; and finally, what he has to say in his many speeches and writings about the U.S. Constitution.

A final conclusion Lincoln made about the Bible did not come from Holy Writ. Rather, they sometimes came from other sources, independent of the Bible itself. One example is the end of his Gettysburg address and its language of "by the people and for the people." These words were actually borrowed from John Wycliffe, who completed the first great English translation of the biblical text in the mid-fourteenth century. In his preface to the introduction of his Old Testament translation, he emphasizes the importance of reading Holy Scripture in the "language of the people." Wycliffe writes, "The Bible is for the Government of the people, by the people, and for the people."[4]

Abraham Lincoln constantly employed passages from the Bible to communicate many of the ideas in his speeches and writings. In this chapter of this study, we shall examine a number of those instances where the sixteenth president quoted directly from Holy Scripture. At the close of this fourth chapter, we also will describe and discuss a number of Bibles that served roles in the life of Mr. Lincoln.

As early as his address to the Young Men's Lyceum in Springfield in 1838, Mr. Lincoln adopted biblical allusions and metaphors to characterize American ideals, by quoting Psalm 137:5–6, which tells us, "May my right hand lose its cunning and my tongue cleave to the roof of my mouth, If ever I prove false to those teachings" (KJV).[5] Here Mr. Lincoln seems to be concerned about remaining loyal to the biblical teachings that he ties to the principles of the founding documents of America.

The sixteenth president later employed the same verses, during the Civil War period, in his claim that America was the "new Jerusalem," and he understood himself as a kind of "new Moses," or a "new Joshua," who led the Jews after Moses's death. Many slave preachers, and Northern abolitionists, saw him that way, as well.

4. Wycliffe, *Wycliffe Bible*, 7.

5. Lincoln, address to the Young Men's Lyceum, January 27, 1838.

We will begin this chapter, then, by looking at twelve to twenty places in Holy Scripture where Lincoln quotes directly from the text. Half of these are from the New Testament and the others from the Old Testament. The first of these New Testament passages, Revelation 16:7–8, tells us this:

> And they heard another out of the altar say, "Even so, Lord Almighty, true and righteous are Thy judgments." And the fourth angel poured out his vial upon the Sun; and the power was given unto him to scorch men with fire. (KJV)

Mr. Lincoln uses this passage from Revelation within the context of the Civil War. Here, he reminds the participants in the war that God's judgments are "righteous," and power may still be meted out to "scorch men with fire." In another New Testament passage from the Gospel of Matthew 16:8, Lincoln likens himself to Saint Peter. The text tells us, "And I say unto thee, that thou art Peter, and upon this rock I shall build my church; and the gates of hell shall not prevail against it" (KJV). In conjunction with his employment of Matthew 16:7–8, Lincoln also uses Psalm 19:9, which in the King James Version tells us, "The fear of the Lord is clean, enduring forever; the judgments of the Lord are true and directed altogether."

Mr. Lincoln, during the Civil War years, frequently turned to apocalyptic passages of Scripture, full of tribulations and descriptions of the end times and the second coming of Jesus, in places like the book of Daniel and the book of Revelation. Indeed, the New Testament book most quoted by President Lincoln is the book of Revelation. This was most likely because the president understood the Civil War period as a time of great turmoil, and, in his mind, this turmoil would be followed by a time of great tribulation and punishment, of both the North as well as the South, for the sins of slavery and the Civil War.

Again, the context of Mr. Lincoln quoting this line is the midst of the American Civil War. In speaking of the Union, Lincoln proclaims that "The gates of hell shall not prevail against it." The church, of course, plays the part of the Union in the analogy, and Lincoln stands for Saint Peter, upon whom the church/Union will survive. Lincoln employed Acts 7:6–7 and Genesis 15:14 for similar purposes. In the first of these, the KJV gives us: "And God spoke to this effect—that his offspring would be sojourners in a land belonging to others, who would enslave them and inflict them for four hundred years. 'But I will judge the nation they serve,' said God, and after that they shall come out and worship me in this place."

The references to enslavement and sojourning are clear connections of the Jews in Egypt to America, the new Jerusalem. Mr. Lincoln uses a similar passage, Genesis 15:14, for similar purposes. The King James Version of the verse tells us, "But I will bring judgment on the nation that they serve, and afterwards they shall come out with great possessions."

A third New Testament passage of Mr. Lincoln's was one he quoted to Illinois Senator Stephen Douglas during the 1858 senatorial campaign, and which we have employed as an epigram to this chapter. The president said, "My friend has said to me that I am a poor hand to quote Scripture. I will try it again, however." Mr. Lincoln goes on to quote the words of Matthew 5:48 to Mr. Douglas: "Be ye therefore perfect, even as your Father which is in heaven, is perfect" (KJV).

The perfection to which Mr. Lincoln refers is clearly moral perfection. He enjoins Americans to attempt to achieve it as God has achieved it. The president also refers to the "house divided" passage in the fifth chapter of Matthew's Gospel. More will be said of Lincoln's uses of this verse later in this essay.

In another of the 1858 debates with Stephen Douglas, President Lincoln makes a comment about human nature in relationship to the Bible. He observed, "The Bible says somewhere that we are desperately selfish. I think we would have discovered that fact without the Bible. I do not claim that I am any less so than the average of men, but I do claim that I am not more selfish than Judge Douglas."[6]

Witnesses to the debate report that this comment was followed by a roar of laughter and applause coming from the crowd present. It is not clear where in the Bible Mr. Lincoln was referring to selfishness, but it may well have been at the Epistle of James 3:16, which tells us in the King James Version translation, "For where selfishness and strife is, there is confusion and every evil work."

As we shall see in a later chapter of this essay on ethics, chapter 5, Mr. Lincoln, among other theories, assented to a belief in what is sometimes called "ethical egoism," a view that maintains that human beings always act with their self-interest in mind, and that they ought to act that way. This view was popularized by books like Ayn Rand's *The Virtue of Selfishness*, published in 1964.

In the Peoria debate on October 16, 1854, Mr. Lincoln expressed his opposition to continue slavery in the Western Territories of the nation. In the final sentence, Lincoln expresses his major point—"slavery extension is wrong." In the middle of his comments that day, the sixteenth president provided a biblical reference that corresponds to Luke's version of the Sermon on the Mount, at 6:43–45. The King James Version of Lincoln's use of the text tells us:

6. Lincoln–Douglas debate in Alton, October 15, 1858.

For a good tree bringith not from corrupt fruit; neither doth a corrupt tree bring forth good fruit. For every tree is known by its own fruit. For of thorns, men do not gather figs, nor of a bramble bush do they gather grapes. A good man out of the good treasures of his heart bringith forth that which is good; and an evil man out of the evil treasure of his heart bringith forth that which is evil; for of the abundance of the heart his mouth speaketh.

Mr. Lincoln clearly assented to the belief that good men do not bear bad fruit and bad men do not bear good fruit. The president may also have been implying here that Judge Douglas, who he believed was a good man, may have been suggesting a morally bad thing—the spread of slavery into the Western Territories. Again, what better way to do that, on Mr. Lincoln's part, than to quote Holy Scripture in his favor.

William J. Johnson, in his work *Abraham Lincoln: The Christian*, cites a letter from Lincoln that the president sent from Petersburg, Illinois, in 1843 and was later published in the *Springfield Journal* of May 16, 1874. Mr. Lincoln is reported to have quoted the King James Version of 1 Corinthians 15: 22, to wit: "As in Adam all die, even so in Christ shall all be made alive."[7]

Johnson says that Lincoln "Followed this proposition that whatever the breach or injury of Adam's transgression to the human race was, which no doubt was very great, it was made just and right by the Atonement of Christ."[8] If Lincoln did, in fact, utter these words, then at least in 1843 Mr. Lincoln ascribed to the doctrine of the atonement.

William Herndon, however, disagreed with this assessment, suggesting that Lincoln at the time did not have a belief in such a central idea of traditional Protestant Christianity. At any rate, if Mr. Johnson was correct, then 1 Corinthians 15:22 was another important New Testament passage in the belief system of Abraham Lincoln.

On another occasion, Clarence Macartney, in his work *Lincoln and the Bible*, describes a dying woman asking the president to read to her from the Bible. Rather than reading, however, Lincoln is said to have recited from memory the Twenty-Third Psalm, as well as Jesus's farewell speech to his disciples, "Let not your hearts be troubled," from the Gospel of John 14:1–3.[9]

Mr. Lincoln refers to a version of the "hoisted by his own petard" theme in an August 24, 1855, letter to his friend Joshua Speed. He quotes

7. Johnson, *Abraham Lincoln, the Christian*.
8. Ibid.
9. Macartney, *Lincoln and the Bible*, 17–18.

the Geneva Bible version of Esther 7:9–10, when he wrote that Persian Haman was "hanged upon the gallows of his own building." Haman had prepared those gallows for Mordecai and was executed on those same gallows.

Indeed, far more often, however, our sixteenth president quoted from the Old Testament. We turn next to several examples, some of which are still in the context of the Civil War. Mr. Lincoln makes reference, for example, to the third chapter of Genesis. After Senator Douglas has mentioned Adam and Eve in their debates, Mr. Lincoln responded, "God did not place good and evil before man, telling him to make his choices. On the contrary, he did tell them there was one tree, of the fruit of which he should not eat, upon pain of certain death."[10]

This comment tells us something of how acutely aware President Lincoln was of the ethical dimensions of the narrative found in Genesis 3. The tree from which Adam and Eve were not supposed to eat, of course, was the tree of the knowledge of good and evil; and if they were to eat it, "in that day they surely would die," as it tells us in verse 3 of the third chapter of Genesis. Mr. Lincoln's response to Mr. Douglas was a subtle one, far more so than Judge Douglas's understanding of Genesis 3. Douglas believed the passage in Genesis 3 was about human free will and the ability to choose between right and wrong; but, more properly, Mr. Lincoln saw the passage as the product of the grace of God, and the consequences of human sin.

Mr. Lincoln is said to have added about the narrative in question, "I should scarcely wish so strong a prohibition against slavery in Nebraska," a reference to the question of slavery in the Western Territories, the topic of the Lincoln-Douglas Debates, and Mr. Lincoln's opposition to that proposition.[11]

Scholar Elton Trueblood writes of Lincoln's relationship to the Bible in his early life. Trueblood says:

> While it is generally recognized that young Lincoln heard many passages from the Bible, both in his cabin home and in the Baptist Meeting House, it is not equally known that he also encountered it in his fragmentary schooling. In this, as in many aspects of his development, our most reliable evidence is that provided by the man himself.[12]

Mr. Trueblood goes on to describe a scene at the Lincoln White House, where the president is speaking with Senator John B. Henderson. "Henderson," the president asked the senator, "Did you ever attend an old blab

10. Lincoln–Douglass debate in Alton, October 15, 1858.

11. Ibid.

12. Trueblood, *Abraham Lincoln: Lessons in Spirituality*, 147.

school?" "Yes." "Well so did I. I attended such a school in a log schoolhouse in Indiana, where we had no reading books or grammars, and all our reading was done from the Bible."[13] Mr. Lincoln continued: "We stood in a long line and read in turn, one by one, from it."[14]

"Blab school" is a term used in the nineteenth-century in America, where students recited or "blabbed" their lessons out loud, separately, or in a chorus with others, to accentuate or enhance learning. William Mentor Graham, in his New Salem schoolhouse, employed this educational method. It is most likely the school of Mr. Graham to which President Lincoln refers in this passage.

It appears, then, that Mr. Lincoln had read the Bible and listened to it being recited, long before his father was able to afford to purchase one for his family. Indeed, Lincoln's cousin Dennis Hanks tells us that a family Bible was not purchased until the year 1819, when Lincoln was only ten years old.[15] This Lincoln family Bible was a copy of the three-volume Geneva Bible, as we have indicated earlier.

Mr. Lincoln had a tendency to search the Scriptures for an image or a metaphor to help describe the nation's situation at any given time. He employed Exodus 22:21; Deuteronomy 16:15; Jeremiah 7; and Isaiah 1:4, for examples, to describe the sins of the nation during the Civil War, on both sides. Lincoln used Proverbs 25:11–12, and its image of an apple of gold set in a picture of silver, to describe the U.S. Constitution.

In Mr. Lincoln's reference to a "return to the fountain whose waters spring close by the blood of the Revolution," in his "Lewistown Speech" from August 17, 1858, he may have been referring to the Song of Songs 4:15; Jeremiah 2:13; or, possibly Isaiah 58:11.[16]

At the close of the same address, Lincoln mentions "vanity and vexation of spirit," an obvious reference to Ecclesiastes 4:1–4, and its pervasive use of the Hebrew term *hevel*, or "vanity," employed throughout the book.[17]

In a letter to Thurlow Weed from March 15, 1865, Lincoln also refers to Psalm 19:9, which tells us in the King James Version, "The fear of the Lord

13. Ibid.

14. Ibid, 148.

15. Donald, *Lincoln*, 26–27.

16. All of these texts refer to fountains, or "fountains of living waters," as the verse in Jeremiah tells us.

17. The classical Hebrew word *hevel*, or *hebel*, is employed in the Hebrew Bible in a variety of ways. It sometimes means "vanity," "breath," "emptiness," "futility," "uselessness," "vapor," "worthlessness," and a variety of other concepts. It is one of the most elusive terms in the Old Testament.

is clean, enduring forever; the judgments of the Lord are true and righteous altogether," to indicate the inevitable judgment to follow after the Civil War.

Mr. Lincoln employed the language of America as a "New Jerusalem" in his comments at Gettysburg in regard to "bring forth a new nation." This echoes 2 Chronicles 6:5, "I brought forth my people out of Egypt," and verses 24–25 of the Gospel of Matthew's first chapter, which tells us in the KJV:

> Then Joseph being raised from sleep did as the Angel of the Lord had bidden him, and took unto him his wife; and he knew her not until she brought forth her first-born son: and he called his name Jesus.

In Psalm 137:4–5, Mr. Lincoln again found a metaphor for seeing America as the "New Jerusalem." The KJV's rendering of the couplet asks us, "How shall we sing the Lord's song in a strange land; if I forget then, O Jerusalem, let my right hand forget her cunning." In many times throughout his adult life, our sixteenth president searched the Old and New Testaments to find just the perfect image to aid him in a current struggle, or a given situation.

Mr. Lincoln, along with Rabbi David Einhorn, used Genesis 1:27–31, where man is made in God's image and likeness, as an argument against slavery; he employed Deborah's words in Judges 5:31, during the Civil War years, during the Battle of Antietam, that "Our worst enemy is laid low"; and he quoted the book of Job 2:28 and the Acts of the Apostles 2:17, in an exchange with Canadian Christian Zionist Henry Wentworth Monk, "Your old men shall dream dreams and your young men shall have visions."

Even Mr. Lincoln's famed "House Divided Speech," delivered during his Illinois Senate campaign in 1858, was actually occasioned after thinking of the third chapter of Mark and Matthew 12:25, which tells us, "And Jesus knew their thoughts, and said unto them, 'Every kingdom divided against itself is brought to desolation; and every city or house divided against itself shall not stand'" (KJV). This line later became particularly important to Mr. Lincoln during the Civil War. In the speech, Mr. Lincoln begins by quoting Matthew 12:25. Then he continues:

> I believe that this government cannot endure, permanently, half slave and half free. I do not expect the Union to be dissolved—I do not expect the house to fall—but I do expect it will cease to be divided. It will become all one thing, or all the other. Either the opponents of slavery will arrest the further spread of it, and place it where the public mind shall rest in the belief that it is in the course of ultimate extinction; or its advocates will push it

forward, till it shall become alike lawful in all states, old as well as new—North as well as South.[18]

Mr. Lincoln suggested here that America will either be free in every state, or slavery will be allowed throughout America in the future. But he firmly believed that the current situations in the North and the South would not survive much longer. Clearly, he was prescient about that matter.

This comment is important, as well, because we begin to see a shift in focus right before and during the war years. In the beginning, Lincoln's goal was the integrity and preservation of the Union, but by the middle of the war the goal had shifted to the abolition of slavery and the establishment of the rights of Black Americans.

The origin of the "House Divided Speech" may also be the Gospel of Luke 11:17, which tells us in the King James Version, "But he, knowing their thoughts, said unto them, 'Every kingdom divided against itself is brought to desolation; and a house divided against itselfshall falleth.'"

The "with malice toward none" passage of the "House Divided Speech" may have been inspired by the King James Version's translation of 1 Peter 2:1, which says, "Wherefore laying aside all malice, and all guile, and hypocrisies, and envies, and all evil speakings." And the references to "widows" and "orphans" in that address may well have come from James 1:27, which tells us, "Pure religion and undefiled before God and the Father is this, to visit the fatherless. And widows in their affliction, and to keep him unspotted from the world."

Nevertheless, Mr. Lincoln appears to have had a number of favorite passages from the Old Testament. Among these were: 1 Samuel 22:2; Proverbs 13:10; Genesis 3, mentioned earlier; and Psalm 56:–78, which says in the King James Version, "Shall they escape by iniquity? In thine anger cast down the people, O God. Thou tellest my wanderings: put though my tears into thy bottle: are they not in Thy book?"

About these verses, Mr. Lincoln says, "Record my lament; list my tears on your scroll—are they not on Your record?" He adds, "Tears are prayers too. They travel to God when we cannot speak." This comment may be related to the Old Testament and Quranic belief that the thoughts and actions of human beings are recorded on a scroll, or on a record, long before they actually occur. In Islam, the job of recording these human deeds is assigned by Allah to angels, or mala'ika in Arabic—one records the good deeds, and aother the evil ones. We mentioned these malakayn, the dual form for angels, in our earlier analysis.

18. Lincoln, "House Divided Speech," June 16, 1858.

Indeed, in Islam these angels will read out loud the deeds they had recorded at the resurrection of the dead. The Qur'an, the holy book, at 36:12 tells us, "It is We indeed who bring back the dead to life, and write down what they send ahead (of their deeds), and traces that they leave behind. We keep account of all things in a lucid Register."[19]

The "lucid register" mentioned in the above quotation is a "Book of Deeds" of an individual recorded by the *malakayn*, which they will read out loud on the resurrection of the dead, also called the "Day of Doom" or the "Day of Reckoning" in Islam, to signify the end of time. This reading is to take place before Allah and the other *mala'ika*, or angels, in Arabic.[20]

The sixteenth president's knowledge of the Bible was so great that when he heard that only four hundred people attended a rally in Ohio, he searched through his Old Testament to find a passage that told of King David and the men who gathered around him at the cave of Adullam when they were pursued by King Saul. The passage Mr. Lincoln was searching for was 1 Samuel 22:2:

> And everyone that was in distress, and everyone that was in debt, and everyone that was discontented, gathered themselves unto him; and he became a Captain over them; and there were with him about four hundred men. (KJV)

Thus, "Mr. Lincoln employed his knowledge of the Bible to describe and to ridicule his critics, complainers, and malcontents who had gathered about Fremont," wrote Clarence Edward McCartney, in his work *Lincoln and the Bible*.[21] In a discussion with the secretary of war, Edwin Stanton, Mr. Lincoln accused Stanton of not carrying out an order he had given him. Lincoln said:

> If you get your Bible and turn to the 13th chapter of Proverbs, the 10th verse, you will read these words, "Accuse not a servant unto his master, lest he curse thee, and thou be found guilty."[22]

Mr. Stanton (1817–1869) is reported to have said to the president, "There is no such passage!"[23] The following morning, after consulting his Bible in the private residence of the White House. When he appeared a few moments

19. See Lang, *Christian Historical Devotional*, 256.

20. Qur'an 36:12 (author's translation).

21. Macartney, *Lincoln and the Bible*, 84.

22. Quoted in Basler, *Collected Works of Abraham Lincoln*, 501.

23. Ibid.

later with his Bible in hand, he read the identical passage that Mr. Stanton believed did not exist.[24]

On another occasion, Mr. Lincoln refers to chapter 19 of the book of Exodus. He asks, "Do you remember when the Lord was on Mount Sinai getting out a commission for Aaron, that same Aaron was at the foot of the mountain making a false god for the People to worship. Yet Aaron got his commission, you know?"[25]

In his Gettysburg address, Mr. Lincoln speaks of the possibility of the guilt of the Civil War passing on to subsequent generations by quoting Exodus 20:5; 34:7; and Deuteronomy 5:9, which speak of "guilt to the third and fourth generation." Mr. Lincoln speaks in somber tones of this possibility, and hopes to God that it does not come to pass. The famous passage in the opening of the Gettysburg address, "Four score and seven years ago, our fathers brought forth, upon this continent, a new nation," is actually an indirect quotation of the King James Version of Psalm 90:10. This verse tells us, "The days of our years are three score years and ten; and if by reason of strength they be four score, yet is their strength labor and sorrow; for it is soon cut off, and we fly away."

The expression "fourscore" also can be found at Genesis 16:16; Exodus 7:7; 2 Samuel 19:32; and Joshua 14:10–11, as Mr. Lincoln surely must have known. Like many of his other speeches, Mr. Lincoln wanted to give the address a certain kind of gravity and solemnity. What better way to do that than to cloak the speech in the garb of the Bible. In the third paragraph of the Gettysburg address, the president continued the biblical allusions by speaking of a "new birth of freedom . . . a government by the people and for the people, that shall not perish from the earth."[26] This government was to be a "New Jerusalem," a new "Promised Land," made up of people "all created equal and endowed with certain inalienable rights."

At other times, Mr. Lincoln's references to Holy Scripture were in regard to a particular topic. Recalling a dream that foretold his death, for example, the sixteenth president gave a brief sermon on dreams in the Bible. He observes:

> It seems strange how much there is in the Bible about dreams. There are, I think, some sixteen chapters in the Old Testament, and four or five in the New, in which dreams are mentioned; and

---

24. Ibid.

25. See Exodus 19:9–25.

26. Lincoln, Gettysburg address, November 19, 1863.

there are many other passages scattered throughout the book
which refers to visions.[27]

In point of fact, Mr. Lincoln was entirely correct about the number of "chapters" in the Old Testament devoted to dreams—sixteen. These passages
come at:

1. Abimlelech's dream at Genesis 20:3

2. Jacob's dream at Genesis 28:12–16

3. Jacob's dream at Genesis 31:10

4. Laban's warning at Genesis 31:24

5. Joseph's grain at Genesis 37:5–7

6. Joseph's stars at Genesis 37:9

7. The dream of Pharoah's chief cupbearer at Genesis 40:9–11

8. The dream of Pharoah's chief baker at Genesis 40:16–17

9. Pharoah's dream at Genesis 41:1–7

10. Midianites conquered by Gideon in Judges 7

11. Solomon's blank check at 1 Kings 3:5–15

12. Nebuchadnezzar's dream in Daniel 2

13. Nebuchadnezzar's dream in Daniel 4

14. Daniel's dream on his bed in Daniel 7

15. Daniel's vision in Daniel 8

16. Daniel's vision at Daniel 10:7–14

Mr. Lincoln also was correct about the number of dreams in the New Testament, which actually is six. These are: Joseph being told in a dream to marry
Mary at Matthew 1:20; his fleeing to Egypt, at Matthew 2:13; his return, at
Matthew 2:19; a dream that told him to go to Galilee, at Matthew 2:22; the
magi being warned in a dream not to return home the same way they had
arrived, at Matthew 2:12; and Pontius Pilate's wife, who has a nightmare
about Jesus' trial because she knows he is innocent, at Matthew 27:19.

27. See Moss, "Lincoln's Dreams." William Hill Lamon, friend and body guard of
Mr. Lincoln, and one of the early biographers of the sixteenth president, suggests that
Mr. Lincoln had a premonition of his own assassination on April 14, 1865. Mr. Lamon
says that the president revealed that he walked into the East Room of the White House
to find a covered corpse guarded by soldiers. When Lincoln inquired from one of the
soldiers, "Who died?," the soldier reportedly answered, "The president. He was cut
down by an assassin."

Mr. Lincoln adds this exposition of these passages:

> In the olden days, God and His angels came to men in their sleep
> and made themselves known in dreams. Nowadays, dreams are
> regarded as very foolish, and are seldom told, except by old
> women and by young men and maidens in love.[28]

Not long after the time of Lincoln, of course, Western Europe began to see
the application of another interpretive tool for interpreting dreams—the
psychoanalytic theory of Sigmund Freud and his positing of the unconscious. In his *The Interpretation of Dreams*, Freud sketches out his view that
one way that the repression of one's impulses may be played out is in dreams,
for they have a way, Freud maintains, of coming to the surface in disguised
forms. One way that these urges and impulses are released is through one's
dreams. Because the content of the unconscious mind may be extremely
disturbing or harmful, Freud believed that the unconscious expresses itself
in symbolic language through dreams.

At any rate, other Old Testament passages employed over the years
by Mr. Lincoln included Genesis 3:19; 2 Samuel 19:32; Joshua 14:10–11;
and 2 Chronicles 6:5. This reference to the "apple of gold" is a reference
to Proverbs 25:11, which, in the King James Version, tells us, "A word fitly
spoken is like apples of gold in pictures of silver." Mr. Lincoln employed this
verse in an exchange of letters with Alexander H. Stephens (1812–1883),
who implored the president to say something about the preservation of the
Constitution. In his "Fragment on the Constitution and the Union," in January of 1861, the sixteenth president responded by saying:

> The expression of that principle, in our Declaration of Indepen-
> dence, was most happy and fortunate. Without this, as well as
> with it, we could not have declared our independence of Great
> Britain . . . The assertion of that principle, at that time, was the
> word fitly spoken, which has proved an apple of gold to us.[29]

In this speech, Mr. Lincoln likens the Declaration of Independence and the
U.S. Constitution to "apples of gold in a silver frame." For him, these were
the most valuable documents, with their basic human rights, that the republic was in possession of at his time—an apt use of the biblical reference.

Mr. Lincoln employed Genesis 3:19 on four different occasions, principally to bolster the idea that all men should profit from the benefits of their
own labor. Lincoln uses the verse for these purposes in his "Fragment of a
Tariff Discussion, from December 1, 1847; in a "Response to the Preamble

28. Schwartz, "Poor Hand to Quote Scripture."

29. Lincoln, fragment on the Constitution and Union, January 18, 1861.

and Resolutions of the American Baptist Home Missionary Society," on May 30, 1864; to the *Washington Daily Chronicle*, from December 6, 1864; and in his second inaugural address, on March 4, 1865.

In this latter source, as we have pointed out in an earlier chapter of this essay, Mr. Lincoln said, "It may seem strange that any men should dare to ask a just God's assistance in wringing their bread from the sweat of the other men's faces."[30] The sixteenth president follows this up with a moral judgment from Matthew 7:1: "But let us judge not that we not be judged" (KJV). Mr. Lincoln refers to the Gospel of John 1:47 to speak of an "Israelite without guile" in the same address.

Mr. Lincoln also makes references to the book of Joel 2:7—3:1 to Henry Wentworth Monk,[31] to Daniel 9:25, to Numbers 6:24 and 12:11, and to Deuteronomy 20:8. The latter text occurred in the context of a Jewish soldier having deserted the Union army and Baltimore Rabbi Benjamin Szold (1829–1902) appealing to the president for clemency for the young man. The rabbi quoted Deuteronomy 20:8, "What man is fearful and faint-hearted? Let him go and return unto his house lest his brother's heart faint, as well as his own."[32]

Mr. Lincoln is reported to have responded to the rabbi, "If I were to follow the instructions laid down here, I would not have a man in the field in a week's time."[33] Curiously enough, Lincoln sent the rabbi to speak to the commanding officer of the accused, but he denied the appeal for clemency. As the time for the Jewish soldier's execution neared, Rabbi Szold is said to have clung to the man and kissed him gently.[34]

In the brief letter from November 4, 1862, penned on official letter-head of the "Executive Mansion, Washington," Mr. Lincoln told Rabbi Szold that if he followed his advice he would soon have no soldiers left. Therefore, as mentioned above, he denied the Rabbi's request.

On another occasion, in a letter to Ohio governor Salmon Chase, Mr. Lincoln invoked the apocalyptic language of the book of Daniel 9:25, which speaks of "these troub'lous times" (GB). In his second inaugural address, Mr.

---

30. Lincoln, second inaugural address, March 4, 1865.

31. Henry Wentworth Monk (1827–1896) was a Canadian-born Christian Zionist. He was educated in London and spent considerable time in Palestine. See Peter A. Russell's article on Monk in the *Dictionary of Canadian Biography*, vol. 12 (2003).

32. Rabbi Benjamin Szold (1829–1902) was born in Hungary, studied at a Yeshiva in Eastern Europe, and then moved to Baltimore, where he became the chief rabbi at Oheb Shalom Synagogue. His papers are owned by the Maryland Jewish Museum, where they can be found as MS 37 and MS 38.

33. Ibid.

34. Ibid.

Lincoln employs Numbers 6:24, which tells us in the King James Version, "May the Lord bless thee and keep thee." The sixteenth president turns to Numbers 12:11 after months of frustration with General Robert H. Milroy (1816–1890) for being disobedient and for battlefield failures. The president chose this text because Moses had faulted in his judgment upon striking the rock in the desert, after being instructed by God to do so. Lincoln tells Milroy, "This, my dear General, is, I fear, the rock on which you have split."[35]

Like the disobedient Moses, General Milroy's mistakes thus have had irrevocable consequences, thereby sealing his irreversible fate. General Robert H. Milroy (1816–1890) was a lawyer, a judge, and a military general. He studied at the Captain Partridge Academy, affiliated with Norwich University. He is best known for commanding Union troops at the Battle of McDowell, also known as the Battle of Sitlington's Hill, fought on May 8, 1862.

One final reference to Abraham Lincoln's view of the Bible comes from Elizabeth Keckley (1818–1907.) Keckley was a former slave and seamstress for Mary Lincoln, and the author of the autobiography *Behind the Scenes: Or, Thirty Years a Slave and Four Years in the White House*, published in 1868. Keckley, called "Lizzy" by the Lincolns, was born into slavery in Virginia. Eventually she bought her freedom from her Saint Louis, Missouri, master for twelve hundred dollars. She made her way to Washington, DC, and in 1860 she began working for Mrs. Lincoln.

In her autobiography, Lizzy Keckley reports the president returning to the White House after having been to the War Department. The dressmaker wrote, "His step was slow and heavy and his face sad. Like a tired child, he threw himself upon a sofa, and shaded his eyes with his hands. He was a complete picture of dejection."[36] He reported that the news from the War Department was "dark, dark everywhere."[37] Keckley then reports that Mr. Lincoln took a small Bible from a stand near the sofa and began to read.

Fifteen minutes passed, and Keckley observed, "I then glanced at the sofa and the face of the President seemed more cheerful. The dejected look was gone; in fact, the countenance was lighted up with new resolution and hope." Wanting to see what Mr. Lincoln was reading, she went behind the sofa and gazed over Lincoln's shoulder to see what he was reading. She reported:

---

35. Robert Huston Milroy (1816–1890) was a lawyer, judge, and Union general. He is most noted for his defeat at the Second Battle of Winchester in 1863.

36. Keckley, *Behind the Scenes*.

37. Ibid., 20.

> I discovered that Mr. Lincoln was reading the Divine comfort of the Book of Job. He read with Christian earnestness, and the courage and hope that he had derived from the inspired pages also had made him a new man. I almost imagined that I could hear the Lord speaking to him from out of the whirlwind of battle. "Gird up thy loins like a man; I will demand of thee, and declare thou unto me," she wrote.[38]

Mrs. Lincoln's seamstress Lizzy Keckley quotes directly from two different passages from the biblical book of Job 38:1, which that speaks of God speaking "from a whirlwind," and 40:7, where God tells Job to "Gird up his loins like a man . . ."

Lizzy Keckley then added her own sense of wonder. She wrote, "What a sublime picture this was! A ruler of a mighty nation going to the pages of the Bible with Christian earnestness for comfort and courage, and finding both in the darkest hours of a nation's calamity. Ponder it, oh you scoffers of God's Holy Word, and then hang your heads for very shame."[39] Like the biblical character Job, Mr. Lincoln faced his calamities of Willie's death and the war going badly with patience and fortitude—attributes of Lincoln's to which we shall return in chapter 7 of this essay, on the problem of evil.

On another occasion, Mr. Lincoln was visited by his friend Joshua Speed, who found the president reading the Bible, at which Mr. Speed was surprised. Lincoln is reported to have said that his friend still maintained his earlier skepticism, but he, on the other hand, had given it up. The sixteenth president is said to have then made some remarks about the value of reading the sacred Scriptures, particularly its moral aspects.[40] This was the only occasion from 1861 until his death in 1865 when Lincoln saw Joshua Speed and William Henry Herndon personally saw Mr. Lincoln, when he had invited both to the White House.

Abraham Lincoln also quoted Scripture regularly in his letters throughout his adult life. In a letter to J. M. Peck, for example, he wrote, "Whatsoever ye would that man should do to you, do ye even so to them," an obvious reference to the Golden Rule at the Gospel of Matthew 7:12.[41] In a another letter to Williamson Durley, Lincoln included the words, "By the fruit of the tree you shall be known," an adaptation of Matthew 7:15–20.

When Lincoln's father, Thomas Lincoln, was on his deathbed, he wrote to Dr. John D. Johnston, who was treating the father, "Remind him of the

---

38. Ibid.
39. Ibid.
40. Quoted in Carson, Lincoln's Ethics, 302.
41. Lincoln, letter to J. M. Peck, November 21, 1848.

fall of the sparrow and the number of hairs on his head, and that his Maker will not forget the dying."[42] This is a reference to the Gospel of Luke 12:7, in the New Testament. Again, like thinkers of the Enlightenment, Mr. Lincoln refers to God as his "Maker," like the deists.

In another letter to a Mr. Richard Speer, the president writes, "If they hear not Moses and the Prophets, neither will they be persuaded over one who rose from the dead," a clear reference to Jesus Christ.[43] Mr. Lincoln often quoted directly from Scripture in his letters or gave a short summary of a biblical tale he thought appropriate at the moment.

Mr. Lincoln also mentions the Bible in an exchange of letters between Black abolitionist Sojourner Truth (1797–1883) and the sixteenth president. Ms. Truth wrote to the president that his predicament during the Civil War "reminds me of Daniel in the Lion's Den." Mr. Lincoln wrote back to Ms. Truth a letter full of references taken from the book of Revelation. Later, on October 29, 1864, Mr. Lincoln and Ms. Truth met at the White House, where the President showed Ms. Truth the Bible he had been given by the "colored" ministers from Baltimore, which we shall discuss later in this fourth chapter of this essay.[44]

Sojourner Truth was born Isabella Baumfree into slavery in Ulster County, New York, but she escaped to freedom with her infant daughter in 1826. In going to court to recover her son, she became the first African-American woman to be successful in an American court. During the Civil War, she recruited African-American men to fight for the Union. She made the trip to Washington to visit President Lincoln in the fall of 1864, when she was sixty-seven years old.

When Sojourner Truth first met the president, like her letter, she is reported to have said to Mr. Lincoln:

> When you first took your seat I feared you would be torn to pieces, for I likened you unto Daniel who was thrown into the lion's den; and if the lions did not tear you to pieces, I knew it would be God that has saved you; and I said if he spared me I would see you before the four years expired, and he has done so, and now I am here to see you for myself.[45]

Mr. Lincoln is reported to have responded that at times he has felt the kind of despondency that is exhibited by Daniel in the lion's den. This gives us further evidence of just how familiar the sixteenth president of the United

42. Lincoln, letter to John D. Johnston, November 4, 1851

43. Lincoln, letter to Richard Speer, October 23, 1860.

44. Lincoln, letter to Sojourner Truth, October 29, 1864.

45. Ibid.

States was to the content of Holy Scripture, as well as its many uses. On another occasion, Mr. Lincoln was meeting with Secretary of War Edwin Stanton, who was angry with an army officer. Lincoln suggested he write the officer a letter, which the secretary did and showed the angry words to the president. Lincoln is said to have asked Stanton, ""What are you going to do with the letter?" His response: "Send it!" The president then shook his head, and is reported to have said to Mr. Stanton:

> You don't want to send that letter. Put it in the stove. That's what I do when I have written a letter while I was angry. It's a good letter and you had a good time writing it and now you feel better. Now burn it and write another.[46]

The "stove" mentioned here is not an appliance. Rather, it is a reference to the stovepipe hat worn by Mr. Stanton and other gentlemen, including Abraham Lincoln, during the time of the Civil War.

Mr. Lincoln's unsent letter to his generals in the Western Theatre of the Civil War, discussed in a previous chapter of this essay, is an excellent example of this phenomenon. At other times, Mr. Lincoln reported that he carried angry letters around in his stovepipe hat for a few days until he had cooled off.[47] He also says he carried other important papers of state in the same place, many of them sprinkled with biblical quotations. There is also significant evidence, however, that at times Mr. Lincoln was ambivalent about the value of the truth of Scriptures, at least in his skeptical period.

On one occasion he had his photograph taken while he was reading a large book to his son Tad. Mr. Lincoln complained when he saw the picture that some would believe he was reading the Bible to his son, when in fact it was a child's picture book.[48] On another occasion, Lincoln was discussing Holy Scripture with treasury official Lucius Chittendon. The president is reported to have said, "Now let us treat the Bible fairly. If we had a witness on the stand whose general story we knew to be true, we would believe him when he asserted facts of which we had no other evidence."[49]

Lucius Eugene Chittendon (1824–1900) was a Vermont-born author, banker, attorney, and political figure. He served as the register of the treasury under President Lincoln during the Civil War period.

46. Flowers, *Edwin McMasters Stanton*, 109.
47. Ibid.
48. Carter, "Mr. Lincoln's Top Hat."
49. Chittendon, *Recollections of President Lincoln*, 449–50.

Mr. Lincoln adds, "We ought to treat the Bible with equal fairness."[50] But then he adds this hint of skepticism:

> I decided a long time ago that it was less difficult to believe that the Bible is what it claimed to be than to disbelieve it. It is a good book for us to obey. It contains the ten commandments, the Golden Rule, and many others which ought to be followed. No man was ever the worse for living according to the directions of the Bible.[51]

Mr. Lincoln appears to express his ambivalence about the truth of Scripture; but then he also makes some simple observations about the nature of the moral good, buttressed in his view by the Golden Rule and the Ten Commandments. Much more will be said about Mr. Lincoln's views on ethics and morality in a subsequent chapter of this essay, chapter 5.

Another piece of evidence that Mr. Lincoln was ambivalent about the truths of Scripture is the letter written to Mary Speed about the Bible that her mother Lucy G. Speed had given to Lincoln during a bout of melancholy over the breakup of his engagement with Mary Todd in the winter of 1841. At the end of the letter, Lincoln wrote, "I doubt not that it [the Bible] is really, as she says, the best cure for the blues, could one but take it according to the Truth."[52]

Again, Mr. Lincoln seems to be ambivalent about the value of Scripture, and he goes on to say that the gift of the Bible from Mrs. Lucy Speed could help him overcome his melancholy, if only he could believe it were true.

This is an implicit tone of desperation in the letter to Mary Speed in the words "could one but take it according to the Truth." In other words, the sixteenth president wished to take the Bible at face value, realizing that his life might be much easier if he did so; but his ability to be rational and critically to examine arguments from multiple angles was as much a hallmark of his character as his intellectual might. Confederate military figure Albert Taylor Bledsoe suggests that in the 1840s Lincoln seemed to have deplored his want of faith as a felicity from which he would be glad to be delivered; so there is ample evidence that at times Mr. Lincoln was ambivalent about the value, validity, or the truth of Scripture.

Albert Taylor Bledsoe (1809–1877) was an Episcopal priest, attorney, and professor of mathematics, in addition to being a Confederate general. He also was a graduate of the military academy at West Point—one of the

50. Ibid.

51. Ibid.

52. Lincoln, letter to Mary Speed, September 27, 1841.

many West Point graduates who served as generals in the Civil War, on both sides of the conflict.

Another aspect of Mr. Lincoln's views on Holy Scripture are a number of different copies of the Bible that played roles in the life of the sixteenth president. There is the Bible that Lincoln had received from the Society for the Propagation of Christian Knowledge. In addition to the text of Scripture, the Bible also contained "Arguments prefixed to the different books and moral and theological discourses illustrating each chapter."

These were composed by the Rev. Jean-Frederick Ostervald (1663–1747), a Swiss Protestant professor of divinity. Mr. Lincoln retained this three-volume family Bible until his death. When he is described as reading or discussing the Bible at the White House, it was usually this Geneva family Bible.

There was a Bible that the mother of Lincoln's friend Joshua Speed, Lucy G. Speed, gave the president in the summer of 1841. It was a copy of the Oxford Bible, quite popular in Mr. Lincoln's day. The president had acquired the Bible after his engagement to Mary Todd had been broken off in the winter of 1841, and Mr. Lincoln visited the Speed family in Kentucky while grieving over the event.

In the autumn of that same year, Lincoln wrote to Mary Speed, the daughter of the woman who had given him the Bible, and the brother of Joshua Speed, Mr. Lincoln's close friend. The president wrote, "Tell your mother that I have not got her 'present' with me; but I intend to read it regularly when I return home. I doubt not that it is really, as she says, the best cure for the 'Blues,' could one but take it for the truth."[53] This was during Lincoln's skeptical period, so there is little wonder that he seems to be doubtful of the literal truth of the Scriptures here.

A third Bible related to Mr. Lincoln came into the president's life when he forgot to bring a Bible for his first inaugural in March of 1861. William Thomas Carroll, the clerk of the U.S. Supreme Court, brought a Bible from his office that he kept on hand just for such emergency circumstances. Mr. Lincoln took his oath swearing on this Bible. Since that day, it is known as the "Lincoln Bible." It remained with the Lincoln family until 1928, at which point the widow of Robert Todd Lincoln donated the Bible to the Library of Congress.

The Lincoln Bible was published by Oxford University Press in 1853. It is six inches long, four inches wide, and forty-four millimeters, or two inches, thick. The Lincoln Bible is bound in burgundy red velvet with gilt edges. President Barack Obama, in both 2009 and 2013, as well as president

53. Ibid.

Donald Trump in 2017, were sworn in using this Lincoln Bible. When Carla Hayden, the fourteenth librarian of Congress, was sworn in on September 14, 2016, the Lincoln Bible also was employed at her ceremony.

A final Bible that served a role in the life of Abraham Lincoln was the one presented to Mr. Lincoln by a group of freed slaves from Baltimore in 1864, in the midst of the Civil War. These Protestant ministers, who in the language of the day called themselves "colored men," presented the president with the Bible that is now owned by the Fiske University Library. Robert Todd Lincoln's widow had donated the Bible there in the 1920s.[54]

A September 11, 1864, article from the *New York Times* included a description of the inscription that accompanied the Bible from the Baltimore colored ministers. It reads, 'To Abraham Lincoln, President of the United States, from the loyal Colored people of Baltimore, as a token of respect and gratitude. Baltimore, 4th of July, 1864."[55]

The *Times* article also includes some remarks from the Rev. S. W. Chase, a spokesman for the Black Baltimore ministers. The Rev. Chase said:

> Towards you, sir, our hearts will ever be warm with gratitude. We come to present to you this copy of the Holy Scriptures, as a token of respect for your active participation in furtherance of the causes of the emancipation of our race. This great event will be a matter of history. Hereafter, when our children shall ask what means these tokens, they will be told of your worthy deeds, and will rise up and call you blessed.[56]

Mr. Chase added:

> The loyal Colored People of this country everywhere will remember you at the Throne of Divine Grace. May the King Eternal, and All-Wise, Providence protect and keep you, and when you pass from this world to that of eternity, may you be borne to the bosom of your Savior and to your God.[57]

Upon his receiving this copy of the King James Bible, Mr. Lincoln responded:

> This occasion would seem fitting for a lengthy response to the address which you have just made. I would make one, if prepared; but I am not. I would promise to respond in writing, had not experience taught me that business will not allow me to do so. I can only now say, as I have often before have said, it has

54. "Black Ministers Give Lincoln Bible."
55. Ibid.
56. Ibid.
57. Ibid.

always been a sentiment with me that all of mankind should be free. So far as able, with my sphere, I have always acted as I believed to be right and just; and I have done all I could for the good of mankind generally. In letters and documents sent from this Office I have expressed myself better than I now can. In regard to this Great Book, I have but to say, it is the best gift that God has given to man. All the good that The Savior gave to the world was communicated through this Book. But for it, we could not know right from wrong.[58]

Mr. Lincoln appears to make four relevant points here. First, that he might have given a long speech, but he does not, to the great joy of most of those present; second, that the idea of freedom should be something possessed by all of mankind, including African-Americans; third, that the Bible contains some of the most important gifts that God has given to man; and finally, that all the good that the Savior gave to the world, like the foundations of morality, was given to humans in the Bible.

One final aspect of Abraham Lincoln's relationships with Holy Scripture is that at times, particularly when he was president, Mr. Lincoln would make up or invent lines that claimed to be, or appeared to be, Holy Writ, when, in fact, they were not. Clarence Macartney tells us in this regard, "The ordinary, daily speech of Lincoln was salted with timely and apt quotations from the Bible."[59] Mr. Macartney cites the example of Mr. Lincoln's response to General George McClellen's complaint about the weather bogging down activities on the battlefield. Mr. Lincoln told his Secretary, John Hay, "The general seems to think, in defiance of Scripture, that heaven sent its rain only on the just, and not on the unjust."[60] Mr. Lincoln frequently was at odds with many of his generals over military strategy, including General McClellen—and he sometimes employed the Bible to make arguments against those generals.

When treasury official Hugh McCulloch introduced a delegation of New York bankers to the president, Mr. McCulloch is said to have uttered, "Where the treasure is the hearts will also be." Mr. Lincoln then responded, "Yes, and where a carcass is, there also will be vultures gathered together."[61] Lincoln frequently responded, as if he were directly quoting Scripture, when in fact, he was making it up on the spot.

58. Ibid.
59. McCartney, *Lincoln and the Bible*, 29.
60. Ibid.
61. Donald, *Lincoln*, 551.

When the British ambassador Lord Lyon (1817–1875), Thomas Drummond, came to Mr. Lincoln to inform him that Queen Victoria's son, the Prince of Wales, was to marry Princess Alexandra of Denmark, Mr. Lincoln is said to have said to the bachelor ambassador, "Go Thou and do likewise."[62] Often, then, Mr. Lincoln appeared to be quoting from Scripture, when in fact he made it up on the spot—often to the amusement of himself or to others present.

Julia Taft Bayne, a young babysitter in the Lincoln White House, also wrote about Mr. Lincoln's relationship to the Bible. She says:

> It is well known, of course, that Mr. Lincoln was a great reader of the Bible, but I have a notion, without knowing exactly why I have it, that at the beginning of the war, he read the Bible quite as much for its literary style as he did for its religious or spiritual content. Perhaps I have this notion from his attitude while reading it. He read it in a relaxed, almost lazy attitude of a man enjoying a good book . . . Only once do I recall him saying anything about the Bible or Religion and that was in reply to Tad's plea as to why he had to go to Sunday School. "Every educated person should know something of the Bible and the Bible stories," Tad, answered his father.[63]

Ms. Bayne, who was hired by Mrs. Lincoln to care for their son Tad, makes three points regarding Mr. Lincoln and the Bible. First, he admired the Scriptures for their literary value as much as for their meaning; second, he read the Bible like any man reading a "good book"; and finally, any educated person should be familiar with the Bible, and Tad could get that familiarity of the "Good Book" at Sunday School.

One final aspect of Mr. Lincoln's views on and uses of the Bible pertains to another quotation that frequently is credited to the sixteenth president. He is reported in many sources to have said, "The Bible is not my book nor Christianity my profession. I could never give assent to a long, complicated statements of Christian dogma."[64]

Although this passage is attributed to Mr. Lincoln, we can find no independent confirmation that he actually said it. In other words, it appears that at times the sixteenth president is reported to have said things that, in

62. Ibid., 300.

63. Julia Taft Bayne Taft (1845–1933) helped to watch Tad and Willie Lincoln, along with her own two boys, Bud and Holly. Mrs. Lincoln asked Mrs. Taft to keep her boys home the day of Willie's funeral.

64. See, for example, Wall, "Was President Lincoln an Atheist?," which uses the quote in question.

fact, he never uttered. This is far from the only example of this phenomenon in Mr. Lincoln's public life. Frequently, the sixteenth president was reported to have said something that, in fact, he did not utter.

Two other examples will show this phenomenon. Lincoln is often quoted as saying, "It's not the years of your life that count, it's the life in your years." Unfortunately, there is no evidence that the sixteenth president ever uttered these words. On July 4, of 2017, CNN put a number of patriotic quotations on air, including one from—you guessed it—Abraham Lincoln. He is reported by CNN to have said, "Let the people know the facts, and the Country will be safe."[65] In checking sources at Mount Vernon, the University of Virginia, and other reliable sources online, there is no reason to believe that this quotation came from the mind, or the lips, of Abraham Lincoln, our sixteenth president.

These final few comments of Mr. Lincoln on the Bible naturally move us in the direction of a discussion of what may be called "Mr. Lincoln's ethics," the topic of chapter 5 of this essay, to which we now turn.

65. "Quotations from Patriots," CNN, July 4, 2017.

CHAPTER 5

President Lincoln on Ethics

When I do good, I feel good. When I do bad, I feel bad.
That's my religion.

—ABRAHAM LINCOLN, personal letter[1]

Lincoln strongly opposed the Kansas-Nebraska Act of 1854
because it implied that enslaving fellow human beings was right,
and contravened the principle of Liberty.

—GARY SCOTT SMITH, "Abraham Lincoln and Slavery"

When Abraham Lincoln said in 1858 that the real issue of slavery
was the eternal struggle between right and wrong throughout the
world, he spoke the language of natural law.

—HERMAN BELZ, "Abraham Lincoln and the
Natural Law Tradition"

IN THIS FIFTH CHAPTER of this essay on Abraham Lincoln's religion our central aims are the following. First, to explore the four major theories of the nature of the moral good, as expressed in the history of Western philosophy. Secondly, we will examine the many uses of President Lincoln in his writings and speeches, where he directly made comments on ethics, moral theory, and the nature of the moral good.

1. Quoted in Morris, *Wellness Words of Wisdom* (blog), April 13, 2012.

Finally, in this fifth chapter of this essay, we will explore a set of core moral characteristics exemplified in the life of Abraham Lincoln. Mr. Lincoln, as we shall see, believed both that all good men should exhibit these characteristics, and that God had placed this core collection of attributes into the bosom of all human beings.

In regard to ethics, moral theory, and moral goodness, President Abraham Lincoln made a number of very general comments in his speeches and writings. For example, he appears to have held that "It is better to be sometimes right than at times wrong."[2] On another occasion he said, "You may deceive all the people part of the time, and part of the people all the time, but not all the people all the time."[3] In regard to a particular man's character, Mr. Lincoln is reported to have observed, "I don't like that man. I must get to know him better."[4] In another speech, the sixteenth president made the moral pronouncement, "God grant me the serenity to accept things I cannot change; courage to change the things I can; and wisdom to know the difference."[5]

Historian Joseph R. Fornieri tells us this about Mr. Lincoln's theory of the moral good:

> Lincoln interprets American History as the unfolding of the implications within the Declaration. The document is foundational in the following ways. (1.) It commemorates the birth of a nation; (2.) It defines the creed of the collective American identity.; (3.) It represents a moral covenant.; (4.) It guides the nation's political institutions.; (5.) It constitutes a bulwark against despotism.[6]

Mr. Fornieri certainly is correct that Mr. Lincoln saw the Declaration of Independence and the U.S. Constitution as the foundation of the ethics of his moral view, as well as that of the nation. Mr. Lincoln would most likely add the Ten Commandments and the Golden Rule to enhance that foundation of ethics, as we shall see later in this fifth chapter of this essay on the sixteenth president's religion.

Mr. Fornieri also observes that "Mr. Lincoln transformed the ethos of the nation in the following ways: (1.) He subverted the Constitution by interpreting the Declaration as a Moral Covenant; (2.) He identified equality

2. *Sangamon Journal*, March 9, 1832.

3. Attributed at https://quoteinvestigator.com/2013/12/11/cannot-fool/.

4. Peraino, *Lincoln in the World*, 370. Philemon 4:13 may have been the original source for this quote.

5. Fornieri, *Abraham Lincoln's Political Faith*, 116.

6. Ibid.

as the central idea of the nation; (3.) He internalized the Declaration's assertion of equality by applying it to all individuals."[7] We will say more about Mr. Lincoln's views on these founding moral principles of America, but first we will make some general comments on theories of the moral good in the history of Western philosophy, and how Mr. Lincoln's views may have been related to these theories.

Lincoln scholar William Lee Miller understood him as the most important moral and ethical interpreter of American government. Miller writes, "Abraham Lincoln is the greatest of all interpreters of America's moral meanings."[8] Mr. Miller goes on to observe:

> In the first place because he stated it with rare eloquence. Secondly, he was the primary voice giving the American idea received from the Founders its necessary reinterpretation and fresh critical application because he dramatized the centrality of equality—particularly of racial Equality—as part of the nation's essence.[9]

Mr. Miller maintains that in doing this, Lincoln was able to avoid the bane, scourge, curse, and disease that threatened all statements about moral claims and national ideals—self-righteousness, invidiousness, moral pride, and condescension. Lincoln was able to preserve the moral nation, as well as the ideals on which it was founded; and the central ideas of those ideals were the notions of liberty and the equality of all people, of every color and every religion, as well as the right to profit from one's labor.

In the history of Western philosophy there have been four principal ways that philosophers have discerned the moral good. These four views have been supplied by Aristotle in the ancient world, Immanuel Kant in the eigtheenth century, Jeremy Bentham and John Stuart Mill in the nineteenth century, and a fourth view that has come to be known as "ethical egoism," mostly developed in the twentieth century.

Aristotle thought that morality can be ascertained by understanding what he called "moral virtues," which for him was a mean between two vices. Thus, for the ancient Greek philosopher, justice, or getting what one is due, is a mean between injustice, not getting what one is due, and over-justice, or receiving more than what one is due.

Similarly, the virtue of honesty is a midpoint between dishonesty and over-honesty. For Aristotle, courage is a moral virtue to be found between the vices of cowardice, the deficient vice, and rashness, the excessive vice.

7. Ibid., 117.
8. Miller, *Lincoln's Virtues*, 473.
9. Ibid.

Pride, for Aristotle, is a virtue to be discovered between the vices of vanity and humility; and temperance is a virtue between the vices of indulgence and insensibility. For Aristotle, the collection of these moral virtues is what he calls human happiness, or *eudaimonia*.[10]

Aristotle also made a distinction in his moral theory between moral virtues and intellectual virtues. The former are habitual states of character; the latter are used in the context of teaching and learning. Aristotle believed the bridge between moral and intellectual virtues was the idea of prudence. More will be said about this virtue later in this chapter of this essay.

Aristotle believed that moral virtues became character traits. He also believed the expression of moral virtues were habitual. They become behaviors that, over time, become parts of one's moral character. For Aristotle, then, acting morally is nothing more than displaying these moral virtues in everyday life. One acts morally if he or she exhibits or exemplifies these moral virtues.[11]

The eigtheenth-century moral theory of Immanuel Kant is based on moral duties that he believed are universal and without exceptions. For Kant, there are a collection of universal moral duties that he derived from what he calls the "categorical imperative." In the categorical imperative, Kant believed we should always act as though our moral behavior was universal. If I believe that killing innocent people is wrong, then, in Kant's view, it is morally improper for everyone. He also maintains that under the categorical imperative we should always treat people as ends in themselves, as beings with value, duties, and rights, and never as simply a means to an end.[12] Thus, Kant also was against the idea that "the end justify the means."

Immanuel Kant's ethics is sometimes referred to as "deontological ethics," from the Greek word *ontos*, or being. In his view, actions by their natures, or by their beings, are thought to be moral or immoral. Telling the truth, by its very nature, is moral, while telling a lie is immoral. Stealing, by its nature, is morally wrong, but showing compassion, on the other hand, is morally good; not harming innocent people is moral, while harming them is immoral, according to Kant.[13] Thus, Kant's ethics is based on universal moral duties that are tied to universal moral rules that should be followed by all rational beings; and these moral duties, in turn, are derived from the categorical imperative.

---

10. Aristotle, *Nicomachean Ethics*, book 10.

11. Ibid.

12. Kant, *Lectures on Ethics*, 184.

13. Ibid.

In his first inaugural address, Mr. Lincoln showed clear signs that the sixteenth president agreed with Immanuel Kant's system of ethics. He observed, "I hold that in contemplation of universal law, and of the Constitution, the Union of these states is perpetual."[14] It should be clear that the "universal law" to which he refers is connected to the deontological claims in the founding documents that "All men are created equal and endowed with certain inalienable rights," as well as other universal moral duties.

Mr. Lincoln, then, held to a belief in universal moral duties that are embodied in the U.S. Constitution, as well as the Declaration of Independence. Thus, by extension, Mr. Lincoln endorsed Aristotle's virtue theory, as well as Immanuel Kant's categorical imperative, or deontological theory of ethics.

In the nineteenth century, it became clear that the major shortcoming of Kant's moral theory is that sometimes moral duties may be at odds with each other. The duties to tell the truth and to keep from harming innocent people, for example, may not both be kept in certain circumstances, at the same time. The moral theories of Jeremy Bentham and John Stuart Mill arose specifically to respond to this shortcoming of Kant's theory.

Bentham and Mill did this by arguing that when two moral duties are in conflict with each other, one ought to follow the one that produces the best consequences for the most number of people. This theory is called "utilitarianism," or "teleological theory," from the Greek word *telos*, meaning "plan" or "design."

We also will show at the end of this chapter of this essay that President Abraham Lincoln was a believer in a fourth moral theory called "ethical egoism." This theory suggests that all human beings, by their very nature, act in their own self-interest. In other words, the sixteenth president believed that human beings are basically selfish. More will be said about this fourth moral theory later in this chapter.

Like utilitarianism, ethical egoism is a teleological theory of ethics that sets its goal as the benefit, pleasure, happiness, or greatest good of oneself alone. Egoism is contrasted with altruism, which is not, strictly speaking, self-interested, but includes in its goal the interests of others as well. Ethical egoism, or the promotion of one's self-interest, is often identified with twentieth-century writer and philosopher Ayn Rand, whose book *The Virtue of Selfishness* is often cited as the best representative of this fourth theory of ethics.[15]

14. Lincoln, first inaugural address, March 4, 1861.
15. Rand, *Virtue of Selfishness*.

President Abraham Lincoln appears to have been aware of all four of these moral theories from his general reading over the years. There is also some evidence that the sixteenth president employed each of the four moral theories, depending on which he saw as appropriate or applicable, at any given time. We introduce these four moral theories, then, because there is some evidence that President Abraham Lincoln employed all of these points of view when discerning the moral good. It is clear, for example, that Lincoln believed in Kant's view that there were universal moral duties, related to the founding documents of this nation, as Joseph Fornieri has suggested earlier in this chapter of this essay.

For Mr. Lincoln, it is clear that many of these moral duties pertain to freedom, equality, justice, or fairness, honesty, and the value of one's labor, or work. On many occasions in his writings and speeches, Lincoln repeatedly refers to these universal moral duties.

In regard to freedom, for example, in a letter from April 6, 1859, Mr. Lincoln said, "Those who deny freedom to others, deserve it not for themselves; and, under a Just God, can no longer retain it."[16]

In another speech from a year earlier, Mr. Lincoln observed, "As I would not be a slave, so I would not be a master," is clearly a direct application of Kant's moral theory. Lincoln continues, "This expresses my idea of democracy. Whatever differs from this, to the extent of the difference, is no democracy."[17] Again, this appears to be an application of Kant's universal moral duties, or deontological theory.

In regard to the duty to equality, the sixteenth president explained, "Whenever I hear anyone argue for slavery, I feel a strong impulse to see it tried on him personally."[18]

Here Mr. Lincoln appears to be applying Kant's categorical imperative to the situation. If one does not wish to be a slave, then, according to Kant, no one would wish to be a slave. Therefore, the practice of slavery is morally unacceptable in the German philosopher's view.

In one of his debates with Stephen Douglas in 1858, Mr. Lincoln made a remark to introduce his ethical theory. He observed, "Every nation has a central idea from which all minor thoughts radiate."[19] For Mr. Lincoln, this central idea was in the Declaration of Independence and its notions of justice and equality as the basis for republican government. It is the simple

16. Lincoln, letter to Henry L. Pierce, April 6, 1859.
17. Lincoln–Douglas debate in Alton, October 15, 1858.
18. Quoted in Basler, *Collected works of Abraham Lincoln*, 532.
19. Lincon–Douglas debate in Alton, October 15, 1858.

idea that no one has the right by nature to rule over another without the latter's consent.

"We hold these truths to be self-evident, that all men were created equal, that they are endowed by their Creator with inalienable rights, that among these are life, liberty, and the pursuit of happiness. That to secure these rights, governments are instituted among men." Lincoln saw more clearly than his critics that equality is separable from democracy. As he remarked in 1859:

> All honor to Jefferson—to the man, who, in concrete pressure of a struggle for national independence by a single people , had the coolness, forecast, and capacity to introduce into a merely revolutionary document, an abstract truth, applicable to all men and all times, and so embalm it there, that today, and in all coming days, it shall be a rebuke and a stumbling block to the very harbingers of reappearing tyranny and oppression.[20]

Mr. Lincoln begins by crediting the deftness of the founding fathers in constructing the nation's founding documents in difficult times. Then, he refers to the universal moral rights and duties to be found in those documents. It is these rights and duties that are the foundation of the American republic, and these universal moral rights and duties are very much like those that Immanuel Kant derived from his categorical imperative. Mr. Lincoln also clearly believed that the recognizing and respecting of these moral rights and duties was the opposite of tyranny and oppression.

Mr. Lincoln believed these universal moral rights and duties in Kant's moral theory are also "embalmed," or imbedded, as part of human nature; and among those embedded duties are those related to liberty and equality, as expressed in the Constitution and the Declaration of Independence; and Mr. Lincoln added to these fundamental principles the right to profit from one's own labor, as well.

Indeed, it is the idea of equality in the Declaration, not race or blood, that establishes American nationhood, constituting what Abraham Lincoln called "the mystic chords of memory, stretching from every battlefield, and patriot grave, to every living heart and hearthstone, all over this broad land . . . ," as expressed in his Gettysburg address.[21]

In another speech delivered in early July of 1858, Mr. Lincoln clarified the link between the Declaration and America as a nation. His argument was one in this age of multiculturalism we should keep in mind. Lincoln told his listeners in Chicago:

20. Lincoln, letter to Henry L. Pierce, April 6, 1859.
21. Lincoln, Gettysburg address, November 19, 1863.

> We celebrate the founders, our fathers and grandfathers, those
> iron men . . . But after we have done this we have not yet reached
> the whole. There is something else connected with it. We have
> besides these men—descended by blood from our ancestors—
> among us perhaps half our people who are not descendants at
> all of these men, they are men who have come from Europe—
> German, Irish, French, and Scandanavian—finding themselves
> of equals in all things.[22]

The sixteenth president describes the original conditions of the establishment of the republic, as expressed in the founding documents of the nation.
Then, Mr. Lincoln continues his address:

> If we look back through this history to trace their connection
> with those days by blood, they find they have none; they cannot
> carry themselves back into that glorious epoch and make them-
> selves feel that they are part of us; but when they look through
> that old Declaration of Independence they find that these old
> men say, "We hold these truths to be self-evident, that all men
> are created equal.[23]

Mr. Lincoln refers to the idea that American society has imbedded into their
founding documents these moral rights and duties expressed in the Declaration, the Bill of Rights, as well as the U.S. Constitution and other founding
documents.

In a speech on the Dred Scott decision of 1857, President Lincoln
again spoke of the Declaration and this "central idea" of the republic. Lincoln wrote, "I think the authors of the Declaration intended to include all
men, but they did not intend to declare men equal in all respects . . . they
meant equal in certain inalienable rights, among which are life, liberty, and
the pursuit of happiness."[24] But saying that all men are equal is not the same
thing as saying that they are equal in every respect. Lincoln was decidedly
against that latter idea.

In Lincoln's view, the United States was founded on the principles of
justice and equality. No longer would the foundation of political government be that some men were born "with saddles on their backs," to be rid-
den by others born "booted and spurred." In other words, in Lincoln's view,
and those of the founding fathers, no one in *America* had the right to rule

22. Lincoln, Chicago address, July 10, 1858.

23. Ibid.

24. Lincoln, speech on the Dred Scott decision, June 26, 1857.

one another without the latter's consent.[25] From its inception, America had no interest in establishing classes in the society of the United States.

Mr. Lincoln's third law partner, William Herndon, in his biography of the president, tells us, "With him, Justice and Equality were paramount. If to him a thing seemed untrue, he could not in his nature simulate Truth."[26] This applied to morality and to moral disputes in general.

In an address he gave at the Maryland Sanitary Fair in Baltimore, Mr. Lincoln again spoke of his views on liberty. He said, "The world has never had a good definition of Liberty, and the American people just now, are much in want of one. We all declare for liberty, but in using the same word we do not mean the same thing."[27] This address at the Maryland Sanitary Fair was delivered on April 18, 1864, at what was then called the "Baltimore Institute." The address had been organized by Maryland's Unionist Women, who were raising money for relief for the armed forces. Similar meetings were held at the time in other cities such as Chicago and Boston, to help the war efforts of the Union.

Mr. Lincoln's address was given at the opening of the fair in Baltimore, which was conducted from April 18 until April 30. One of the important features of the opening was a parade of three thousand colored soldiers in new blue Union army uniforms with gold buttons. These were mostly volunteers who had served at Gettysburg and other battles. For President Lincoln, the coming to Baltimore presented an opportunity to make amends for a past indiscretion. In March of 1861, on the way to his inauguration by train, Lincoln secreted himself through Baltimore, in response to a rumor that he might be assassinated there, so he avoided the city.

Many residents of Baltimore at the time regarded Lincoln's actions as a slight on the city. Later, Mr. Lincoln said he had made a huge mistake in his actions. By opening the Maryland Sanitary Fair, the president could mitigate that wrong by expressing his confidence in the city's national loyalty. Mr. Lincoln continues the Baltimore speech about liberty. He observes:

> With some the word Liberty may mean for each man to do as he pleases with other men, and the product of other men's labor. Here are two, not only different, but incompatible things, called by the same name—Liberty. And it follows that each of these things is, by respective parties, called by two different and incompatible names—Liberty and Tyranny.[28]

25. Ibid.
26. Herndon, *Life of Lincoln*, 451.
27. Lincoln, address at the Maryland Sanitary Fair, Baltimore, April 18, 1864.
28. Ibid.

Again, in regard to Liberty, Mr. Lincoln asks, "What constitutes the bulwark of our Liberty and independence?" After rehearsing several answers, he settles on, "Our reliance is on our love of Liberty, which God has placed in our bosoms."[29] Mr. Lincoln appears to have ascribed to the view that God placed into the bosoms of all people these collection of moral rights and duties. He then proceeds to tie this liberty to all men when he says, "Our Liberty is the heritage of all men, in all lands, in all times."[30]

Thus, Mr. Lincoln appears to have believed that all human beings have certain universal moral rights and moral duties, and that these are possessed in all places, at all times, and among all people. He also appears to have assented to the view that God placed these moral duties into the hearts of all humans, a view consistent with the writers of the Old Testament.

One of Lincoln's many biographers, William Wolf, wrote about what he sees as two negative values of Mr. Lincoln's. By this I mean values to which he did not ascribe. Mr. Wolf writes, "One of the greatnesses of Lincoln was the way he held to strong moral positions without the usual accompaniment or self-righteousness or smugness."[31] Wolf goes on to say that he often did this in his humor. Thus, Mr. Lincoln was staunchly against the smug and the self-righteous.

In this essay, already we have said several things about President Abraham Lincoln's views on ethics and the moral good. In an epigraph to this chapter, Mr. Lincoln appears to assent to the emotivist theory of the moral good—that is, that one's emotions or feelings will tell when an action is morally proper. Mr. Lincoln hints at his emotivism when speaking to the African-American ministers from Baltimore who gave him a Bible, on September 7, 1864. In this speech he says, "I have always acted as I believed to be right and just, and I have done all I could for the good of humanity in general."[32] Here moral emotions seem to be at the center of Mr. Lincoln's decision-making skills. In the same speech, Mr. Lincoln lauds the Bible because it contains "The Ten Commandments and the Golden Rule," two foundations of Christian morality, as well as the ethics of Abraham Lincoln.[33] Both the Ten Commandments and the Golden Rule, of course, are deontological systems of ethics, for they require one to follow universal moral duties.

29. Ibid.

30. Ibid.

31. Wolf, *Lincoln's Religion*, 79.

32. "African-American Ministers Giving Bible to Mr. Lincoln."

33. Lincoln–Douglas debate in Alton, October 15, 1858.

We also have indicated earlier in this essay that Lincoln assented to a belief in a host of morals rights and duties that are guaranteed by the founding documents of this country—beliefs related to the central idea discussed earlier in this analysis. Chief among these moral rights are five to which the president constantly referred in his speeches, his letters, and his other writings.

We will more specifically enumerate these five moral rights and duties first, and then sketch them out one at a time. They are: equality, fairness or justice, freedom, a principal moral duty—the duty to honesty, and the right to the product of one's labor or work. Throughout Mr. Lincoln's adult life, he most often referred to these five values above all others. He specifically mentioned these values in the context of discussing the moral rights and moral duties of African-Americans.

Mr. Lincoln expressed his belief in the equality of Blacks in his debates with Senator Stephen Douglas in 1858. After quoting the New Testament—"As your Father in heaven is perfect, be ye also perfect," a reference to Matthew 5:48—Lincoln said to Douglas, "So I say in relation to the principle that all men are created equal, let it be nearly reached as we can."[34] While speaking in Chicago on July 10, 1858, Lincoln spoke of the bill to extend slavery into the Western Territories. He said, "I have always hated slavery, I think as much as any Abolitionist [Applause.] I have been an Old Line Whig. I have always hated it, but I have always been quiet about it until this new era of introduction of the Nebraska Bill began."[35]

As indicated earlier, Abraham Lincoln inherited his negative views of the practice of slavery from his father, Thomas Lincoln, as well as from the Separate Baptist church to which his parents belonged in the beginning of the nineteenth century. He said he had remained quiet about his belief until the era of the Nebraska bill and the extension of slavery into the Western Territories had begun, and he was strongly against the idea, as he was all the way back to his childhood.

In another 1858 debate with Senator Douglas, Mr. Lincoln speaks of some of his core values when he says, "There is no reason in the world why the Negro is not entitled to all the natural and the pursuit of happiness."[36]

Perhaps the moral issue that Mr. Lincoln most often addressed in his adult life was the moral wrongness of the practice of slavery. As indicated in an earlier chapter of this essay, Thomas Lincoln and the Separate Baptists split from the Regular Baptists, among other reasons, due to the issue of

34. Lincoln, Chicago address, July 10, 1858.
35. Lincoln–Douglas debate in Quincy, October 13, 1858.
36. Lincoln, letter to Mary Speed, September 27, 1841.

slavery. Lincoln also encountered slavery in the Deep South firsthand when he piloted a flatboat in 1828 and 1831, when he moved loads of goods down the Ohio and Mississippi Rivers to New Orleans. Some scholars suggest that Lincoln saw the sights of the city, including its slave markets, before returning north to his life in Indiana.

In 1841, while travelling on the Ohio with his friend Joshua Speed, Mr. Lincoln encountered a collection of slaves being brought south by way of the river. The president tells us, "They were chained together, six by six. A small iron clevis was around the left wrist of each, and this fastened to a main chain by a shorter one at a convenient distance from the others. So the negroes were strung together precisely like so many fish upon a trot line."[37]

In a letter to Mary Speed, Joshua's sister, from September 27, 1841, Lincoln says more about the encounter on the Ohio River. He writes:

> In this condition, they were being separated forever from scenes of their childhood, their friends, their fathers and mothers, and sisters and brothers, and many of them, from their wives and children, and going into perpetual slavery where the lash of the master is proverbially more ruthless and unrelenting than any other were.[38]

Mr. Lincoln continues his description of the encounter to Mary Speed. He says, "But instead of deep sadness, these people presented to the world a cheerful face. Yet amid all these distressing circumstances, as we would think them, they were the most cheerful and happy creatures on board."[39] As Lincoln biographer Stephen Oates points out, "These images remained fresh in Lincoln's mind and the scene was a 'continual torment to me.' 'Slavery,' Lincoln observed, 'had the power of making me miserable.'"[40] Mr. Lincoln clearly believed that slavery was improper and immoral, and he held those views from childhood until the time of his death.

Even as early as his Peoria address on October 16, 1854, Mr. Lincoln employed the Bible in order to communicate the wrongness of slavery. Near the close of the Peoria address, Mr. Lincoln expressly sets aside law, politics, and religion, and appeals directly to moral intuitionist sentiments. In this speech, the president concluded:

> Argue as you will, as long as you will, this is the naked Front and Aspect of the measure. And in this aspect, it could not

37. Ibid.
38. Ibid.
39. Ibid.
40. Lincoln, Peoria address, October 16, 1864.

but produce agitation. Slavery is founded in the selfishness of man—opposition to it is in the love of justice. These principles are in eternal antagonism, and when brought into collision so fiercely, as slave extension brings them, shocks, and throes, and convulsions must ceaselessly follow.[41]

This reference to selfishness is an indication that Mr. Lincoln assented to the theory of ethical egoism when it came to the question of human nature. He also maintains that this view is a central cause of Slavery. Then, the sixteenth president speaks of the eternal opposition of freedom and equality versus this view of selfishness.

Mr. Lincoln regularly pitted these two values against each other. In the "House Divided Speech" on June 16, 1858, Mr. Lincoln declares, "Either the opponents of slavery will arrest the further spread of it, and place it where the public mind shall rest in the belief that its course is ultimate extinction, or its advocates will push it forward, until it shall again become lawful in all the States, old as well as new, North as well as South."[42]

Beneath the anti-slavery position of his day, Mr. Lincoln understood the values implicit in the founding documents of this nation—that all are created equal, etc. Retired Supreme Court Justice David Souter refers to these national beliefs as a "pantheon of values," not unlike what Joseph Fornieri has earlier called "the American ethos." By this, Judge Souter means the set of national beliefs and fundamental principles that lie at the heart of our democracy—beliefs that the sixteenth president thought God had imbedded into the bosoms of all human beings. The sixteenth president sums up his moral stance against slavery when he wrote, "The institution of slavery is founded on injustice and bad policy."[43] He refers here, of course, to moral badness.

In speaking of this "pantheon of values," or "the American ethos," Mr. Lincoln said at Independence Hall in Philadelphia, on February 22, 1861, "I have never had a feeling politically that did not spring from the sentiments embodied in the Declaration of Independence."[44]

Mr. Lincoln claims that all of his political decisions were made in light of the universal moral rights and duties embodied in the Declaration of Independence, the Bill of Rights, and the U.S. Constitution; and, Lincoln believed, these moral rights and duties are embedded into the bosoms of all men.

41. Lincoln, "House Divided Speech," June 16, 1858.

42. Lincoln–Douglas debate in Ottawa, August 21, 1858.

43. Lincoln, Independence Hall address, February 22, 1861.

44. Lincoln, Peoria address, October 16, 1854.

In one work, Mr. Lincoln asks, "Is the Negro a man . . . ? Does he not have the right to govern himself?" He syllogizes the answers to these questions. He quotes the Declaration twice, the second time alluding to the fact that governments are instituted among men, "deriving their just powers from the consent of the governed."[45] The implication here, of course, is that Black slaves have not agreed to be governed by White masters. Thus, the government is illegitimate, in Lincoln's view.

For Mr. Lincoln, slaves had been denied the right to profit from their own labor since the establishment of slavery in America. For him, this makes slavery, and other forms of captivity, morally wrong. In another place, Lincoln says, "My ancient faith teaches me that all men are created equal . . . according to our ancient faith, the just powers of government are derived from the consent of the governed, without the conclusion that no consent has come from slaves."[46]

In a letter to General George E. Pickett, whose name has become synonymous with the defeat at Gettysburg, Mr. Lincoln wrote, "I have never encouraged deceit, and falsehood, especially if you have a bad memory—that is the worst enemy a fellow can have. Lincoln found deception and the telling of lies to be among the human's greatest sins. The facts of truth are your truest friends, no matter what the circumstances are."[47] Mr. Lincoln's friend Dr. Jason Duncan, whom the president knew in New Salem, later wrote, "If there was one trait of Mr. Lincoln's character that stood out more conspicuously than any other, it was his regard for truth and veracity. He had less prevarication than almost any man with whom I was ever acquainted."[48]

Mr. Lincoln's fondness for the truth is also clear in an episode involving John L. Scripps, a famous Chicago newspaper writer. Scripps had written in a story about Lincoln that he had read Plutarch. Later, he suggested to the president that he acquire a copy and read it, so the report would become true. Lincoln is said to have been amused and repeated the tale many times afterwards.[49] Plutarch (46–125) was one of the best-known Greek biographers and essayists. He wrote extensively about Greek and Roman cultures, influencing many Western intellectuals in Europe and America, as well as many in Byzantium.

---

45. Lincoln, letter to George E. Pickett, August 12, 1860.

46. Dr. Jason Duncan, a physician in New Salem in Lincoln's time, introduced the president to the poem "Mortality," also sometimes called "Immortality," by William Knox. The poem in question begins, "Oh! Why should the spirit of mortal be proud?"

47. Ibid.

48. Horrock, *Lincoln's Campaign Biographies*, 55.

49. Scripps, "Lincoln on Plutarch."

Mr. Scripps suggested that Mr. Lincoln should read Plutarch because the latter wrote extensively on ethics and human behavior. Of his 227 known works, the most famous are his *Moralia*, also known as his *Ethics*, and his *Parallel Lives*, a series of biographies arranged in pairs, highlighting the subjects' virtues and vices. Plutarch focused more on the character of his subjects and not so much on the times in which they lived.

John L. Scripps (1818–1866) was an Missouri-born attorney, journalist, and author. He founded the Chicago Democratic Press, which became the *Chicago Press and Tribune*. Scripps is also important because he was the author of the first good biography of Abraham Lincoln, published a year after the president's death. Mr. Scripps also died in 1866.

Mr. Lincoln's friend Joshua F. Speed also recalled the importance of veracity in the character of his friend. In fact, Speed wrote of Lincoln, "Unlike all other men there was an entire harmony between his public and his private life. He must have believed that he was right, and that he had Truth and Justice with him, or he was a weak man. But no man could be stronger if he thought he was right."

During the Quincy debate in 1858, German-American politician Carl Schurz observed about Mr. Lincoln:

> There was, however, in all he said, a tone of earnest truthfulness, of noble, elevated sentiments and of kindly sympathy, that added greatly to the strength of his argument, and became in the course of his speech, he touched upon the moral side of the question of the debate, powerfully impressive.[50]

Mr. Schurz continued his analysis:

> Even when attacking his opponent with keen satire or invective, which coming from any other speaker, would have sounded bitter and cruel, there was still a certain something in his utterance making his hearers feel that those thrusts came from a reluctant heart, and that he much rather would have treated his foe as a friend.[51]

Carl Christian Schurz (1829–1906) was a Cologne-born writer and reporter who emigrated to the United States. He was a Republican and campaigned for Mr. Lincoln when the latter ran for congress. He wrote for a number of years for the *New York Tribune*.

Another pair of principles, or moral duties, that were central to Mr. Lincoln were hard work and the right to keep the proceeds of it. In an

50. Schurz, "Quincy Debate."
51. Ibid.

address delivered on March 21, 1864, to the members of the New York Republican Association, the sixteenth president spoke of the products of one's labor. He said:

> Property is the fruit of labor . . . property is desirable . . . is a positive view in the world. That some should be rich shows that others may become rich, and hence is just encouragement to industry and enterprise. Let not him who is houseless pull down the house of another; but let him labor diligently and build one for himself, thus by example assuring that his own shall be safe from violence when built.[52]

Indeed, at times Mr. Lincoln expressed his belief in the equality of Negroes specifically in what he said about labor. In an early letter to Mr. Williamson Durley from October 3, 1845, the future president declared, "The Negro may not be my equal, but in the right to eat the bread, which his own hand earns, he is my equal . . . and the equal of every living man."[53] Williamson Durley (1810–1901) was a Kentucky-born owner of a dry goods store in Sangamon County, Illinois. Durley served in the Black Hawk War in 1831. He knew Mr. Lincoln when the latter was in Springfield, and carried on a correspondence with him.

In a speech of Mr. Lincoln's in Springfield, after the Dred Scott decision, Mr. Lincoln remarked, "When the fathers declared all men equal in certain inalienable rights, they did not mean to confer such rights on all men immediately."[54]

Mr. Lincoln added:

> This meant simply to declare the right, so that the enforcement of it might follow as fast as circumstances could permit. They meant to set up a standard maxim for free society . . . and even though never perfectly attained, constantly approximated, and thereby constantly spreading and deepening its influence, and augmenting the happiness and value of life to all people of all colors everywhere.[55]

The sixteenth president points out that the universal rights expressed in the Declaration of Independence and in the U.S. Constitution are simply an "ideal" state. Circumstances may not have dictated, however, that these

52. Lincoln, address to the New York Republican Association, March 21, 1864.

53. Lincoln, letter to Williamson Durley, October 3, 1845.

54. Lincoln, speech on the Dred Scott decision, June 26, 1857.

55. Ibid.

rights may not be achieved in the present circumstances. The ideal and the practical, in Lincoln's view, must be balanced.

Indeed, on countless occasions, Mr. Lincoln expressed the belief that all human beings have the moral duty to respect the products of another's labor. One way to see this value at work in Lincoln's life is another letter from a stepcousin who asks for Lincoln's financial help, even after the man had asked for the same, and received it, many times before.

Mr. Lincoln's beliefs and dedication to freedom, equality, justice, honesty, and the right to one's labor are expressed through his major speeches and writings, such as his Gettysburg address, the "Emancipation Proclamation" of 1863, and his first and second inaugural addresses in 1861 and 1865; but he also sketches out a number of other negative virtues, like not being smug and self-righteous, mentioned earlier in this chapter of this essay.

Earlier, William Wolf mentioned the sixteenth president's desire for speakers not to be smug or self-righteous. Wolf also alludes to Lincoln's belief about those who think they are better than others when the president wrote, "I would inculcate this idea, so that we may not, like the Pharisees, set ourselves to be better than other people."[56] The Pharisees, of course, were a first-century Jewish religious party. They insisted in the binding force of the oral tradition, the "unwritten Torah." They had many controversial things to say about Jewish law in the Second Temple Period.

In a discussion with the secretary of war, Edwin Stanton, President Lincoln quoted Proverbs 13:10, which indicates what the chief executive thought of making accusations: "Accuse not a servant unto his master, lest he curse thee, and thou should be found guilty" (GB). Thus, Mr. Lincoln suggests we not be accusatory, smug, or self-righteous, nor think we are better than others.

Two other values that seem to have been central in Mr. Lincoln's moral views are forbearance and respect. William Lee Miller, in his book *Lincoln's Virtues: An Ethical Biography*, calls the president's moral view "moral realism," an "ethic of responsibility of prudence and realism."[57] Mr. Miller argues, however, that Mr. Lincoln's theory was not simply made of principles. He says, "There are principles that determine actions decisively, but absent those, the moral case should be determined by the consequences, the results, the fruits."[58]

Here Mr. Miller alludes to the two most important modern philosophical theories of the moral good—Kant's theory of universal moral duties and

56. Wolf, *Almost Chosen People*, 83.
57. Miller, *Lincoln's Virtues*, 17.
58. Ibid.

Bentham's theory of "best consequences for the most number of people."[59] In fact, speaking in Cincinnati in February of 1860, President-Elect Abraham Lincoln observed:

> I hold that while man exists, it is his duty to improve not only his own condition, but to assist in the ameliorating mankind; and therefore, without entering upon the details of the question, I will simply say, that I am for those means which give the greatest good for the greatest number.[60]

Mr. Lincoln's early belief in utilitarian, or teleological, theory can also be seen in a letter to Joshua Speed on August 24, 1855, when the president wrote, "Much as I hate slavery I would consent to its extension rather than see the Union dissolved, just as I would consent to any Great evil, to avoid a Greater one."[61]

Mr. Lincoln begins by expressing his lifetime hate of slavery, and then maintains that it is better to experience a greater evil at the simple expense of a lesser evil, in line with utilitarian principles.

By the war years, Lincoln still tied his views on slavery to the preservation of the Union and a utilitarian view of ethics. In a letter to Horace Greeley from August 22, 1862, Lincoln tells him:

> My paramount object in this struggle is to save the Union, and is not either to save or destroy slavery. If I could save the Union without freeing any slave, I would do it, and if I could save it by freeing all the slaves I would do it; and if I could save it by freeing some and leaving others alone, I would also do that.[62]

Horace Greeley (1811–1872) was the founder and editor of the *New York Tribune*, one of the great American newspapers of the nineteenth century. Greeley also vigorously expressed the North's abolitionist sentiments of the 1850s and 1860s.

At times, rather than expressing his ethical views under the cloak of utilitarianism, Lincoln employed the idea of what he called "pragmatism" to express his idea of producing the best consequences. Historian Walter McDougall speaks of Lincoln's ethics in just these terms. McDougall observes, "It is futile to debate whether a pragmatic Lincoln made a pretense

---

59. Ibid.
60. Lincoln, Cincinnati address, February 19, 1860.
61. Lincoln, letter to Joshua F. Speed, August 24, 1855.
62. Lincoln, letter to Horace Greeley, August 22, 1862.

of pragmatism. He was a brilliant, subtle, troubled man, feeling his way through a national identity crisis."[63]

Mr. Lincoln often sought novel ways to pursue his core principles. In December of 1862, for example, he argued at length the moral rightness of compensating emancipation, and he then threw in the following remarks: "As our case is new, so we must think anew, and act anew. This is the theory of Pragmatism in a nutshell."[64] It is likely that here Mr. Lincoln was speaking of the balance between rights and practicalities. Often, he suggested, new circumstances require new moral decisions in those circumstances.

Mr. Miller continually points to the role that prudence played in Abraham Lincoln's ethics. Miller believes that prudence was, at least for Lincoln, the bridge between moral virtue and intellectual virtue. Prudence was necessary, Miller contends, in Mr. Lincoln's learning and teaching, as well as his praiseworthy conduct.[65] Aristotle also held prudence to be the link between moral and intellectual virtues, as mentioned earlier.

Another value of great importance in the ethic of Abraham Lincoln was humility. In one of his letters, the sixteenth president speaks of the value in question. He says, "It behooves us, then, to be humble, and to humble ourselves before the offended Power to confess our national sins and to pray for clemency and forgiveness."[66] Again, it is clear that Lincoln is speaking of the "sins" that both sides of the Civil War had committed, and he calls for both sides to ask Almighty God, "He Whom had been offended," for forgiveness. Again, Lincoln eschews the word "God," in favor of "He Whom had been offended."

Other moral virtues to which Abraham Lincoln often referred include prudence and honesty, already mentioned, as well as pride, steadfastness, silence, mercy, and economy. About the latter Mr. Lincoln wrote, "Teach Economy. That is one of the first and highest virtues. It begins with saving money."[67] Fellow Springfield attorney Samuel Parks, whose law office was adjacent to Lincoln's, later wrote that "The greatest feature in Mr. Lincoln's character was his Honesty and Integrity, in the longest sense of that term. His devotion to Truth and Justice and Freedom in every department of human life and under every temptation. I have often said that for a man who

---

63. See Goldman, "Neither American, nor Civil, nor a Religion," a review of Walter McDougall's book *The Tragedy of American Foreign Policy: How America's Civil Religion Betrayed the National Interest.*

64. Ibid.

65. Miller, *Lincoln's Virtues*, 20.

66. Lincoln, Presidential Proclamation 97, March 30, 1863.

67. Lincoln, address to the National Education Association, quoted in the *Los Angeles Herald*, March 24, 1916.

for a quarter century both a lawyer and a politician, he was the most honest man I ever knew."[68]

In regard to silence, the sixteenth president tells us, "I am rather inclined to silence, and whether that be wise or not, it is not more unusual nowadays to find a man who can hold his tongue than to find one who cannot."[69]

In giving advice to his son Tad's teacher, Lincoln again mentions silence when he writes, "Teach him the secret of quiet laughter."[70] The president appears to have believed silence was valuable for himself, as well as for others—especially for his own son Tad.

About the need to remain steadfast, Mr. Lincoln observes:

> I have not permitted myself, gentlemen, to conclude that I am the best man in the Country; but I am reminded in this connection, of the story of an old Dutch farmer who remarked to a companion once that "it was not best to swap horses while crossing streams."[71]

Mr. Lincoln made a number of references to the virtue of pride in his letters, speeches, and writings. In a letter to Mrs. Lydia Bixby, for example, a woman who had lost five sons in the Civil War, Mr. Lincoln wrote:

> I pray that our Heavenly Father may assuage the anguish of your bereavement; and leave you only with the cherished memory of the loved and lost, and the solemn pride that must be yours, to have laid so costly a sacrifice upon the altar of Freedom.[72]

In speaking to a crowd in Wisconsin on September 30, 1859, Mr. Lincoln tells the tale of an Eastern monarch who once charged his wise men to invent a sentence to be ever in view, and which could be true and appropriate in any time or situation. They presented the words that said to the king, "And this too shall pass." Lincoln adds, "How chastening in the hour of pride. How consoling in the depth of affliction."[73] Thus, Mr. Lincoln seems to bow to the moral virtue theory of Aristotle, and among his core moral virtues, the sixteenth president included: prudence, honesty, pride, steadfastness, silence, and economy.

68. Parks (1820–1917) had a law practice in New Salem, and later in Mt. Poluski, Illinois. This quote appears in Herndon, *Abraham Lincoln*, 1:166.

69. Holzer, "Sound of Lincoln's Silence."

70. Lincoln, advice to Tad's teacher, February 5, 1862.

71. Lincoln, letter to the National Union League, June 9, 1864.

72. Ibid.

73. Ibid.

Joseph Gillespie, the attorney general of Illinois, quotes Lincoln on the importance of practicing mercy. He says Lincoln said, "My impression is that mercy bears richer fruits than any other attribute."[74] This certainly was the case in Mr. Lincoln's life.

Joseph Gillespie (1809–1885) was a New York-born lawyer, judge, and politician, mostly in the state of Illinois. He served during the Black Hawk War, and later served in the Illinois General Assembly and as a judge in that state's circuit court.

It was also during the Douglas debates in 1858 that historian Douglas Wilson argues that the sixteenth president first understood the nature and value of honor, and the importance of honorable behavior to all people at all times. Wilson also suggests it was in these debates that Mr. Lincoln first comprehended that honor was a necessary element of a moral Life; and Aristotle made the same claim.[75]

In addition to the moral principles and virtues mentioned above, and Lincoln's concern for the best of consequences, he also exhibited exemplary leadership characteristics—another central part of Mr. Lincoln's overall ethical views. More specifically, Mr. Lincoln, in his major speeches and writings, regularly exhibited a collection of leadership qualities. We will point to six in particular that characterized his leadership model.

First, it appears that Mr. Lincoln always kept his vision in constant focus. For him, this vision was the preservation of the Union. This allowed the president to set his personal differences, egos, and personal ambitions to the side. If others came up with better suggestions to further the vision, he was only too accommodating. Related to this point about the vision was Mr. Lincoln's ability to manage his emotions. He was very good about not retaliating or lashing out in anger. When he felt angry, he wrote a letter about it and then slept on it for an evening. Rarely did he send those angry letters later.

Sometimes, however, Mr. Lincoln appears to have changed his vision. At the beginning of the war, for example, Lincoln's primary goal was the keeping of the integrity of the Union. About halfway through the war, though, his goal seems to have shifted to the abolition of slavery and the enforcing of the view that all men are created equal, even Black Americans.

One good example of this phenomenon was when Mr. Lincoln wrote an angry letter to Generals Halleck and Buell, commanders of the Western Theatre. In the letter, the president expresses his consternation over a number of military decisions they had made in direct opposition to the

74. Ibid.

75. Wilson, *Lincoln's Sword*, 278.

president. Although Lincoln wrote the letter, he never actually sent it. Apparently, Mr. Lincoln did similar things about strategy throughout the war.

Third, Mr. Lincoln was a great communicator. He was a good listener and those around him always felt heard. He had a knack for speaking in plain language and was a superb story-teller. He had an uncanny ability to take very complex ideas and render them in the simplest of language. He usually kept criticisms from his major speeches.

Fourth, Mr. Lincoln was very much attuned to the needs and feelings of others. He had the ability to bring people of differing opinions together. At the end of the Civil War, Lincoln went to great lengths not to humiliate the defeated South. He treated their leader, General Robert E. Lee, with dignity and respect. He resisted calls from some members of his cabinet and others to deal harshly with the South. Rather, he focused on ways that he could heal old wounds and foster reconciliation.

Fifth, Mr. Lincoln was flexible, humble, and was always ready to learn from his mistakes. He was open to new ideas. He was fully aware that he was fallible. When he made mistakes, he neither tried to hide them nor to deny them. Instead of dwelling on his mistakes, Mr. Lincoln acknowledged them and then moved on as quickly as he possibly could. Mr. Lincoln's ethics, then, was made up of an understanding of moral duties and moral rights, an understanding of the consequences for all concerned, as well as a host of five leadership characteristics that frequently were embodied in the life of the sixteenth president, characteristics that Mr. Lincoln also found, or should have found, in the best of men.

Finally, Mr. Lincoln was known for his uncanny ability to display compassion, even in the most difficult of circumstances. In a later chapter of this essay, chapter 7, on the problem of evil, we examine one particular case of the sixteenth president's use of compassion to the daughter of a Civil War Union soldier friend who had died in battle.

General William Sherman (1820–1891), in a meeting with President Lincoln on March 27, 1865, attempted to summarize the nature of Lincoln's moral character, in relationship to the Civil War. Sherman remarked, "I left more than ever impressed by his kindly nature, his deep and earnest sympathy with the afflictions of the whole people, resulting from the War, and his honest desire to end the war speedily, without more bloodshed and devastation, and to restore all the men of both sections to their homes."[76] The "both sections," of course, meant the North and the South.

Journalist Ellis Henry Roberts visited Illinois in 1860. In speaking to Mr. Lincoln's neighbors, Robert wrote, "I heard but one exception of

76. "Lincoln, Sherman and Grant Meet."

unqualified praise of Mr. Lincoln among his neighbors. No man living is more profoundly praised and respected. Everywhere I heard him spoke of as the best of husbands, the kindest of parents, and the most irreproachable of citizens."[77]

Ellis Henry Roberts (1827–1918) served in the House of Representatives from the state of New York. Later, Roberts became the publisher and editor of the *Utica Morning Herald*. He was writing for that paper when he visted Illinois in 1860 to speak with family and friends of Mr. Lincoln.

Mr. Lincoln also appears to have been a fervent believer in a moral theory known as "ethical egoism," mentioned earlier in this chapter. This theory asserts that all human beings primarily act from the standpoint of their own self-interest. One day the president remarked to a fellow passenger on an old-time mud coach. He had just explained to the companion his views on egoism, when the coach crossed a bridge. As they crossed, Lincoln discovered that a number of pigs were stuck in the mud on the shore. Lincoln called to the driver to stop, and the president proceeded to free the animals.

After doing so, and returning to the carriage, the president's companion asked, "Now where is the selfishness in that ?" Lincoln responded that the episode was the essence of selfishness. "I would have had no peace with myself if I had not freed those pigs.[78] By and large, Mr. Lincoln's major moral decisions during his administration were spot on. He handled some matters correctly right, most notably Fort Sumter, the cases of Fremont and Hunter, the "Emancipation Proclamation," and the abolition of slavery. In the words of Frederick Douglass about Mr. Lincoln, "Infinite Wisdom has seldom sent any man into a world better fitted for his mission than Abraham Lincoln."[79]

Both the Fremont and Hunter cases involved insubordination from a general. Major General David Hunter (1802–1886) was an 1822 graduate of West Point. He served on the Western frontier and eventually in the Mexican War, and commanded what was known as the "Department of the South." General Hunter abolished slavery in his department on May 9, 1862.President Lincoln reversed the action. He thought the general had surpassed his authority. Later, General Hunter raised the First South Carolina, an all-Black regiment that congress has approved. The Confederacy called Hunter "a felon to be executed if captured."

General John Christian Fremont (1813–1890) issued a proclamation on August 30, 1861, in St. Louis, during the early months of the war. The

---

77. Roberts, "Lincoln's Friends and Neighbors."

78. A version of this tale can be found at snopes.com from May 13, 2010.

79. Douglass, *Life and Times of Frederick Douglass*, 111.

proclamation placed the state of Missouri under martial law and decreed that all property of those bearing arms in rebellion would be confiscated, including slaves, who would be set free. Fremont had been a career army officer, frontiersman, and politician.

General Fremont was in command of the Department of the West from July to October of 1861. He claimed his proclamation was intended as a means of deterring secessionists in Missouri, but his policy had national repercussions. Potentially, the "Fremont Emancipation," as it was called, set a precedent that the Civil War was a conflict of liberation. In that regard, Mr. Lincoln was not happy with General Fremont.

For the sixteenth president, the Fremont Proclamation created a difficult situation, as he attempted to balance the agendas of the radical Republicans, who favored abolition, and slave-holding Unionists in the American border states, whose main aim was keeping Missouri, Kentucky, and Maryland in the Union. Consequently, President Lincoln saw both Hunter and Fremont as insubordinates, and he may have handled both cases in a much better manner than he did. *a mind-bogglingly fallacious*

At times, however, the sixteenth president showed some moral flaws. He did not argue for the full rights of Black citizens nearly early enough. He was harsh and outright vicious to General McClellan and Secretary of the Treasury Salmon P. Chase; and Lincoln should not have favored the idea of colonization. Still, as W. E. B. Du Bois said of Mr. Lincoln in his 1922 work "The Crisis," "I loved him not because he was perfect but because he was not."[80] In the same work, Mr. Du Bois remarked in the context of observations about the sixteenth president: *statement*

> The scars and foibles and contradictions of Great Men do not diminish but enhance the meanings of their upward struggles . . . It was his true history and antecedents that proved Abraham Lincoln a "Prince of Men."[81]

One final aspect of President Abraham Lincoln's view of ethics has to do with his understanding of America's place in the world. For Lincoln, the concept of justice had a value just beneath that of survival, not only of the nation's physical survival, but also its system of democratic government. Lincoln appears to have identified this system, as he thought the founding fathers did, with the survival of democracy throughout the world.

For Lincoln, the United States was the supreme demonstration of democracy; but the United States did not exist just to make men free in

80. Du Bois, "Crisis."
81. Ibid.

America. It had an even greater mission—to make people free everywhere. Lincoln saw a clear responsibility to the principle of liberty, not just in America, but in the world, as well. America's world-historical mission was crucial to Mr. Lincoln, as he quoted criticisms from "the liberal party of the world," and declared in his Peoria address that "Our Republican robe is soiled."[82]

Thus, in this fifth chapter of this essay on Mr. Lincoln's ethical views, we have maintained that the sixteenth president of the United States, Abraham Lincoln, knew and employed the moral theories of Aristotle, Immanuel Kant, and the nineteenth-century teleological theory of the utilitarians, as well as the theory of ethical egoism. We also have shown that President Lincoln was known for several moral traits that he frequently exhibited to others. These included: prudence, honesty, mercy, and humility, among many others. We also have maintained that President Lincoln saw the survival of the United States after the Civil War as an exemplar for democracy everywhere.

Finally, we also have suggested in this chapter of this essay that Mr. Lincoln's core values included: freedom, justice, reason, mercy, honor, prudence, and gratitude. This brings us to the sixth chapter, on what we have labeled "the Conversion of Abraham Lincoln."

---

82. Lincoln, Peoria address, October 16, 1854.

CHAPTER 6

The Conversion of Lincoln and the Role of Religion in the Civil War

I do not believe a word of it. It could not have been true while he was here, for I had frequent intimate conversations with him on the subjects of the Bible and the Christian Religion.

—REV. PHINEAS GURLEY, "Reflections on Abraham Lincoln"[1]

Finally, he spoke not in arrogance but in winsome humility . . . Instead of rallying his supporters, he asked his listeners to imitate the ways of God.

—RONALD C. WHITE, *Lincoln's Greatest Speech*

May God live in all . . . My poor boy, he was too good for this earth. God has called him home. I know that he is much better off in heaven.

—ABRAHAM LINCOLN, upon the death of his son Willie[2]

AS THE TITLE OF this chapter indicates, we shall deal with two separate issues in this chapter. In this sixth chapter of this work we first shall deal with the phenomenon held by some Lincoln scholars that the sixteenth president

---

1. In Gurley, *Assasination of Abraham Lincoln,* 17–18.
2. Qouted in "Death of Willie Lincoln."

of the United States, Abraham Lincoln, went through a period of religious conversion at the end of his life. This conversion, if indeed it did happen, was the result of a convergence of events.

These events include the most difficult period of the American Civil War and the deaths of two of Mr. Lincoln's sons, but most especially Willie Lincoln in February of 1862, from typhoid fever, which is caused by the *Salmonella* typhi bacteria, and may have existed in the White House's water supply.

These remarks on Lincoln's conversion will be followed in this chapter by a second topic, with some thoughts and observations on the role that religion played for the two sides of the American Civil War. As we shall see, religion played a pivotal role in the lives of people in the North and the South, as well as in the lives of slaves, during the Civil War period, from 1861 until 1865.

The minister of the New York Avenue Presbyterian Church, Dr. Phineas Gurley, in Washington, DC, which Lincoln and his family attended at the end of his life, wrote that on the following Sunday after the President's assassination he was to declare himself a believing member of the Presbyterian congregation. A number of other individuals close to Mr. Lincoln, around the same time, also allege that the president became more religious after the death of the president's two sons, particularly that of Willie, in February of 1862.

William Wallace Lincoln (1850–1862) was the third son of Abraham Lincoln. The blue-eyed boy was named after Mary Todd Lincoln's brother-in-law, Dr. William Wallace (1802–1867), who also was the Lincoln family physician when they lived in Springfield. When Willie and his younger brother, Tad, lived with their parents in Springfield they were said to be "hellions." Abraham Lincoln's third law partner, William Herndon, wrote that the boys turned their law office into chaos, pulling law books off the shelves and running around the office making noises, while their father appeared oblivious to their behavior.[3] With their father's election in 1860, the boys moved into the White House, which became their new playground.

In early 1862, both Willie and Tad became ill. Tad was only mildly affected by the illness, but Willie's condition was serious. On Thursday, February 20, 1862, shortly after 5:00 p.m., Willie died at the White House. The cause of death was typhoid fever brought on by tainted water or food. At the time, the White House drew its water from the Potomac River, though much of the land between the river and the White House was swampland and may easily have fostered disease.

3. Herndon, *Life of Lincoln*, 139.

Many historians suggest that this event may have been the most difficult personal crisis for Mr. and Mrs. Lincoln to endure. Willie was the president's favorite son and also the boy most like the sixteenth president, according to many close to the family, including both servants and friends.

After the funeral of Willie, Lincoln attempted to resume his schedule, but with very little success. For the next four days, he wrote no correspondence. In fact, this was the only period in his presidency when Mr. Lincoln did not write any letters. Elizabeth Keckley, a slave attendant to, and dress maker for, Mrs. Lincoln, reported that the president wept for days at a time. After Willie's death, Mrs. Lincoln was equally affected. In fact, they employed the services of mediums and spiritualists to try to contact their two dead sons.

Twelve years earlier, in 1850, Eddie Lincoln (1846–1850), another son, had died just a few days short of his fourth birthday.[4] After the death of her son Willie, Mrs. Lincoln isolated herself in her bedroom in the White House, spending her time reading tarot cards. Reportedly, she did the same thing after the death of her husband, as well.

After Willie's death in early 1862, both Mary Todd and Abraham Lincoln were devastated. Mrs. Lincoln appears to have found some comfort in mediums and what was called "spiritualism." She thought that the souls of departed loved ones could be contacted by "lifting a very slight veil," as William James called it, between the living and the dead, through seances. Between 1862 and 1865, at least four and as many as eight "sessions" were held at the White House, and one at the Soldier's Home. Mrs. Lincoln also attended several sessions at the home of Mr. and Mrs. Cranston Laurie, both well-known spiritualists in Georgetown.

"The Soldier's Home" was an armed forces retirement home established on March 3, 1851, when Congress passed a law to found a "Military Asylum for the relief and support of invalid and disabled soldiers of the Army of the United States." The séance at the Soldier's Home was conducted by a medium named "Lord" Charles J. Colchester, whose spiritual gifts were as fake as his supposed noble pedigree. He claimed to be an illegitimate son of an English duke.

Mr. Lincoln asked Dr. Joseph Henry, the first head of the Smithsonian, to investigate the royal medium. When Mr. Henry was unable to determine the cause of the rapping sounds, he asked Noah Brooks, a local writer, to attend the séance at the Soldier's Home. Later, Mr. Brooks gave an account of what went on that evening at the home in northwest Washington. In Mr.

4. See Wheeler, "Mystery of Eddie Lincoln."

Brooks' account, he clearly showed how the thumping noise came from a small drum. Thus, the son of a duke was a fraud.

Later, Mr. Colchester attempted to blackmail Mary Todd Lincoln, but Mr. Brooks again intervened. Even though the séance at the Soldier's Home might have been an embarrassment for the first lady, nevertheless, she continued to consult spiritualists throughout the remainder of her life. Several contemporary writers, including Herbert Mitgang, Daniel Mark Epstein, and Kenneth J. Winkle, give accounts of the séance at the Soldier's Home.[5]

The most famous of these spiritualist sessions, however involves the Laurie's daughter, Mrs. Belle Miller, who made a piano move and jump while Lincoln and two other men, reportedly, sat on the piano. The Lincolns also were involved with a medium named Nettie Colburn, who later wrote a 1891 book entitled *Was Abraham Lincoln a Spiritualist?* Mrs. Colburn claimed that she and the spirits she summoned influenced the president in regard to the "Emancipation Proclamation," as well as the establishment of the Freedmen's Bureau, a U.S. federal government agency established in 1865 to aid freed slaves in the South during Reconstruction.

Mr. Lincoln attended at least one of Mrs. Colburn's sessions in Georgetown. Nettie at the time was a twenty-one-year-old woman. In her book, Nettie described the result of her session with the president. She said:

> He turned to me, and laying his hand upon my head, uttered these words in a manner I shall never forget: "My child, you possess a very singular gift; but that it is of God, I have no doubt. I thank you for coming here tonight. It is more important than perhaps anyone present could understand."[6]

Mr. Lincoln's response to the medium was an ambivalent one. On the one hand, he says Mrs. Colburn's message is "of God." On the other hand, Mr. Lincoln's skepticism seems to lie just below the surface of the conversation.

On the occasion of the death of Eddie, as well, Mr. Lincoln was distraught. He turned at the time to Presbyterian clergyman the Rev. James A. Smith for aid. Dr. Smith had emigrated from Scotland and became the pastor at the First Presbyterian Church in Springfield. The two met, counseled, and prayed, and slowly, unsteadily, a change began. Lincoln scholar Stephen Mansfield suggests the beginning of this change was the death of Eddie.

As Mansfield put the matter, "It was the bugle call of Lincoln's epic battle of faith. Though Mr. Lincoln never joined a church and seldom spoke of Jesus Christ publically, he became our most spiritual Chief Executive, at

---

5. See Mitgange quoted in Brooks, *Washington in Lincoln's Time*, 66–68; Epstein, *Lincolns: Portrait of a Marriage*, 385–86; Winkle, *Abraham and Mary Lincoln*, 123–25.

6. Colburn, *Was Abraham Lincoln a Spiritualist?*

times becoming more Prophet than President."[7] Indeed, when Mr. Lincoln did refer to Jesus, it was usually as "My" or "Our Savior." Although Lincoln seems to have rejected survival after death in his skeptical period, in the above passage he appears to have endorsed immortality of the soul. He may, of course, also have been mindful of the general views of his constituents and been hedging his bets in this incident.

The death of Willie twelve years later intensified this new movement to religion. Indeed, several people at the time reported that Mr. Lincoln told them that his beliefs about religion changed at this time. When Willie died, Lincoln is reported to have said about Willie, "May God live in all. He was too good for this earth. The good Lord has called him home. I know that he is much better off in Heaven."[8]

Bishop Matthew Simpson, who gave the address at Lincoln's funeral, quoted the president asking a soldier, "Do you ever find yourself talking to the dead? Since Willie's death, I catch myself every day, involuntarily talking to him as if he were with me."[9] Matthew Simpson (1811–1884) was an American bishop in the Methodist-Episcopal Church. He moved from Ohio to Evanston, Illinois, in 1859. Bishop Simpson got to know Mr. Lincoln in the winter of 1860–1861. Later, he became a trusted confidant of the president.

Another aspect of this new movement to religion on the part of Mr. Lincoln was developments in the war. It was not going well for the Union.[10] General George McClellen (1826–1885) had failed in the Peninsula Campaign, shortly after Willie's death. General Robert E. Lee and his Confederate army were victorious at the Second Battle of Bull Run; after this event, Mr. Lincoln is reported to have said, "I have been driven many times to my knees by the overwhelming conviction that I had nowhere else to go."[11] Salmon Chase (1808–1873), Lincoln's secretary of the treasury, reports that while Mr. Lincoln was preparing the "Emancipation Proclamation" he commented, "I made a solemn vow before God, that if General Lee was driven back from Mary-land, I would crown the result by the declaration of freedom to the slaves."[12]

---

7. Mansfield, *Lincoln's Battle with God*, 63.

8. Donald, *Lincoln*, 251–52.

9. Crooks, *Life of Bishop Matthew Simpson*, 5–6.

10. Donald, *Lincoln*, 267–368.

11. This quote appears to be among the many spurious remarks that it has been recorded that Mr. Lincoln said. More is said of these remarks in the concluding chapter of this work, chapter 8.

12. Donald, *Lincoln*, 281–82.

Mr. Lincoln appears to be referring here to the Battle of Antietam, fought on September 17, 1862, near Sharpsburg, Maryland, at Antietam Creek. Robert E. Lee's troops were turned back at the battle, securing the victory for Mr. Lincoln and his Union army.

Indeed, from the time of Willie Lincoln's death until Mr. Lincoln's assassination, he appears to have been far more religious than at any other time in his adult life. His address at Gettysburg in July of 1863, his decision along with the secretary of the treasury to include "In God we trust" engraved on all U.S. coins, and the many references to God in his second inaugural address are all indications of this new conversion experience at the end of his life.

Scretary of the Navy Gideon Welles (1802–1878), also recorded what he saw as Mr. Lincoln's late conversion in his life. After the Battle at Antietam, Welles records Mr. Lincoln as saying, "God has decided this question in favor of the slaves."[13] Welles adds, "He was satisfied that he was right, and was confirmed and strengthened in his actions and vow [at Antietam,] and the results."[14] Secretary Welles believed that Mr. Lincoln was confident that God had "decided" the battle on the side of the North, and that the Union was on the side of the right in that skirmish.

In September of 1864, Lincoln placed the role of the Civil War squarely within the purview of divine providence. In a letter to a member of the Quakers, the Society of Friends, for example, Mr. Lincoln wrote:

> The purposes of the Almighty are perfect, and must prevail, though we erring mortals may fail accurately to perceive them in advance. We hoped for a happy termination of this terrible war long before this; but God knows best, and has ruled otherwise . . . we must work earnestly in the best light He gives us, trusting that so working still conduces to the great ends He ordains. Surely, He intends some great good to follow this mighty convulsion, which no mortal can make, and no mortal can stay.[15]

Mr. Lincoln clearly believed that God had some great good or "great ends," as he put it, that was to follow the American Civil War, and that no human being could change that divine plan. He also believed that humans were not the *cause* of the war, and that no human could change its course. Lincoln thought that at some point all the suffering and evil of the war would be seen as necessary, in order that the "great ends" might follow.

13. Ibid., 285.
14. Ibid.
15. Lincoln, letter to Mrs. Eliza Gurney, September 4, 1864.

This is an obvious reference to divine plan theory, with respect to the issues of theodicy and the problem of evil. More will be said about the problem of evil later in this chapter, as well as in chapter 8 of this essay, which is dedicated to the issues of theodicy and the problem of evil.

On the day that Mr. Lincoln was shot, he reportedly told his wife that he wished to visit the Holy Land, and "There is no place he so much desired to see as Jerusalem."[16] A pastor from Freeport, Illinois, in November of 1864 said that he had visited the president in the White House, and after conducting other business casually asked Mr. Lincoln if he loved Jesus. The anonymous Illinois pastor said the president buried his face in a red handkerchief as tears came to his eyes. Then, Mr. Lincoln is reported to have responded:

> When I left home to take this chair of state, I requested my countrymen to pray for me. I was not then a Christian. When my son died, the severest trial of my life, I was not a Christian. But when I went to Gettysburg and looked upon the graves of our dead heroes who had fallen in defense of their country, I then and there consecrated myself to Christ. Yes, I do love Jesus![17]

This story from the anonymous Illinois minister has been repeated in a number of versions, and in many venues. Sometimes they say "crosses" rather than "graves," and some have the president saying "Christ" instead of "Jesus." One of these other versions is reported by William Eleazar Barton in *The Soul of Abraham Lincoln*. Mr. Barton's version of the tale tells us this:

> This incident must have appeared in print immediately after Lincoln's death, for I find it quoted in memorial addresses of May, 1865. Mr. Oldroyd has endeavored to learn from me in what paper he found it and on whose authority it rests, but without result. He does not remember where he found it. It is inherently improbable, and rests on no adequate testimony. It ought to be wholly disregarded. The earliest reference I have found to this story in which Lincoln is alleged to have said to this unnamed Illinois Minister, "I do love Jesus," is in a sermon preached in the Baptist Church of Oshkosh, Wisconsin, on April 19, 1865, by the Rev. W.W. Whitcomb, which was published in the Oshkosh *Northwestern*, on April 21, 1865, and issued as a pamphlet in 1907 by John E. Burton.[18]

16. Mansfield, *Lincoln's Battle with God*, 3.

17. Ibid., 4–7.

18. Barton, *Soul of Abraham Lincoln*, 19.

Mr. Barton doubts the validity of this tale, and then he suggests another version of the narrative supplied by the Rev. W. W. Whitcomb of Wisconsin. The Mr. Oldroyd referred to here is Osborn Oldroyd (1842–1930), a Civil War sergeant who served in the Twentieth Ohio Volunteer Infantry in 1861. Later, after the war, Mr. Oldroyd rented a house from the Lincoln family. The Rev. William W. Whitcomb (1838–1900) was a Baptist preacher who served congregations in Wisconsin for over forty years.

What to make of this tale that Mr. Lincoln came to Jesus at the end of his life is not entirely clear. What is unmistakable, however, is that from the death of Eddie Lincoln in 1850 until Mr. Lincoln's assassination in 1865, our sixteenth president had become considerably more religious than he had been earlier in his adult life. Late in Lincoln's life, the skeptical beliefs appeared to have been gone, and in their place was a clear, religious commitment, perhaps a deep commitment to Jesus Christ.

Even earlier, in 1839, while Lincoln was still in Springfield, the Rev. James F. Jacquess suggested that Mr. Lincoln converted to Christianity in his church. Indeed, the minister gave this account of the episode:

> The Church was filled that morning. It was a good sized Church, but on that day all the seats were filled. I had chosen for my text, 'Ye must be born again,' and during the course of my sermon I laid particular stress on 'must.' Mr. Lincoln came into the Church, and after the service had commenced, chairs were put in front of the altar and Lincoln and Governor French and his wife sat near the altar for the entire service. Mr. Lincoln was on my left and the Governor on my right, and I noticed that Mr. Lincoln appeared to be deeply interested in the sermon. A few days after that Sunday, Mr. Lincoln called on me and informed me that he had been greatly impressed with my remarks on Sunday and that he had come to talk with me further on the matter. I invited him in, and my wife and I talked and prayed with him for hours. Now, I have seen many persons converted; I have seen hundreds brought to Christ, and if ever a person was converted, Abraham Lincoln was converted that night in my house.[19]

The text, of course, that the minister had chosen for his sermon was the Gospel of John 3:7, from which came one of the key ideas of the Second Great Awakening—the notion of being "born again." The Rev. Jacquess went on to describe meeting Mr. Lincoln after the service that day to discuss theological issues further. The minister was also a member of that school

---

19. The Rev. Jacquess, quoted in ibid., 309–13. The remarks appear as an appendix to Barton's volume.

that believes that the sixteenth president had a conversion experience—far sooner, in 1839, than other thinkers have suggested.

Dr. James F. Jacquess (1836–1902) was a Methodist minister and war hero. He helped to organize the Seventy-Third Regiment of Illinois, rising to the rank of colonel. After the war, he served a number of Methodist congregations in and around Springfield. Late in life, he received a twelve-dollar-a month-pension from the army. The Seventy-Third Regiment of Illinois was known as the "Parson's" or "Preacher's Regiment" because of the number of ministers who had joined the unit.

The Governor French referred to in the above passage is Augustus French (1808–1864), the ninth governor of the state of Illinois. He served as governor from 1846 until 1852, several years after the events described in this narrative. These comments from 1839 by the Rev. Jacquess come more than twenty years before the death of Willie Lincoln.

Other Lincoln scholars find Jacquess's claim unlikely to be true. Indeed, a number of writers claim that if the sixteenth president went through a conversion, it was at the end of his life. Contemporary historian Allen C. Guelzo, for example, comments on this move to religion by Mr. Lincoln late in life. He observes:

> This was no mean feat, coming from a man who had been suspected of agnosticism or atheism most of his life. Yet, by the end, while still a religious skeptic, Lincoln too seemed to equate the preservation of the Union and the freeing of the slaves with some higher mystical purpose.[20]

This remark of Mr. Guelzo is quite similar to the end of Mr. Lincoln's second inaugural address, which speaks of "mystical cords" that keep the Union together. Presbyterian minister the Rev. James Armstrong Reed (1830–1921), while preparing a series of lectures on Lincoln's religion, asked a number of the president's friends and colleagues about whether Lincoln was an infidel. Pastor Phineas Gurley, of New York Avenue Presbyterian Church in Washington, DC, said about the alleged infidelity, "I do not believe a word of it. It could not have been true while he was here, for I had frequent and intimate conversations with him on the subjects of the Bible and the Christian Religion."[21]

The Rev. Gurley, then, also seems to believe that Mr. Lincoln was planning to return to the church the Sunday following his assassination, and purportedly sent the minister a letter to inform him that he was to join the

---

20. Guelzo, *Redeemer President*, 328.

21. See Barbee, "President Lincoln and Dr. Gurley."

church the Sunday after his assassination, Easter Sunday 1865. This supposed letter, however, has never surfaced since Gurley's time.

The Rev. James A. Smith, who had emigrated from Scotland to assume the position of Pastor at the First Presbyterian Church in Springfield, was the author of *The Christian Defence*, a book that is said to have had an influence on Mr. Lincoln. Later, in a letter from Smith to William Herndon that later appeared in the *Springfield Journal*, in March of 1867, the minister wrote to Lincoln's law partner:

> It will no doubt be gratifying to the friends of Christianity to learn that very shortly after Mr. Lincoln became a member of my congregation, at my request, in the presence of a large assembly at the annual meeting of the Bible Society of Springfield, he delivered an address the object of which was to inculcate the importance of having the Bible placed in the possession of every family of the state. In the course of it he drew a striking contrast between the Decalogue and the moral codes of the most eminent lawgivers of antiquity, and closed, as near as I can recollect in the following language: 'It seems to me that nothing short of infinite wisdom could by any possibility had devised and given to man this excellent and perfect moral code. It is suited to men in all conditions of life, and includes all the duties they owe to their Creator, to themselves, and to their fellow men.[22]

If the Rev. Smith is correct about this episode, and if Mr. Lincoln did, in fact, have a conversion experience—a return to his Baptist roots—then it may have occurred during his time in Springfield, and Dr. Smith attributed that conversion to be a product of the grace of God; but other reports by the Rev. Gurley and others say that the President's conversion came much later, if it happened at all.

William Barton, another Lincoln biographer, mentions a lawyer in Springfield named Thomas Lewis, who had an office near that of Herndon and Lincoln. In November of 1898, Mr. Lewis, who by then lived in Kansas, wrote a letter in which he mentioned the alleged conversion and lecture of Mr. Lincoln's in Springfield. Mr. Lewis wrote:

> Some months later the session of the church invited Mr. Lincoln to give an address on the Bible. When it became known that Mr. Lincoln was to lecture in the Presbyterian Church it assured a full house. It was said by divines and others to be the ablest defense of the Bible ever uttered in public.[23]

22. Anonymous, in the *Springfield Journal*, March 27, 1867.
23. Barton, *Soul of Abraham Lincoln*, 23–25.

If Mr. Barton and Mr. Lewis are correct about this episode in Mr. Lincoln's life, then this letter would be further evidence that if the president did, indeed, return to his Christian roots, he may have done it far before his time as president in the 1860s. Other scholars, however, such as David Herbert Davis, for example, have doubts that the lecture, or the conversion, took place in the Springfield years, if at all.[24]

Still other critics maintain that Mr. Lincoln was ever the pragmatist, whose reed bent in whatever political and desirable wind was blowing at the time. Mr. Lincoln knew how to take the temperature of his political environment, and the sentiment of the lecture, if it did take place, may well have been what Mr. Lincoln believed he thought the audience wanted to hear. This is the position, for example, of John Burt, in his biography of Mr. Lincoln, published by Harvard University Press in 2013.[25]

Nevertheless, Mrs. Sidney Lauck, in February of 1928, reported that the Rev. Gurley told her after Lincoln's death that the following Sunday the president was to join the Presbyterian congregation. Mrs. Lauck said she was about thirty years old when she was told this about Mr. Lincoln. Later, in 1928, Mrs. Lauck signed an affidavit under oath in Essex County, New Jersey, in which she again stated that the Rev. Phineas Gurley, pastor of New York Avenue Presbyterian Church in Washington, DC, told her the president had made arrangements to join the church "by confession of his faith in Christ." The event was to take place on Easter Sunday, but Lincoln was shot on Good Friday and died at 7:22 on Sabbath morning.[26]

Although it is possible that this story was true, Dr. Gurley mentioned nothing of it at Mr. Lincoln's funeral in the White House, nor in his reply to the Rev. Reed mentioned above; and Dr. Gurley never produced the letter from Mr. Lincoln informing the minister of his intention to declare himself as a member of Gurley's Presbyterian church.[27] It seems likely that this story is an apocryphal one.

Further proof of Lincoln's conversion and faith is provided by the tale of visiting Quaker Mrs. Eliza Gurney and three friends to the White House on October 26, 1862. As Quakers, they were quite different from other visitors, for they had no axe to grind in the war. In what amounted to a short sermon, Mrs. Gurney said she wanted to assure the president that he was "an instrument of God," that his efforts to see the oppressed go free "would bear

24. Davis, *Lincoln*, 354–76.

25. Burt, *Lincoln's Tragic Pragmatism*, 670–83.

26. See Deckle, *Prairie Defender.*

27. Ibid.

fruit," and that he should "continually seek to be in consort with the W God."[28]

Mr. Lincoln is reported to have been visibly moved by her sincerity, and thanked the visitors with these words:

> I have desired that all my words and actions may be in accordance with His Will; but if after endeavoring to do my best with the light which He affords me, I find my efforts have failed, then I must believe that, for some purposes unknown to me, He wills it otherwise. If I had had my way, this war would never have been; but, nevertheless, it came. If I had had my way, the war would have ended before this; but, nevertheless, it still continues. We must conclude that He permits it, if I am able to comprehend it; for we cannot but believe that He Who made us is glad always.[29]

The mention of "purposes unknown" is another reference to the view that God's will will be the final word on the war and, in Lincoln's view, God's unknown purposes will eventually come to full fruition, either in history or beyond the grave. Mr. Lincoln also appears here to be expressing a genuine religious belief, while at the same time also expressing belief in two Christian responses to the problem of evil—that God has a divine plan, and that the Divine "permits" evil, while not "causing" it. A year or so after the Eliza Gurley meeting, the Rev. John H. Barrows claimed that Mr. Lincoln became a Christian in 1863.

The Rev. Barrows reported about Mr. Lincoln at Gettysburg:

> In the anxious uncertainties of the great war, he gradually rose to his full height, where Jehovah became to him the sublimest of realities, the ruler of nations . . . When darkness gathered over the brave armies fighting for the nation's life, this strong man in the early morning knelt and wrestled in prayer with Him who holds the fate of empires. When the clouds lifted above the carnage of Gettysburg, he gave his heart to the Lord, Jesus Christ.[30]

The Rev. Barrows, then, seemed to have believed that if Mr. Lincoln had a conversion experience, it took place at Gettysburg. Barrows said it was a dedication to "Jehovah," the name that God gave himself at Exodus 6:2–3. In most English Bibles, the word *Jehovah* is translated as "Lord," though

28. Gurley, letter to Abraham Lincoln, October 26, 1862.

29. Lincoln, letter to Mrs. Eliza Gurley, November 9, 1862.

30. The Rev. John H. Barrows later would become president of Oberlin College, beginning in 1899.

Jehovah is not an ancient Hebraic name for God; rather, it is a derivative of the name *Yahweh* that was developed by sixteenth-century Christians.

The portrait painter Francis Bicknell Carpenter (1830–1900), in his book *Six Months at the White House*, told the Rev. Reed that the president had a "change of heart," and intended at some suitable time to make a profession of his religion.[31] Mr. Carpenter resided at the Lincoln White House for a period of six months while he was working on his now-famous portrait called *First Reading the Emancipation Proclamation of President Lincoln*. The painting now resides at the United States Capitol.

These comments made above by Allen Guelzo point out that some Lincoln scholars in contemporary America also believe that Mr. Lincoln found religion at the end of his life; but whether or not this was actually true, there is not nearly enough evidence at this point in the scholarly materials to verify this fact.

Finally, contemporary Lincoln scholar Ronald C. White, in his book *Lincoln's Greatest Speech*, as well as in his essay in the journal *Christian History*, takes a positive view about the question of Mr. Lincoln's conversion. About the end of Lincoln's second inaugural address, Mr. White observes:

> Finally, he spoke not in arrogance but in winsome humility. In the final paragraph of the Second Inaugural, Lincoln offered the ultimate surprise. Instead of rallying his supporters in the name of God to support the War, he asked his listeners, quietly to imitate the ways of God.[32]

The paragraph in question tells us:

> With malice toward none, with charity for all, with firmness in the right as God gives us to see the right, let us strive on to finish the work we are in, to bind up the nation's wounds, to care for him who shall have borne the battle and for his widow and his orphan, to do all which may achieve and cherish a just and lasting peace among ourselves and with all nations.[33]

Like Allen Guelzo, F. B. Carpenter, the Rev. John Barrows, and William Barton, Ronald White also believes that the sixteenth president of the United States, Abraham Lincoln, went through a religious conversion of sorts at the end of his life; and like these other men, we too think it is advisable to take this same point of view on the matter. In the last three years of Mr. Lincoln's life, William Herndon had very little contact with the president. If the latter

31. Carpenter, *Six Months at the White House*.
32. White, *Lincoln's Greatest Speech*.
33. Ibid., 6.

had a conversion experience, the former may not even have known it had occurred of the latter.

Mr. Lincoln pointed out in his second inaugural address that "strange men should dare to ask a Just God's assistance in wringing their bread from the sweat of other men's faces"—an allusion to Genesis 3:19, as well as the practice of using slave labor in the South. This is followed, immediately, by quoting the Sermon on the Mount, "Judge not, lest we be judged," from Matthew 7:1–2 (KJV). By his second inaugural in March of 1865, Lincoln's religious conversion, from the childhood belief in the law of necessity, through his period of skepticism, and then finally to the mature belief in divine plan theory, was now complete.

In regard to the other topic of this chapter of this essay, the religious and theological ideas that helped to shape the origins of the Civil War, as well as President Abraham Lincoln's actions during that conflict, to this we shall now turn.

In the process of Northern abolitionists and Southern slaveholders clashing over the question of slavery, Mr. Lincoln kept to his vision, to keep the Union together. At the same time, both sides of the conflict turned to the Bible to argue their causes. Frederick Douglass, at the time, despaired that people who called themselves Christians could defend the uses of violence on both sides of the war.[34]

Over and against this positive evidence that Mr. Lincoln went through a religious conversion at the end of his life, we still have the claims of his law partner, William H. Herndon. To those who claim that the sixteenth president was converted to Christianity, Mr. Herndon asks:

> Do you mean to say that Mr. Lincoln was converted and that he so declared? If so, where, when, and before whom did he declare or reveal it? Do you mean to say that Mr. Lincoln joined a Church? If so, what Church did he join. Do you mean to say that Mr. Lincoln was a secret Christian, acting under the cloak of the devil to advance Christianity? If so, what is your authority? [35]

Both sides of the Civil War were convinced that God was on their side. Meanwhile, Mr. Lincoln, who had put his faith in reason over revelation, in his period of skepticism, had to come to grips with the mounting casualties, as well as the death of his young son Willie. In his anguish, as we have argued earlier in this essay, Lincoln began a religious transformation or conversion that changed his ideas about God and the ultimate meaning of the war.

34. Douglass, *Life and Times of Fredereck Douglass*, 113.
35. Herndon, *Life of Lincoln*, 263.

The Civil War was both a political and a theological crisis. There were sharp disagreements over what God might be doing in and through the war. For some Americans, the turmoil of the war years called into question the belief that America was a chosen nation with a special destiny. The war also occasioned Lincoln to reexamine his own understanding of God's purposes and the role of divine providence, or divine necessity, in the affairs of men.

A mere forty-one days after President Lincoln delivered his stirring second inaugural address on March 4, 1865, with its Old Testament language, deep moral sentiments, and conciliatory language, Lincoln was shot dead by an assassin. For many, Mr. Lincoln immediately became an American martyr, cut down on Good Friday, ironically enough!

The Civil War began with the Battle at Fort Sumter, a skirmish whose only fatality was the horse of a Confederate officer. The theological points of view of the Confederate States of America—the Southern point of view—largely rested on the truth of two philosophical propositions: first, that individual states were sovereign, even to the point of secession from the Union; and second, that the peculiar practice of slavery was not only expedient, but it also was ordained by God, and explicitly upheld by Sacred Scripture.

More specifically, people in the South believed that the Old Testament outlines the parameters under which slavery could be practiced, and the rules under which it may be conducted. Exodus 21:2–6; Leviticus 25:39–55; and Deuteronomy 15:12–18 were among the sacred texts most often pointed to as a theological justification for slavery.

The first of these Old Testament passages, the one from Exodus, speaks only of the rules pertaining to Hebrew slaves. The second passage, Leviticus 25:39–55, talks about the conditions under which slaves may be redeemed in the Old Testament. It is only in the third passage, Deuteronomy 15:12–18, that we find rules under which slaves may be freed. Ironically, Deuteronomy 15:18 tells us that slaves are worthy of freedom after they have served a master for six years. If the American South followed this provision, of course, there would have been few captives left on the plantation. Most slave families stayed put for decades in the American South.

Nevertheless, the South claimed to be a uniquely Christian nation. In fact the new Constitution of the Confederate States of America, which was adopted on February 8, 1861, and ratified a month later, announced its Christian identity, "invoking the favor and guidance of Almighty God."[36] This is something the U.S. Constitution does not do.

Indeed, the Southern states chose as their national motto the Latin expression *Deo Vindice*, or "God will avenge!!" At the time of the ratification

36. Constitution of the Confederate States, February 8, 1861.

of the Southern states' constitution, President Jefferson Davis proclaimed that "The time has come to recognize our dependence upon God . . . and to supplicate His merciful protection."[37]

At the same time, the Confederates saw themselves to be at odds with the "godless" government of the North, a government that ignored the divine in its constitution. The South also maintained that the North put secular concerns above the sacred duties of Christian service and above a divine commission.

Vindication that God's will was on the side of the South was seen in the victory at First Manassas, also called the First Battle of Bull Run by the Union, on July 21, 1861, in Prince William County, Virginia. The Battle of Bull Run is considered by many to be the first great battle of the Civil War. A large Union force under the command of General Irvin McDowell was routed by a Confederate army under General Pierre G. T. Beauregard.

General Beuregard (1818–1893) was a native of Louisiana. He served in the U.S. army until his resignation in February of 1861, at which time he began serving the Confederacy. He was instrumental in the victory at the Battle of Bull Run, in July of 1861.

In a sermon on gratitude preached that same day as the Battle of Bull Run, at St. John's Episcopal Church in Richmond, by Rev. William C. Butler, the Southern minister declared:

> God has given us of the South today a fresh and golden oppor-
> tunity—and so a most solemn command—to realize that form
> of government in which the just, constitutional rights of each
> and all are guaranteed to each and all . . . He has placed us in the
> front rank of the most marked epochs of the world's history. He
> has placed in our hands a commission which we can faithfully
> execute only by holy, individual self-consecration to all of God's
> Plans.[38]

The Rev. Butler speaks of the Battle at Bull Run being a "golden opportunity" for the South. He praised the Confederate form of government, suggesting it was among the greatest governments in human history. Certainly, these were grandiose claims and there is little evidence that any of them were true.

Declarations such as this one became regular occurrences in the Southern religious press, as well as in the pulpit. It was the belief of those in the South that God was ultimately on their side. Even the secular press got in on the spin. The *Richmond Daily Express*, to cite one example, reported in

37. Some translate it, "God brings retribution."

38. The Rev. William C. Butler, "Sermon on Battle of Bull Run," July 22, 1861, St. John's Episcopal Church, Richmond, reprinted in Snay, *Gospel of Disunion*.

January of 1864 that "The religious interests in the Army is unchilled by the cold weather."[39] Even the cold weather could not stop Johnny Reb!

One of the ways that the Southern religious press solidified the South's belief that the Confederacy was a "chosen nation" was the mythology that sprung up around Southern leaders like General Stonewall Jackson. Jackson had rallied his troops with his conviction that God would deliver them to victory. When he died on the battlefield, his memory and the strength of most important Southern religious values and beliefs—not unlike Mr. Lincoln was seen in the North after his death—began to wane as well. Like Lincoln, General Jackson was seen as a martyr to the cause.

General Thomas Jonathan "Stonewall" Jackson (1824–1863), after Robert E. Lee, was the best known general of the Confederate army. He was also regarded then, and now by historians, as the greatest military tactician of the cause of the South.

Mrs. Mildred Lynch, of Augusta County, Virginia, drew encouragement from her minister in January of 1861 when he "likened his sermon to the Israelites and earnestly sought deliverance for us," much like the Israelites being brought out of captivity in Egypt.[40] Judith McGuire attended a fast service in Richmond on March 27, 1863. Mrs. McGuire wrote, "The church was crowded with worshippers, who, I trust, felt their dependence on God in this great struggle."[41]

Another religious belief that was common in the American South in the 1860s was the view that God had not abandoned them. Rather, they held that the Divine was disciplining or testing them in a burning fire that would hone them for a higher calling, one that was yet to be revealed. Interestingly enough, at the same time, people in the North were employing precisely the same arguments. Thus, the South often used what we call the "test perspective," or the "moral qualities view," with regard to the issues of theodicy and the problem of evil. More is said about these views in a later chapter of this essay, chapter 7.

For now, it is enough to say that religious people in the South regularly saw the suffering of the war as a "test" of people's character, or a way of improving that character. The South believed that God employed evil and suffering to test the mettle of believers, or even to make moral characters in the South better. Thus, they used two responses to the problem of evil that

39. In the *Richmond Daily Express*, January 19, 1864.

40. Mildred Lynch, Diary, entry from January 20, 1861.

41. Judith McGuire, *Diary of a Southern Refugee During the War*, entry from March 27, 1863.

we will see in chapter 7 of this essay—the test perspective and the moral qualities view.

At the same time, the theological presuppositions of the Northerners were radically different in at least four important ways. First, the North saw America as having a special status in world history. With its republican institutions, democratic ideals, and Christian values, the United States was thought by those in the North to stand on the vanguard of civilization marching forward. The success of the South, in the eyes of the North, would impede that progress. If the South was successful in dismembering the Union, the idea of republican government would be deemed by people everywhere to have been declared a failure.

The Northerners saw themselves, therefore, as struggling on behalf of the preservation of the Union, as well as the advance of liberty elsewhere in the world. In that regard, Mr. Lincoln saw himself as the "keeper of democracy." If it failed in America, it could fail elsewhere, now and in times to come. This would bring doubt among people in the South that their government was the best form of government.

Secondly, Christian Protestant ministers in the North began to portray the struggle with the South in terms of the millennium. They drew from images outlined in chapter 20 of the book of Revelation, as well as other portions of Scripture describing events that depict the end of time with tribulations and the second coming of Jesus Christ. More specifically, these ministers drew on passages such as Romans 12:12; John 16:33; Revelation 11:7 and chapter 20; Matthew 7:21–23; 19:28; and 24:21; and Luke 21:22.

These ministers in the North began to characterize the war as a victory that preceded the kingdom of God on Earth. In this scheme, this time will come after the thousand-year period described in Revelation already has happened.

Thirdly, these theological presuppositions caused the North to begin to understand the issue of slavery in profoundly different terms. At the beginning of the war, Northern ministers exhibited an entire spectrum of theological points of view in regard to slavery. These perspectives ran from a desire for emancipation because slavery is an immoral institution, to those who suggested that slavery was morally acceptable because it was sanctioned by the Bible, such as in the above analysis.

Those who held this latter extreme said that contemporary Christians had no business condemning slavery as sinful, for it is sanctioned by Holy Writ. Most Northern Protestant ministers fell somewhere between these two extremes. They considered slavery to be less than ideal, but that it would eradicate itself by slow and peaceful means. At the same time, they abhorred the abolitionist's attacks on slaveholders as sinners.

The abolitionist ministers began to formulate a response to the biblical sanctioning of slavery found principally in the Old Testament. They pointed to one New Testament letter in particular, in which slave owner Philemon is told by Saint Paul to welcome back a certain Onesimus, "No longer as a slave, but more as a beloved brother . . . both in the flesh and in the Lord" (Philemon 1:16, KJV).

In another passage in the New Testament, at the Gospel of Luke 12:47–48, the text seems to confirm that the beating of slaves is acceptable. The New Testament Greek word for "slave" is *doulos*. It usually is accompanied by the word *despote*, or "master." These terms are employed at Luke 17:7–10; Romans 7:22–23; 1 Peter 2:16; Matthew 8:9; and 11:28–30, as well as a variety of other places in the New Testament.

For these Northern Protestant ministers in this Pauline text, they found a theological justification for the proposition that Black slaves were to be afforded the same status as White slave owners. Rather than encouraging slaves to embrace and accept their captivity, the abolitionist perspectives urged them to seek their freedom. Some debate what purposes Saint Paul had in this passage in question, but it is clear that there were a number of first-century Jews and Christians who resisted the practice of slavery.

The community responsible for the Dead Sea Scrolls, for example, the Essenes, forbade their members from owning slaves.[42] Revelation 18:13 lists slaves among a group of luxury items that Roman soldiers generated by exploiting other societies. Luxuries, of course, were frowned upon in the early church.

In fact, many early ancient Christian documents indicate that some early Christians sold themselves into slavery in order to redeem others. One good example of this is 1 Clement 54:4–5. Other early Christian communities collected funds to buy the freedom of slaves, as is indicated in Ignatius of Loyola's letter to Polycarp of Smyrna.[43]

In addition to these presuppositions of the South and the North during the Civil War, there is also a third point of view to be considered—that of the slaves. Within the privacy of the Southern slave quarters, the Bible was employed for entirely different purposes. The slaves had their preachers too, as well as their own secret gatherings. On many Southern farms, Black preachers were among the only literate captives. This created powerful narratives and stories of redemption and retribution against their White owners.

42. The Essenes were a first-century Jewish party living near the Dead Sea.

43. Ignatius, *Letters*, 4:8–10.

These slave preachers frequently likened the role of the Southern slaves to be like Moses leading the Israelites out of Egypt to freedom, or Joshua who led the tribes of Israel after Moses' death. Indeed, many slaves in the period of the Civil War saw Mr. Lincoln as a "new Moses" or a "new Joshua."

Like both of the competing sides in the Civil War conflict, African-American slaves also saw God to be on their side. This resolve gave rise to a number of slave phenomena in mid-nineteenth-century America. One development is the Underground Railroad, by which many slaves sought freedom in the North, by way of a clandestine passage to freedom. A second phenomenon is the existence of runaway slave advertisements that began to appear in American newspapers like the *Virginia Gazette* and the *Maryland Gazette* in the third quarter of the eigtheenth century. These advertisements continued in the South until the close of the Civil War.[44]

Another way that freed Blacks and slaves began to participate in the Civil War to fight was the number of men who joined both the North and the South during the Civil War. News from Fort Sumter set off a rush of free Blacks to enlist in U.S. military units. Altogether, some 180,000 African-Americans fought in the conflict. These men served 163 different units in the Union army, and many other in the navy, as well. In 1861, only 1 percent of all Black people in America were in the North. Although African-Americans fought for the North from 1861 on, in the South slaves and freed men only began serving the Confederate army in 1865.[45]

Figures exist that suggest that nearly 80,000 Black men served in the Union army: close to 25,000 alone from the state of Kentucky; 9,000 in both Maryland and Pennsylvania; 8,000 from Missouri; 5,000 in Ohio and New York; and 4,000 from both Massachusetts and the District of Columbia.[46] In the South, the state with the most Black volunteers into the Confederate army was Louisiana (25,000), followed by Tennessee (20,000), Mississippi (18,000), Virginia (6,000), and North and South Carolina (5,000 each).[47]

When all was said and done, it was crystal clear that religion played a significant role in the Civil War period, for the South, the North, and for the slaves in captivity in America. Religion took part in the shared culture and language that developed among African-Americans. Religion also fueled the entrance of African-Americans into leadership positions, in Civil Rights contexts, and in the arts and education venues in America.

44. The *Virginia Gazette* began publishing in 1736, nine years after the *Maryland Gazette*.

45. "Black Civic War Soldiers."

46. Ibid.

47. Ibid.

One final aspect of the religious underpinnings of the Civil War period has to do with an environment of pessimism and negativity that began to appear in all three contexts discussed in this chapter of this essay. Indeed, all three aspects of the conflict—the North, the South, and the slaves—began to exhibit negative and pessimistic pronouncements in regard to how the war was going. Many of these points of view came in the context of the ever-rising number of deaths in the Civil War. Indeed, by its end nearly 700,000 Americans died in the conflict—more than in all of America's others wars combined.

One way to see this negativity in the Confederate army of 1861 was to see General Stonewall Jackson's reply to being told that God was on the side of the South. Jackson is said to have replied, "I am afraid that our people are looking to the wrong source for help, and ascribing our successes to those to whom they are not due." The general is said to have added, "If we fail to trust in God and give Him all the glory our cause is ruined. Give to our friends at home due warning on this subject."[48] General Jackson clearly was ambivalent about God's role in the Civil War. He seems to have been cautious in saying, "God is on our side."

At any rate, many in the North also were becoming negative and pessimistic about the outcomes of the war—no man more so than President Lincoln himself. One way to see Mr. Lincoln's pessimism and negativity about the war is to look at his words from his September 2, 1862, work, "Meditation on the Divine Will." In that essay, he wrote:

> The will of God prevails. In great contests each party claims to act in accordance with the will of God. Both may be, and one must be, wrong. God cannot be for and against the same thing at the same time. In the present Civil War, it is quite possible that God's purpose is something quite different from the purpose of either party; and yet the human instrumentalities, working just as they do, are the best adaptation to effect this purpose. I am almost ready to say that this is probably true, that God wills this contest, and wills that it should not yet end. By his mere and great power on the minds of the now contestants, He could have either saved or destroyed the Union without a human contest. Yet the contest began. And having begun, He could give the final victory to either side, and day. Yet the contest proceeds.[49]

In this passage, Mr. Lincoln believes that God has willed the war to continue; and, by his great omnipotence, he may "save or destroy" the Union,

48. Stonewall Jackson, quoted in Cozzens, "Shenandoah Valley Campaign."
49. Lincoln, "Meditations on the Divine Will," September 1862.

and he may bring victory to either side of the conflict. Mr. Lincoln, however, is convinced that ultimately the will of God will prevail in the war, and his providence will show that all evil and suffering has been part of a greater divine plan.

Historian Allen Guezlo identifies "pain, desertion, and remoteness" as characterizing the faith of Mr. Lincoln in this work. Yale scholar Henry Stout, in his 1998 book on *Religion in the Civil War*, makes the same claim that the sixteenth president's mind was full of anguish and despair over the War.[50] In 1861, on his way to his first inauguration, Mr. Lincoln said in a speech:

> I am exceedingly anxious that this Union, the Constitution, and the liberties of the people shall be perpetuated in accordance with the original idea for which the struggle was made. And I shall be most happy indeed if I shall be a humble instrument in the hands of the Almighty, and of this, His almost chosen people, for perpetuating the object of that great struggle.[51]

Mr. Lincoln begins in this passage with the Constitution and the liberties that are guaranteed there. Next, he suggests that God may be using him as an instrument for the good in the war. Finally, Mr. Lincoln, in this 1861 passage, calls America God's "almost chosen people," certainly a pessimistic and negative judgments about the Union he was about to lead.

Later in the war, his views appear to have become even more filled with pessimism and negativity; but we have suggested in a previous chapter of this essay that around the same time Mr. Lincoln may have experienced a kind of conversion experience, one where he seems to have come to rely more and more on divine providence in conducting the business of the nation.

Another way to see negative and pessimistic attitudes in the war by 1861 is to examine the lyrics of Mrs. Julia Ward Howe's classic hymn, "The Battle Hymn of the Republic." These lyrics are the following:

> Mine eyes have seen the glory of the coming of the Lord: He is trampling out the vintage where the grapes of wrath are stored; He hath loosed the fateful lightning of this terrible swift sword: His truth is marching on.[52]

---

50. Stout, *Religion in the Civil War*.

51. Lincoln, first inaugural address, March 4, 1861.

52. Howe, "Battle Hymn of the Republic," *Oxford Learner's Dictionary*. Mrs. Howe (1819–1910) was also a noted abolitionist and poet.

stanzas of the hymn are full of apocalyptic language quite similar the book of Revelation. The words express a concern with the sacredness of human life and a belief that God's purposes ultimately will be served. Historian Paul Boyer says of Mrs. Howe's words, "The simple and yet moving lines with their Old Testament vocabulary and cadence captured the somber emotions of a country at war." Mr. Lincoln is said openly to have wept upon first hearing the song sung.[53]

It is clear, as we have shown in this chapter, that Mr. Lincoln went through a period of skepticism, beginning in his early adulthood, and that he gave up his Baptist upbringing in favor of a more rational and logical approach to questions of religion and the Bible. What is not clear, however, is at what point the sixteenth president gave up this period of skepticism. William Herndon maintains he never did. Other thinkers, however, whom we have mentioned earlier in this chapter, like the Rev. Smith and the Rev. Gurley, suggest that Lincoln gave up this skepticism in favor of a new conversion—a readopting of his Baptist and Calvinist roots.

As indicated earlier in this essay, the strongest evidence suggests that if Mr. Lincoln went through a conversion experience, it happened, we believe, with the death of Lincoln's sons in 1850 and February of 1862, and accompanying of some of the worst suffering in the Civil War period. In that period, Mr. Lincoln refers to being "brought to his knees" by the carnage of the war, and that the resources of the day left him little chance of doing anything to improve the situation of the nation.[54] At the time, Mr. Lincoln felt powerless, and said so.

It is also clear that by 1863 Mr. Lincoln's primary vision also had begun to change. It was no longer the preservation of the Union. Rather, this goal gave way to the freeing of the slaves, ending with the passing of the "Emancipation Proclamation" and the Thirteenth Amendment to the U.S. Constitution, in 1863 and 1864, respectively.

Although William Herndon is convinced that Abraham Lincoln did not have a religious conversion of sorts at the end of his life, other Lincoln scholars are much more open, or even positive, about that possibility. Allen Guelzo, for example, leaves open the possibility that in the crucible of the war, Lincoln's skepticism was softened, perhaps allowing him to develop a more personal relationship with God.

Mr. Guelzo never reaches a final conclusion that the sixteenth president became a believing Christian. Professor Guelzo's best guess is that

53. Paul Boyer, quoted in Hawn, "Battle Hymn of the Republic."

54. As indicated earlier in this essay, this quote in which Mr. Lincoln speaks of being brought to his knees is a spurious passage. No reputable source contains the quotation in question.

Mr. Lincoln very much wanted to become one. While at Ford's Theatre the night of his assassination, Mrs. Lincoln reported that the president, after his time in the White House, expressed a desire to travel, particularly to the Holy Land.[55] Professor Richard Carwardine, an American history professor at Oxford University in England, also suggests that Lincoln may have been evolving a religious sincerity. Carwardine points out, however, that his strong use of religious language at the end of his life may well have been to please his constituents.[56]

Professor Carwardine also points out, however, that the United States since the 1740s was experiencing several waves of religious revivals in what is known as the Great Awakening, discussed in the opening chapter of this essay. To this point, the jury is still out on this matter, to the point where there is not sufficient evidence one way or the other to establish whether Lincoln became a Christian or not. It is also quite possible that Mr. Lincoln remained a religious skeptic from his time in Springfield and New Salem until the time of his death, as Mr. Herndon suggested. It again is simply not something we can say one way or the other at this point.

One thinker who was convinced that Mr. Lincoln went through a conversion experience at the end of his life was the Rev. John Blake Falkner (1832–1916) of Christ Church in Bridgeport, Connecticut. The Sunday following Mr. Lincoln's death, the Rev. Blake gave a homily entitled, "Sermon on the Services and Death of Abraham Lincoln."[57] Blake received his BA and DD degrees from New York University. In between, he attended the Episcopal Theological Seminary in Alexandria, Virginia. Blake began his remarks this way:

> We are accustomed at Easter to come to the house of God, and, while our souls are overflowing with joy, to mingle our voices in triumphant sound . . . But on this Easter, His hand so heavy upon us that we are constrained to hang our harps upon the Willows and sit down and weep.[58]

Later, in the same Sermon, the Rev. Blake spoke of Mr. Lincoln's conversion. He spoke, in cogent and clear fashion, of a tale we have seen earlier in this essay:

55. Heuser, "Lincoln and the Holy Land."

56. Carwardine, *Lincoln: A Life of Purpose and Power*, 261–62.

57. Blake, "Sermon on the Services and Death of Abraham Lincoln," April 19, 1865, Christ Church, Bridgeport, Connecticut.

58. Ibid.

A gentleman, having recently visited Washington on business with the President, was, on leaving home , requested by a friend to ask Mr. Lincoln whether he loved Jesus. The business being completed, the question was kindly asked. The President buried his face in his handkerchief, turned away, and wept. He then turned and said, "When I left home to take this chair of state, I requested my countrymen to pray for me; I was not then a Christian. When my son died, the severest trial of my life, I was not a Christian. But when I went to Gettysburg and looked on the graves of our dead heroes who had fallen in defense of their country, I then and there consecrated myself to Christ. Yes, indeed, I do love Jesus."[59]

There can be little doubt that the Rev. Blake was certain of the veracity of this tale. Most of the major Lincoln biographers, however, have doubts that this episode did, in fact, occur. The Rev. Gurley of New York Avenue Presbyterian Church in Washington, DC, as we have indicated earlier, reported that Mr. Lincoln had sent him a letter informing him that the president wished formally to become a member of the Rev. Gurley's Presbyterian congregation the following Sunday, Easter Sunday, after his assassination on Good Friday. Whether or not this was true, we cannot say, nor did the Rev. Gurley ever produce the phantom letter for viewing.

Another way to see Mr. Lincoln's final points of view about religion is to reexamine what he says about theological responses to the evil and suffering that the war had brought. Earlier in this chapter of this essay, we have mentioned that both the North and the South employed the test perspective, as well as the moral qualities view and divine plan theory, when it came to understanding the evil and suffering of the war.

We have devoted chapter 7 of this essay entirely to the issues of theodicy and the problem of evil, and what the sixteenth president of the United States had to say about these issues. It is to Mr. Lincoln's views on the problem of evil, then, to which we now turn in chapter 7 of this essay. This will be followed by the conclusions we have made in this work.

59. Ibid.

CHAPTER 7

Lincoln on the Problem of Evil

Without the assistance of the Divine Being, I cannot succeed,
and with His assistance, I cannot fail.

—ABRAHAM LINCOLN, Farewell Address,
Springfield, February 11, 1861

The general knowledge of this great truth is that God always acts
the most perfect and most desirable manner possible.

—G. W. LEIBNIZ, *Discourse on Method*

That was a sacred effort.

—FREDERICK DOUGLASS, on hearing Mr. Lincoln's second inaugural
address, in *The Life And Times of Frederick Douglass*

THE CENTRAL AIM OF this seventh chapter of this work on President
Abraham Lincoln's religion is to explore the traditional Judaic-Christian-
Islamic tradition's quandary known as the problem of evil or theodicy, a
term invented by G. W. Leibniz in his book by the same name, published
in 1710.[1] Indeed, the word "theodicy" has been employed since the time of
Leibniz to indicate a response, or a solution, to the traditional problem of

1. Leibniz, *Theodicy*. The word "theodicy" was coined by Leibniz as a combination
of two classical Greek terms, *Theos*, or "God," and *dike*, or "justice." Thus, for him the
word means the showing of the justice of God in the face of evil and suffering. Later
Western philosophers, like Immanuel Kant in Germany, also employed the term.

evil, in Western religious thought. To wit, if God is all-good, all-knowing, and all-powerful, then why is there so much evil and suffering in the world?

A second aim in this seventh chapter of this study is to describe and discuss the many places in the sixteenth president's speeches and writings where he seemed to address the problem of evil—most especially in regard to what he tells us about the meaning and causes of the evil and suffering brought about by the Civil War. A third aim of this seventh chapter of this work is to explore ten to a dozen answers or responses to the classical problem of evil as employed in the history of Western philosophy, in Judaism, Christianity, and in Islam, and Mr. Lincoln's employment of these responses.

In earlier chapters of this study, we have maintained that President Abraham Lincoln went through a conversion experience of sorts, directly tied to the death of his son Willie in 1862, as well as the Civil War turning bad under his leadership. In 1862 to 1865, facing the worst evil and deepest tragedy of American history, the president somehow moved from his earlier law of necessity or fatalism to a view of divine providence, or divine plan theory. In this view, the many sins of the Civil War, Mr. Lincoln argued, came about through this divine providence—and who are we to say there is "therein any departure from those Divine attributes to which the living God is always to be identified"?

What Mr. Lincoln ultimately appears to have meant by this remark is, "Who would dare call into question the traditional attributes that God is all-good, all-knowing, and all-powerful, in the face of the evil and suffering of the Civil War period?" Certainly, Mr. Lincoln would have seen this as heresy.

The problem of evil in classical Western philosophy can be expressed in very simple terms. If the God of the Judeo-Christian-Islamic tradition is all-good, all-knowing, and all-powerful, then why is there so much evil and suffering in the world? Usually, in the West distinctions are made among three separate kinds of evil—natural, moral, and psychological. Natural evils are what are sometimes called "acts of God." They are examples of evil and suffering caused by the natural world, like cancer and earthquakes, as well as other diseases and natural disasters. Moral evils are those that human beings bring on each other, like murder, rape, stealing, dishonesty, etc.

The third type of evil, which we will label here "psychological evil," is those examples of evil and suffering that are the products of psychological conditions, like worry, fear, dread, or anxiety. In some ways, this third type of evil is often the most intense variety.

The problem was first formulated in these terms, in Western history, by fourth- and third-century-BCE Roman philosopher Epicurus. John Milton, in the first book of his *Paradise Lost*, also raises the issues of theodicy and the problem of evil, when he writes:

> Of man's first disobedience, and the fruit
>
> Of that forbidden tree, whose mortal taste . . .
>
> I may assert eternal providence,
>
> And justify the ways of God to men.[2]

In these lines, Mr. Milton seeks to "justify the ways of God to men," or correctly to identify the proper ways of providence, or God's divine plan. Milton begins with the cause of man's fall. He argues that the fall was fortunate, although its outcome would be very bad. Human beings can endure, however, if we know that God has his purposes, even though as humans we cannot know them now.

Later David Hume, in the eigtheenth century, in his book *Dialogues Concerning Natural* Religion, offered this terse and elegant version of the problem of evil: "Is He [God] willing to prevent evil, but not able? Then He is impotent. Is He able, but not willing, then He is malevolent. Is He both able and willing? Whence then is evil?"[3]

Over the course of the history of Western philosophy and theological thought, there have been a number of primary responses to the problem of evil, as outlined by Epicurus and David Hume. Some of those response look backward for the meaning or the source of evil, and suggest original sin theory, the influence of demonic forces, the activity of human free will, or retributive justice, either individual or collective, to explain why there is so much evil and suffering in the world. In contemporary parlance, retributive justice is the philosophical position that is connected to responses like "What comes around, goes around" or "Karma's a bitch." God visits evil and suffering, in this view, on those who have committed grave sins. It is also the philosophical view that lies beneath the question, "What have I done to deserve this?"

Retributive justice suggests that the reason for evil and suffering is punishment for sin, either of individuals or a collective—the sins of a family, clan, or nation, for example. The influence of demonic forces response to the problem of evil essentially says that Satan or the devil, and his minions, sometimes have attempted to persuade or coax human beings to commit sin. In fact, in the Islamic tradition, the Arabic term employed to describe the actions of *Shaytan* or *Iblis*—the two names for the demonic in Islam—is

---

2. Milton, *Paradise Lost,* book 1.

3. Hume, *Dialogues Concerning Natural Religion.*

the word *was was*, which is also the word for "whispering," one of the many onomatopoeia in the Semitic tongue.

The free will defense view says that God created humans with free will and they sometimes freely choose to use it to do immoral actions, or for evil purposes. Often, the activity of the serpent in chapter 3 of Genesis has been interpreted in Judaism and Christianity in just these terms. The serpent is seen as the devil, and he coaxes Adam and Eve to commit disobedience to God.

Sometimes these backward-looking responses are used at the same time. Some exegetes interpret the account of Genesis 3 and the fall of Adam and Eve to say that the serpent, who is really Satan, tempted the first parents to sin after God told them not to eat from the fruit of a certain tree. Adam and Eve went on, through their free will, to eat the fruit anyway; and then they were punished and banished from the garden for doing so. Thus, these exegetes combine the free will defense, the demonic influence view, original sin theory, as well as retributive justice, all that the same time.

Other responses, however, look forward to explain evil and suffering in the world. Among these responses are the contrast view, the moral qualities perspective, what is called the test view, which we have seen earlier in this essay, and an overall perspective called the divine plan point of view.

The contrast view says we have to have evil to know the good. Logically, this position maintains that we cannot know one without the other. This theory first was employed by Plato in the West, when it was known as the "theory of opposites." The test perspective, which we have introduced earlier, suggests that God uses evil and suffering as ways to test people's characters.

The moral qualities view, which we also already have introduced earlier in this essay, argues that certain essential moral human qualities, like patience and fortitude, for examples, can only be developed through evil and suffering. God uses evil and suffering in the world, then, to improve the characters of human beings, or to test those characters, or what we have called the test perspective and the moral qualities point of view, as well.

The divine plan theory, which we have spoken of several times in this essay, claims that something may appear to be evil and suffering in the short run, but in the long run everything will be shown to work out for the good. Later, we will see that Lincoln speaks of this view of God having "purposes" not known to human beings.

The closest that Abraham Lincoln came to dealing directly with the classical problem of evil was in a speech to the U.S. House of Representatives that he delivered on June 28, 1848, in Washington, DC. What he had to say about evil that day has pragmatic or utilitarian overtones. Mr. Lincoln said to the congressmen:

> The true rule in determining to embrace or reject anything is not whether it has any evil in it, but whether it has more evil than good. There are few things wholly evil or wholly good. Almost everything . . . is an inseparable compound of the two, so that our best judgment of the preponderance between them is continually demanded.[4]

Something is better or worse morally, then, in President Lincoln's view, depending on the relative amounts of Good and Evil in any particular situation. This committed him to a Utilitarian account of ethics in regard to the issues of Theodicy and the Problem of Evil. We have introduced the Theory of Utilitarianism back in chapter 5 of this essay.

At other times, Mr. Lincoln appeared to suggest that life is often a battle that pits justice against injustice, as in the Alton debate with Stephen Douglas, in 1858. In that debate, Lincoln observed, "That is the real issue. That is the issue that will continue in this country where these poor tongues of Judge Douglas and myself shall be silent. It is the eternal struggle between these two principles—right and wrong—throughout the world."[5]

For Mr. Lincoln, then, the extension of slavery in America to the Western Territories, which was the subject matter of the debate with Mr. Douglas, was simply a moral question, a debate of nothing less than good versus evil. Mr. Lincoln continues his analysis:

> They are the two principles that have stood face to face from the beginning of time; and will ever continue to struggle. The one is the common right of humanity and the other the divine right of kings. It is the same principle in whatever shape it develops itself. It is the same spirit that says, "You work and toil and earn bread."[6]

In this speech, Mr. Lincoln appears to contrast individual rights against the idea of tyranny, in whatever form that tyranny takes. For Lincoln, of course, he believed he was on the side of the good, while tyranny was on the side of evil. The side of individual rights, of course, was the side of the good. Mr. Douglas favored the extension of slavery into the Western Territories, so in Mr. Lincoln's mind Douglas was on the side of tyranny.

In the corpus of President Abraham Lincoln's speeches and written works, he often employs four of these major responses to the problem of

---

4. Lincoln, speech to Congress, June 28, 1848.

5. Lincoln–Douglas debate in Alton, October 15, 1858.

6. Ibid.

evil. These are a collective form of retributive justice, the test perspective, the moral qualities view, and the divine plan point of view. The latter view, in Lincoln's mind, was associated with divine providence, or what he called the "law of necessity," introduced earlier in this essay. Mr. Lincoln also endorses the idea of compassion in discussing questions related to evil and suffering, as we shall see later in this chapter of this essay. Indeed, Mr. Lincoln proposed that we add compassion and humility, and to imitate the behavior of Jesus in his treatment of the poor and the lame, when dealing with evil and suffering—a very practical approach to suffering, much like Jesus' response to the issue in the Gospels.

Mr. Lincoln also employed a number of other philosophical and theological responses to explain evil and suffering, as we shall see later in this seventh chapter of this study. Earlier in this work, in chapter 6, we made some comments about how Mr. Lincoln responded to the issues of Evil and suffering. We will return to some of these now and then supplement them with additional perspectives.

One response of President Lincoln to the issues of evil and suffering is related to the eulogy that the Rev. Phineas Gurley gave at Willie Lincoln's funeral, in Washington in February of 1862. In the eulogy, Dr. Gurley said, "What we need in this hour of trial, and what we should seek by earnest prayer, is confidence in Him who sees the end from the beginning and doeth all things well."[7] Mr. Gurley's language of "hour of trial" is little more than the test view in regard to the issues of theodicy and the problem of evil. We also discussed this view back in chapter 6 of this work. God sometimes uses evil and suffering to test the moral characters of people.

The Rev. Gurley's comment about "Him who sees the end from the beginning and doeth all things well" is nothing more than a reference to the divine plan theory with respect to the issues of theodicy and the problem of evil. Shortly after the funeral, the president asked the Rev. Gurley for a copy of the eulogy. Gurley's comment about Willie's death being a "trial" is an indication that Mr. Lincoln ascribed to the view that God sometimes uses evil and suffering as a way of testing one's character, or a means to improve one's moral resolve.

These views are sometimes referred to as the test perspective and the moral qualities answer to the problem of evil, mentioned earlier. The latter view suggests that the only way certain human moral characteristics, like patience and fortitude, may be developed is by God using evil and suffering in history to develop these moral characteristics in humans, particularly in good men.

7. Gurley, funeral sermon for William Lincoln, Washington, DC, February 24, 1862.

The moral qualities perspective is also the philosophical view that lies beneath Frederich Nietzsche's comment in his book *Twilight of the Idols*, where he wrote, "*Was mich nicht umbringt macht mich starker*," that is, "What doesn't kill you makes you stronger."[8] Nietzsche employed a similar line in an 1888 essay called "Why I Am So Wise," in his *Ecce Homo*, or "Behold the Man."[9] Nietzsche's line was also used as a motto for Hitler's Nazi youth camps.

Mr. Lincoln also referred to these two responses to evil and suffering in the letter he wrote to his son Tad's teacher. Among the small pieces of advice he sent to the teacher were three of interest to us. First, Lincoln says the teacher should "Try to give his son strength on the bandwagon." Presumably by this he meant that one should give his son verve in the face of embarrassment, or courage in the face of shame. Secondly, the sixteenth president advises that teacher to, "Let him [Lincoln's son Tad] have the courage to be impatient and let him have the patience to be brave."[10] These are, of course, two important moral virtues in both Aristotle and among the Stoic philosophers.

Lastly, he recommends that the teacher "Treat his son gently but not cuddle him, because only the test of fire makes fine steel."[11] The first two of these pieces of advice are versions of the moral qualities view, while the third, where steel is tested by fire, is an example of the test perspective of the problem of evil and theodicy.

Lincoln scholar Ronald White also understands Willie's eulogy as a pivotal moment for Mr. Lincoln. White observes:

> Your son had died; you listen to this sermon; this Pastor whom you have respected comes into the White House and suggests to you that you need to trust in a loving God with personality, who acts in History.[12]

In September of 1862, still in the darkest moments of the war, Lincoln begins his "Meditation on the Divine Will" with the words, "The Will of God prevails."[13] In his second inaugural address, Mr. Lincoln reminds us that "The Almighty has His own purposes," again indicating that he ascribes to the divine plan perspective with reference to the classical problem of evil in

---

8. Nietzsche, "Maxims and Arrows," in *Twilight of the Idols*.

9 Nietzsche, *Ecco Homo*.

10. Lincoln, advice to Tad's teacher, February 5, 1862.

11. Ibid.

12. White, *Lincoln's Greatest Speech*, 132.

13. Lincoln, "Meditations on the Divine Will," September 1862.

Western philosophy.[14] The conversion of Mr. Lincoln is now complete. He has moved from the law of necessity and fatalism, or *moirai* in Greek, to being a believer in divine plan theory, as expressed in God's overall providence.

Earlier in this essay, in the chapter on Lincoln's uses of the Bible, we described an experience of Mr. Lincoln reading the Bible in the face of intense suffering in the Civil War. Elizabeth Keckley, Mrs. Lincoln's dressmaker, speaks of Mr. Lincoln turning to the book of Job, in the Old Testament. The figure of Job, of course, is known for his patience and fortitude in the face of his great suffering. This may well be another case where the sixteenth president employed a version of the moral qualities answer with respect to the issues of theodicy and the problem of evil.

Other places in the book of Job that discuss the moral qualities and test views in regard to the problem of evil include: 5:17 (moral qualities); 7:18 (test view); 11:7–11 (a combination of divine plan and the moral qualities view); 22:29–30 (a combination of the test view and moral qualities answer); 34:2 (test view); 34:36 (test view); and 36:10 (moral qualities theory).

Indeed, Mr. Lincoln also employed something like the divine plan answer to the problem of evil in his Gettysburg address (1863) in his "Meditation on the Divine Will" (1862), in his "Thanksgiving Proclamation," which he delivered on October 20, 1864, as well as in both his inaugural addresses, in 1861 and 1865. He also used this approach in his departing speech to the people of Springfield, on February 11, 1861, at the Great Western Depot in that city, before going to Washington.

In his "Thanksgiving Proclamation," he asks God to "Heal the wounds of the nation and to restore it as soon as may be consistent with the Divine purposes to the full enjoyment of peace, harmony, tranquility and Union."[15] "Divine purposes," of course, is the language of divine plan theory, which the sixteenth president often employed.

Additionally, Mr. Lincoln makes an allusion to the divine plan perspective on the problem of evil in one of his many references to the Psalms. This one comes in relationship to Psalm 54:4, which tells us, "God is my helper, the Lord is the upholder of my life" (GB). Another place to see Mr. Lincoln's commitment to divine plan theory, even early on, is in remarks he made in his 1852 eulogy of Henry Clay (1777–1852), lawyer, planter, and statesman. Ostensibly, the sixteenth president was speaking of Mr. Clay, but on a second look, he may have been referring to himself. Lincoln said that day:

> Such a man the times have demanded, and such in the Providence
> of God as given to us. But he is gone. Let us strive to deserve, as far

14. Ibid.

15. Lincoln, Presidential Proclamation 118, October 20, 1854.

as mortals may, the continued care of Divine Providence, trusting that, in future national emergencies He will not fail to provide us with the instruments of safety and security.[16]

The bottom line on theodicy, for Mr. Lincoln, especially after Willie's death, is the sixteenth president's dedication to, and belief in, the divine plan perspective. Above all, Mr. Lincoln seemed worried about the overall effect that evil and suffering may have on the Union. In an address in Cleveland, Ohio, delivered on February 15, 1861, the president expressed that concern this way: "If all do not join now to save the good ship of the Union, this voyage nobody will have a chance to pilot her on another voyage."[17]

In this metaphor of the nation as a ship, Mr. Lincoln worries about the continued survival of the Union, of which he is now the captain—something he is not entirely sure will come about in the long run—there may not be any more voyages! In addition to Mr. Lincoln's employment of the test view, the moral qualities perspective, and divine plan theory with respect to the issues of theodicy and the problem of evil, in the final three years of his life there is also ample evidence that the sixteenth president also used one other classical response to these issues. The name of this final theory is retributive justice, as mentioned earlier.

The theory of retributive justice, is, perhaps, the oldest response to the issue of evil, suffering, and theodicy in the Old Testament. Indeed, this view was employed throughout the major empires of the ancient Near East in biblical times. It can be found among the Egyptians, the Babylonians, the Greeks, and many other cultures in the ancient Near East.

In short, as indicated earlier, this theory says that the reason that people experience evil and suffering is because they must have done something morally wrong. In Scripture this is sometimes known as "*lex talionis*," or "the law of retribution," and is associated with Old and the New Testament passages that say, "An eye for an eye and a tooth for a tooth," like at Exodus 21:24 and Matthew 5:38, for examples.[18]

Mr. Lincoln's employment of retributive justice theory is a collective form. In the second inaugural, as well as his "Meditation on the Divine Will," we see Mr. Lincoln's most mature theological response to the issues of theodicy and the problem of evil. The citizens of America were sick of the Civil War and both sides were earnestly yearning for victory. Yet, in these two documents, Mr. Lincoln tells these people it is God's will that the war

---

16. Lincoln, eulogy for Henry Clay, July 6, 1752.

17. Lincoln, Cleveland address, February 15, 1861.

18. Also see: Deuteronomy 19:16–19, Leviticus 24:19–21, and the Qur'an 2:178, for other examples of *lex talionis*.

shall continue until an additional penance has been enacted for the evils of slavery.

Retribution, in Mr. Lincoln's view, will be collective. It is punishment to be enacted on the nation as a whole, not simply the South. It is collective punishment for the sins of slavery and the violence of the Civil War, on both sides of the conflict, for both sides were causes of that violence.

Near the beginning of his second inaugural, Mr. Lincoln speaks of this collective retributive justice. After suggesting that many sins, or what he calls "offenses" that have been committed in the Civil War, the sixteenth president goes on to say:

> If we shall suppose that American slavery is one of those of-fenses, which, in the Providence of God, must needs come, but which, having continued through His appointed time, He now wills to remove; and that he gives to both North and South this terrible War as the woe due to those by whom the offense came, shall we discern therein any departure from those divine attributes which the believers in a living God always ascribe to Him?[19]

Again, the attributes of God that Mr. Lincoln has in mind here are omnipotence, omniscience, and omnibenevolence, or being all-powerful, all-knowing, and all-good. Mr. Lincoln, then, saw the Civil War as God's punishment to both the North and the South for the practice of slavery. For him, this is to be understood as a collective punishment. The words "as the woe due to those by whom the offenses came," of course, refer to nothing more than the punishment God has meted out for the collective sins of the war.

At the close of his second inaugural address, Mr. Lincoln turns to the issues of forgiveness and reconciliation. He wishes that we may "achieve and cherish a just and lasting peace, among ourselves, and with all nations."[20] He adds the line, "As God gives us to see the Right."[21]

This final remark refers to Mr. Lincoln's belief that God instills the good into the hearts of all human beings. Again, this view is akin to the ancient Jewish theory of the two *yetzerim*, whereby God places in all human hearts the capacities for good and for evil.

The place where Abraham Lincoln most clearly employed the retributive justice, or *lex talionis*, theory was in his "Order of Retaliation," from July of 1863. The full text of that Executive Order 252 reads this way:

19. Lincoln, second inaugural address, March 4, 1865.
20. Ibid.
21. Ibid.

It is the duty of every government to give protection to its citizens of whatever class, color or condition , and especially to those who are duly organized as soldiers in the public service. The law of nations and the usages and customs of war as carried on by civilized powers, permit no distinction as to color in the treatment of prisoners of war as public enemies. To sell or enslave any captured person, on account of his color, and for no offense against the laws of war, is a relapse into barbarism and a crime against the civilization of the age. The government of the United States will give the same protection to all its soldiers, and if the enemy shall sell or enslave anyone because of his color, the offense shall be punished by retaliation upon the enemy's prisoners in our possession. It is therefore ordered that for every soldier of the United States killed in violation of the laws of war, a rebel soldier should be executed; and for every enslaved by the enemy or sold into slavery, a rebel soldier shall be placed at hard labor on the public works and continued at such labor until the other shall be released and receive the treatment due to a prisoner of war.[22]

The continuation of slavery, in Lincoln's view, would be a "relapse into Barbarism." Mr. Lincoln speaks specifically of the rights of Black soldiers, pointing out that they have the same rights as White soldiers. The precedent for this Executive Order 252 goes back to as early as November of 1862. At that time, Confederate soldiers captured four Black soldiers wearing Union uniforms.

Both Confederate Secretary of War James Seldon (1815–1880) and Confederate President Jefferson Davis (1808–1889) approved of the "summary executions" of the four and hoped the incident would serve as an example to others who had ideas of joining the Union forces.

A month later, President Davis issued an infamous Christmas Eve proclamation. In that proclamation, Mr. Davis made a number of promises. The most important for our purposes were these:

That all negro slaves captured in arms be at once delivered over to the executive authorities of the respective States to which they belong to be dealt with in according to the laws of said states.

That the orders be executed in all cases with respect to all commissioned officers of the United States when found serving in

22. Lincoln, Executive Order 252 ("Order of Retaliation"), July, 1863.

company with armed slaves in insurrection against the authorities of the different States of the Confederacy.[23]

According to Mr. Davis, former slaves would be returned to slavery, while
White officers who commanded them would be executed. On May 30, the
Confederate congress sanctioned the policy, but added one caveat—that
captured officers were to be tried and punished in military courts. This
policy was not strictly enforced. Many Confederate officers took matters
into their own hands. A number of atrocities followed at the orders of these
Confederate officers. Rumors of these atrocities spread to the North, including all the way to Washington.

This prompted the Union's war department to draft an "Order of Retaliation." On this date in 1863, President Abraham Lincoln signed his name to
Executive Order 252, and in it we see Lincoln's display of retributive justice
described earlier, and in force.

For the most part, however, as indicated earlier, the most often employed response that Mr. Lincoln used to respond to the issues of evil and
suffering was the divine plan response. This overall view of Mr. Lincoln's,
which proclaims, "The Almighty has his own purposes," is most closely
aligned to the philosophical work of G. W. Leibniz, at least according to a
recent essay by David Shavin entitled, "Abraham Lincoln's Leibnizian Second Inaugural Address."[24]

In this essay, which was published in the online journal *EIRHistory*,
Shavin suggests:

> The Second Inaugural Speech is unmistakably infused with
> the theology of Gottfried Wilhelm Leibniz (1646–1716.) Now,
> Lincoln's particular genius could have fashioned His theodicy,
> his justification of the ways of God toward mankind, without
> having to work through Leibniz's particular version.[25]

Dr. Shavin goes on to suggest that Lincoln arrived at his use of Leibniz by
reading the first great English translation of the German's *Essays on Human
Understanding*, completed by John Milton Mackie (1813–1894) in 1845.
Mackie also completed an English biography of the German philosopher,
called *The Life of Godfrey William Von Leibniz*, around the same time.[26] Indeed, in a footnote to his essay, Dr. Shavin says:

23. Ibid.
24. Shavin, "Abraham Lincoln's Leibnizian Second Inaugural Address."
25. Ibid.
26. Mackie, *Life of Godfrey William Von Leibniz.*

Lincoln may well have read Mackie's biography of Leibniz in the favorable review in Silliman's 1845 "American Journal of Science and the Arts." . . . Edgar Allen Poe read Silliman's journal, and also made notice of the biography of Leibniz in *Graham's Magazine* (volume 27, 1845).[27]

Whether or not Mr. Lincoln read Mackie's biography, or read Leibniz directly in his Springfield period, is not entirely clear. If he did, however, it is clear that the sixteenth president would have discovered a philosophical view in accord with his words, such as these from his "Farewell address in Springfield on February 11, 1861:

> Without the assistance of the Divine Being who ever attended him, I cannot succeed. With that assistance, I cannot fail. Trusting in Him who can go with me and remain with you, and be everywhere for good; let us hope that all will yet be well.[28]

The comment that "all will be well," of course, is nothing more than a reference to divine plan theory—that all will work out for the good in the end. Similarly, in the close of his Gettysburg address, given in the autumn of 1863, President Lincoln said, "That we hear highly resolve that these dead shall not have died in vain; that this nation under God, shall have a new rebirth of freedom . . ."[29]

Mr. Lincoln appears to have believed that this "new rebirth of freedom" was related to what Lincoln believed was a divine plan that God had for America. At the close of his second inaugural address, the sixteenth president alluded to this divine plan when he wrote and said, "The Almighty has His own purposes."[30]

In both his *Theodicy* as well as his *Discourse on Method*, G. W. Leibniz assented to a similar theological point of view. In section 30 of the *Discourse*, Leibniz first suggests his conviction that "This is the best of all possible worlds." Every case of apparent Evil must be judged teleologically in terms of how it contributes to the greatest possible whole. For Leibnitz, as for Mr. Lincoln, God's omni- attributes remain whole in Leibniz's view, for what we see as evil God actually understands as part of some greater good, or what Lincoln means by "the will of God prevails."

Leibniz puts the matter this way in the *Discourse*:

27. Shavin, "Abraham Lincoln's Leibnizian Second Inaugural Address."

28. Lincoln, farewell address, Springfield, February 11, 1861.

29. Lincoln, Gettysburg address, November 19, 1863.

30. Ibid.

The general knowledge of this great truth that God always acts in the most perfect and most desirable manner possible, it is in my opinion the basis of the love which we owe God in all things, for he who loves seeks his satisfaction in felicity or perfection of the object loved, and in the perfection of his actions.[31]

This view that God always acts in the best way possible, and that all is good when seen from a larger teleological, or divine, perspective, in the early eighteenth century came to be known as "optimism." In the poetry of Alexander Pope (1688–1744), we find another enthusiastic adherent to this divine plan, or optimism, view to the problem of innocent suffering. In Pope's *Essay on Man,* in the final stanza of that poem, he observes:

All Nature is but Art, unknown to thee.
All chance, Direction, which thou canst not see.
All Discord, Harmony not understood;
All partial Evil, universal Good:
And spite of Pride, in erring Reason's spite.
One truth is clear, WHATEVER IS, IS RIGHT.[32]

A number of other eighteenth-century European philosophers were devoted to the philosophy of optimism. Others, like Voltaire and Pierre Bayle, for examples, argued staunchly against the view. Voltaire became acquainted with the ideas of optimism when he befriended Alexander Pope in the former's exile in England, between 1726 and 1728. Voltaire savagely attacks the optimism philosophy in his novel *Candide*, exemplified in the character Doctor Pangloss.

French philosopher Pierre Bayle (1647–1706) revived the Manichean point of view, suggesting that evil was caused by a bad God, of equal power with the good God. The approach is akin to the ancient Persian religion of Zoroastrianism, as well as to the Manichean movement in the Roman Empire in the third to fifth centuries CE.[33] In fact, Saint Augustine, before his conversion to Christianity, in the spring of 386, was a member of the Manichean sect for nearly a decade.

Other eigtheenth-century European philosophers who took part in the optimism debate were Montesquieu (1689–1755), Condillac (1715–1780), Diderot (1713–1784) d'Alembert (1717–1783), the Baron d'Holbach (1723–1789), and Jean-Jacques Rousseau (1712–1778). Each of these thinkers, in

31. Leibniz, *Discourse on Method*, section 30.
32. Pope, *Essay on Man.*
33. Bayle, *Great Contests of Faith and Reason.*

their own ways, had various degrees of confidence or criticism of the optimism view of the eigtheenth century.

Albert Camus, as well, in his novel *La Peste*, or *The Plague*, published in 1947, also criticized the divine plan answer in the character of Father Paneleaux, a Jesuit Priest who gives two sermons in a town inundated with the plague.

In the first sermon, the priest simply says, "You have sinned, so now you are suffering from the Plague, a version of Retributive Justice"; but in the second sermon, the priest says, "My brothers, a time of Testing has come for us all. We must believe everything, or deny everything. And who among you, I dare ask, would dare to deny everything?"[34] Like many thinkers in the West, Father Paneloux had moved from retributive justice theory to a view of the test theodicy and then, finally, to the divine plan theory.

At any rate, as we have shown, like Leibniz and Alexander Pope, Mr. Lincoln's most fundamental response to the problem of evil is the perspective we have called divine plan theory. This is clear in comments like "The Will of God prevails" and "The Almighty has His own purposes." President Lincoln appears firmly to have believed that the evil and suffering of the war would in the long run be seen as part of some greater good, devised by the Divine.

This is precisely the point of view that Mr. Lincoln endorsed in a September 4, 1864, letter to Quaker Eliza Gurney, in which the president begins by saying, "The purposes of the Almighty are perfect and must prevail, though we erring mortals may fail to accurately perceive them in advance," which are morally perfect, as a whole."[35] The sixteenth president here refers to the omniscience of God and the ignorance of men when it comes ultimately to understand God's purposes. Mr. Lincoln continues his letter:

> We hoped for a happy termination of this terrible war long before this; but God knows best, and has ruled otherwise. We shall yet acknowledge His wisdom and our own error therein. Meanwhile, we must work earnestly in the best light He gives us, trusting that so working still conduces to the great ends He ordains. Surely, He intends some great good to follow this mighty convulsion, which no human can deter.[36]

The expression "great ends," of course refers to divine plan theory, while "God knows best," however human suffer from their "own errors," is an

---

34. Camus, *The Plague*.
35. Lincoln, letter to Mrs. Eliza Gurney, September 4, 1864.
36. Ibid.

indication of how much Lincoln thinks humans are unaware of the overall divine plan, despite evil and suffering.

Again, Mr. Lincoln refers here to an emphasis on the omniscience of God and the lack of knowledge on the part of mortal men in regard to God's purposes. Even as late as 1864, the sixteenth president continues to proclaim that he ordains "great ends" to come. In the second inaugural, Mr. Lincoln ties this divine plan perspective with the idea of America as a "second Jerusalem." He observed about the war:

> Yet if God wills that the war continue, until all the wealth piled up by the bond-man's two hundred and fifty years of unrequited toil shall be sunk, and until every drop of blood drawn with a lash shall be paid by another drawn with the sword, as it was said three thousand years ago, so still it must be said, "The judgments of the Lord, are true and righteous altogether."[37]

The "two hundred and fifty years" referred to here, of course, is the number of years slavery had been practiced in America to that point. The "three thousand years" figure, on the other hand, is a reference to Moses leading the Israelites out of Egypt. In the above quotation, Mr. Lincoln also appears to be putting the emphasis on retributive justice, as punishment for the collective sins of the Civil War.

Interesting enough, the narrative about the book of Job and Mr. Lincoln mentioned above by Mrs Lincoln's dressmaker, Lizzie Keckley, also ends the same way as the biblical book does. Mr. Lincoln, in Keckley's tale, begins to feel better after perusing the book of Job. At the end of the biblical book, in chapters 38–41, God addresses Job out of a "whirlwind," or a *cuphah* in the original Hebrew text.[38]

Indeed, at Job 38:4–7, God asks Job:

> Where were you when I laid the foundations of the Earth?
> Tell me if you have understanding.
> Who determined its measurements—surely, you know!
> Or who stretched the line upon it?
> On what were its bases sunk,
> Or who laid its cornerstone
> When the morning stars sang together,
> And all the sons of God shouted for joy? (KJV)

---

37. Ibid.

38. There are a variety of words for "storm" and "whirlwind" in classical Hebrew, including *sa'ar*, *ca'ar*, and the feminine noun *ctarah*.

With these and similar rhetorical questions, God's speech was an attempt to answer Job about the meaning and cause of his suffering. The overall response we see in these speeches of God in chapters 38–41 of the book of Job is what we have called the divine plan view—the same point of view most fundamentally employed by the sixteenth president of the United States, Abraham Lincoln, during the Civil War years.

Prior to God's speeches in the book of Job, a fourth friend of the patriarch, a young man named Elihu, employs the test view at Job 34:36; the moral qualities perspective at 36:10, 15, and 16; the retributive justice perspective at 37:14; and the Divine Plan Theory at 36:22; 37:5 and 14. Like President Lincoln, then, the writer of the book of Job employed precisely the same responses to the problem of evil that the sixteenth president did—the test view, the moral qualities perspective, a collective form of retributive justice theory, and, above all, the divine plan point of view.

One final aspect of Abraham Lincoln's responses to evil and suffering has been pointed out in an op-ed piece written by historian Harold Holzer in a recent edition of the *Wall Street Journal*, from February 13, 2016. Mr. Holzer speaks of the death of ". . . an obscure Union cavalry Commander who lost his life in a nighttime ambush behind Confederate lines."[39] The officer's name was Lieutenant Colonel William McCullough. Mr. Lincoln had met McCullough years earlier, when the president was a circuit-riding attorney. In those years he came to know McCullough in Bloomington, Illinois, when he was the sheriff and then a clerk at the county court.

Lincoln and McCullough had much in common. Both served in the state militia during the Black Hawk War; both men married a woman named Mary; both became Republicans. When Lincoln heard that McCullough's daughter, twenty-two-years-old, Mary Frances—known as Fanny—was grieving with an alarming intensity, he decided to write her. The grieving Fanny had shut herself up in her room, refusing to take food and pacing the floor in a violent grief, much like the behavior of the president immediately after the death of his son Willie, or Mrs. Lincoln after the death of her son Eddie in 1850.

Indeed, Mr. Lincoln, with his own history of grief and loss, wrote Fanny a 166–word letter. The correspondence shows the sixteenth president's compassion for others in the throes of suffering, in an attempt to console her. Mr. Lincoln wrote to Fanny:

> Dear Fanny:
> It is with deep grief that I learn of the death of your kind
> and brave father; and especially that it is affecting your young

39. Holzer, "Curious Death."

heart beyond what is common in such cases. In this sad world of ours, sorrow comes to all; and to the young, it comes with the bitterest agony, because it takes them unawares. The older have learned to ever expect it. I am anxious to afford some alleviation of your present distress.

Perfect relief is not possible, except with time. You cannot now realize that you will ever feel better. Is not this so? And yet it is a mistake. You are sure to be happy again. To know this, which is certainly true, will make you some less miserable now. I have had experience enough to know what I say; and you need only to believe it, to feel better at once. The memory of your dead Father, instead of the sort than you have known before. Please present my kind regards to your afflicted mother.

Abraham Lincoln.[40]

In the letter, Mr. Lincoln gives us some indication of his deep compassion for the sufferings of others. He tells Fanny McCullough that things will indeed get better, even though it may now seem to be an impossible state of affairs. Lincoln speaks of his own great losses and griefs when writing to Fanny, and he suggests to her that she may well one day be happy again, despite the fact that she sees this to be impossible.

This response with Compassion was a common one in the adult life of Abraham Lincoln when he came upon someone in the throes of suffering or disappointment. It was his principal response to his wife Mary when both of their sons died. Mr. Lincoln's letters also were filled with his display of compassion. Following his defeat in the 1858 senate contest, Lincoln wrote to his campaign manager, Norman B. Judd, "Now you are feeling badly, and this too shall pass away. Never fear."[41] Mr. Lincoln seems to be reminding the grieving Mr. Judd that life is often fleeting and ephemeral, and that nothing is permanent. This particular phrase came from an Eastern folktale erroneously attributed to King Solomon.

Mr. Judd's feelings of sadness would indeed pass away. Within six weeks, Mr. Lincoln would be proposed as a possible presidential candidate in the election of 1860. Nevertheless, Mr. Lincoln showed a great capacity, far beyond what one would consider to be normal, when he encountered the grieving or the disappointed, principally because of the many hardships he had suffered throughout his life.

This capacity for expressing his compassion was a core aspect of Mr. Lincoln's responses to evil and suffering. You find this attribute in his personality in his Cooper Union address, in the "Emancipation Proclamation,"

40. Ibid.

41. Lincoln, letter to Norman B. Judd, October 20, 1858.

in 1863, as well as in his second inaugural address, in 1865. Lincoln's clarity of expression and the confidence of his authority is nothing short of breathtaking.

In his Cooper Union address, delivered on February 27, 1860, Mr. Lincoln's rhetorical gifts were in full display. He carefully showed that each of the "thirty-nine" founding fathers of America had consented to a host of national beliefs as embodied in the Declaration of Independence and the U.S. Constitution. For Lincoln, these men, and these beliefs, were at the very heart of the American republic.

A variety of writers and scholars have pointed out that Lincoln's second inaugural address contains the president's most profound observations about the issues of theodicy and the problem of evil. Indeed, syndicated columnist Garry Wills sees this address, along with the Gettysburg address, as parts of "Lincoln's theodicy of the Civil War."[42] On the day of the second inaugural, Frederick Douglass, noted abolitionist and writer, met the president in the East Room, when Mr. Lincoln was receiving guests. Douglass wrote this about his encounter with Lincoln that day at a reception following the oath and the inaugural address:

> Recognizing me, even before I reached him, he exclaimed, so that all around him could hear, "Here comes my friend Douglass." And taking me by the hand, he said, "I am glad to see you. I saw you in the crowd today, listening to my Inaugural Address; how did you like it?" I said, "Mr. Lincoln, I must not detain you with my poor opinion, when there are thousands waiting to shake hands with you." "No, no," he said, "You must stop a little, Douglass; there is no man in the country whose opinion I value more than yours. I want to know what you think of it?"
>
> I replied, "Mr. Lincoln, that was a sacred effort!" "I am glad you liked it," he said; and I passed on, feeling that any man, however distinguished, might well regard himself honored by such expressions, from such a man.[43]

Lincoln begins by saying it is strange to be speaking of an all-good God in the circumstances of great evil. He continues by employing his deft capacity for compassion, but he ends with his clear assent to the divine plan theory with respect to the issues of theodicy and the problem of evil.

Mr. Lincoln, himself, in a letter to Thurlow Weed (1797–1882), the Republican organizer in New York, says of his second inaugural that he expected it to "wear as well as—perhaps better than—anything that I have

42. Wills, *Lincoln at Gettysburg*, 193–96.

43. Douglass, *Life and Times of Frereck Douglass*, 113.

produced."[44] Mr. Weed was a prominent New York newspaper publisher, Whig Republican, and close friend of William Seward (1801–1872), Mr. Lincoln's political rival and then cabinet member.

Contemporary thinker Caitrin Nicol Keiper, editor of *Philanthropy Magazine*, compares the speech to the "Peeling of an onion, the next casual layer that Lincoln strips back is the idea of a provincial God, even one interested in the clear cause of justice."[45] Ms. Keiper then quotes the second inaugural:

> It may seem strange that any men should dare to ask a just God's assistance in wringing their bread from the sweat of other men's faces—but is it not even stranger that a just God would not have come to the assistance of those who oppose them? Both read the same Bible, and pray to the same God; and each invokes His aid against the other . . . The prayers of both could be answered; that of neither has been answered fully.[46]

Ms. Keiper goes on to make some interesting observations about this paragraph from the second inaugural address of Mr. Lincoln's. She relates, "Buried in this paragraph is the first suggestion of what Lincoln's objective is for this address (which he had begun by announcing what it was not): 'Let us judge not that we not be judged.'"[47]

Mr. Lincoln refers here, of course, to the opening verses of chapter 7 of the Gospel of Matthew. Ms. Keiper adds, "This phrase may sound flip and noncommittal to our ears in this present age of tolerance, but in context it is an extraordinary request."[48] It reminds one of what Mr. Lincoln wrote to Albert G. Hodges, in a letter from April 4, 1864: "If slavery is not wrong, then nothing is wrong."[49] Ms. Keiper points out, "He begins a sentence by indicting Slavery, but concludes by saying we must not judge."[50]

Confederate General Edward Porter Alexander (1835–1910) points out that both sides of the Civil War used the "providence is on our side" argument. Alexander wrote, "It is customary to say that Providence did not intend that we should win, but I do not subscribe in the least to that

44. Lincoln, letter to Thurlow Weed, March 15, 1865.
45. Keiper, "Very Peculiar God."
46. Ibid.
47. Ibid.
48. Ibid.
49. Lincoln, letter to Albert G. Hodges, April 4, 1864.
50. Keiper, "Very Peculiar God."

doctrine. Providence did not care a row of pins about it. If it did, it would be an unintelligent Providence."[51]

Ms. Keiper highlights what only can be referred to as the pessimism of General Alexander's view that "God is on our side." If there is a divine plan, it is the plan of a God without sufficient intelligence for the job. Ms. Keiper here seems to express a similar kind of criticism of the view that God has his purposes, unknown to us.

Ms. Keiper goes on, nevertheless, to maintain that Mr. Lincoln "finally offers a comprehensive but harrowing theodicy of American history stretching back before the nation's founding, that undermines the comforting assurances and vindication that the North would be expecting on the eve of victory."[52] Ms. Keiper says that Mr. Lincoln saw his situation during the war being connected to certain moral values stretching all the way back to the founding fathers—values such as freedom, equality, and the right to profit from one's labor.

The solution that Ms. Keiper suggests that Lincoln offers the nation in his second inaugural—humility and charity—is not much different from Mr. Lincoln's response to Fanny McCullough. As Mr. Lincoln said, "A just and lasting peace" cannot be accomplished unless each side shows humility and charity to each other.

By the close of the second inaugural, Mr. Lincoln turns to how we are to treat each other, after the war. In short, we should treat the other side of the conflict the same way that Jesus suggests we should treat all people—with humility and charity. Mr. Lincoln argues for a practical approach at the end of what many have called his greatest speech. Ms. Keiper ends her essay by concluding that Mr. Lincoln finished his second inaugural by declaring:

> We do not know the ways of the Almighty. We do not know the future, and we may not understand the past, but we know our obligations to each other, drawn from the character of Christian Providence, whatever that ultimately means. This is the final objective of the President who was almost mysteriously appointed to lead America through the Civil War, a national apocalypse with an opportunity to be reborn to the other side.[53]

In this passage, Lincoln begins by mentioning the divine plan theory. Then he mentions the providence of God, followed by his "mysterious" appointment as president, much like the mysterious plan of God's by which everything works out for the good in the end, in his view. Lincoln also speaks of

51. Alexander, *Military Memories of a Confederate*, 207–9.

52. Keiper, "Very Peculiar God."

53. Lincoln, second inaugural address, March 4, 1865.

the obligations that the two sides will have to each other after the close of the war, perhaps a nod in the direction of the practical view of suffering, outlined earlier.

Mr. Lincoln, of course, was shot just forty-one days later, on Good Friday, no less. Instantly, he became a martyr, the holy savior of a nation. Like Jesus, he concluded in a letter to his friend, Mr. Weed, that the war "falls most directly on myself."[54] If there is a just God that governs the world, perhaps Mr. Lincoln was sacrificed not because he was innocent, but rather because, like all Americans, he was guilty.

One other contemporary writer, Alfred Kazin, in an essay entitled "The Almighty Has His Own Purposes," raises an interesting hypothetical: "Let us suppose [Lincoln says in effect] that slavery is an offense that God inexplicably allowed into human history. Let us further suppose, that He allowed just so much time for it. To suppose anything like this is actually to suppose a very peculiar God."[55] Indeed, we may ask whether it is an all-loving God. Mr. Kazin's conclusion:

> But since it all happened as described, and believers hold God responsible for all things, one can only yield to the enigma of having such a God at all. It is clear that the terrible War has overwhelmed the Lincoln who identified himself as a man of reason. It has brought him to his knees, so to speak, in heart-breaking awareness of the restrictions imposed by a mystery so encompassing it can only be called God. Lincoln could find no other word for it.[56]

Mr. Kazin points to some fundamental problems with the Leibniz/Pope/Lincoln point of view when it comes to evil and suffering. If all that happens in the world occurs by the law of necessity, then God predetermined that all the suffering in the Civil War was preordained. It had to have happened that way, and that way only. To use Aristotle's expression, "Things could not have been done otherwise."[57] This is very much like Lincoln's earlier view of the law of necessity.

But this leaves us, however, in a moral environment where we are forced to say that God allows evil, while at the same time not causing it. This distinction between allowing and causing, however, is a morally dubious one. Normally, if we know that evil is about to happen and we allow it, and

---

54. Lincoln, letter to Thurlow Weed, March 15, 1865.
55. Kazin, "Almighty Has His Own Purposes."
56. Ibid.
57. Ibid.

we could have stopped it, then many might say that we are complicit in the moral act.

In the final analysis, Mr. Lincoln seems to have gone from fatalism, or the law of necessity, to the providence of God, or divine plan theory—and who are we to say there is "therein any departure from these divine attributes which the believers in a living God always ascribe to Him?" Again, by this, of course, he meant God's being all-good, all knowing, and all-powerful. To deny the divine plan, Mr. Lincoln wrote to Republican politician Thurlow Weed a few days after the second inaugural, "is to deny that there is a God governing the world."[58]

One might ask just how we are to behave when faced with such a woeful God, while also asking at the same time to believe that he is not malevolent. Mr. Lincoln's clear answer is compassion and charity. Reason has nothing more to say on the questions of evil and suffering. The final message from the sixteenth president is that both sides of the Civil War afterwards are to treat the other side with compassion and charity—much like the Jesus to be found in the Gospels, specifically his attitude toward the poor and the lame.

Indeed, one might say that the predominant characteristics displayed by Jesus in the Gospels when healing the poor and the lame are compassion and charity. If Jesus had a "philosophy of suffering," it may well be to fight suffering wherever one finds it. In the twenty-one major instances of healing in the New Testament, Jesus usually responds to evil and suffering by fighting it wherever he finds it with compassion and charity.[59]

Mr. Lincoln knew of the disastrous consequences that would follow in Reconstruction should they be carried out with a heavy, judgmental hand from either side, instead of one made gently by sorrow and mutual repentance, and the practical view of suffering. Lincoln's final instructions on mutual compassion and charity, read with our knowledge of the assassination, take on an undercurrent of eerie foreboding for the difficult Reconstruction that actually was to take place; but, in a deeper sense, they offer Americans a charge that is never too late to heed:

> With malice toward none; with charity for all; with firmness in
> the right, as God gives us to see the right, let us strive on to fin-
> ish the work we are in; to bind up the nation's wounds; to care

58. Lincoln, letter to Thurlow Weed, March 15, 1865.

59. The healings of Jesus we have in mind here can be found at: Matthew 8:1–4; Luke 7:2–10; Mark 1:23–28; Luke 4:38–39; Mark 2:3–12; Mark 7:31–37; Matthew 9:27–32; Mark 5:22–24; Luke 2:2–3; Matthew 17:14–21; Luke 17:15–19; Luke 22:50–51; John 4:46–54; John 5:2–12; John 9:1–12; John 9:35–37; John 11:19–28; John 11:39–44; Matthew 8:14–15; Luke 6:6–11; Mark 8:22–26.

for him whom shall have borne the battle, and for his widow, and his orphan—to do all which may achieve and cherish a just, and a lasting peace, among ourselves, and with all nations.[60]

But Ms. Keiper, however, in the essay mentioned above, speaks of a similar criticism of Mr. Lincoln's view on the problem of evil to that of Mr. Kazin. In short, she says, "This account of woe lies directly at the feet of the Almighty, and concludes, claiming there is no other conclusion left to draw, that it, like all His other judgments, is 'true and righteous altogether.'"[61]

Again, Mr. Lincon appears to draw the contrast here between human ignorance and the knowledge of God. Ms. Keiper continues her analysis:

> The Lincoln who three decades earlier looked to "cold, calculating, unimpassioned reason" as the bedrock of the future of America had long since disappeared. The Lincoln of 1865 is prostrated by the great and tragic mystery whose scope he cannot comprehend.[62]

In Keiper's view, Lincoln is left alone with the mystery of human suffering in the Civil War, and what some have called the "silence of God," or the "distant God." But Ms. Keiper goes on to ask, what kind of God is one who would "allow" and "preordain" slavery? Her answer is not a deity that is best understood as being all-good, all-knowing, and all-powerful; rather, it is a hidden, distant, and a silent God.

Finally, at the end of Mr. Lincoln's life, from the debates with Stephen Douglas in 1858 on, another response to evil and suffering can be seen in Lincoln's life. In one of the Douglas debates, the judge remarked, "Evil originated when God made men, and placed good and evil before them, allowing them to choose upon his own responsibility."[63]

In this statement, Mr. Douglas seems to call to mind two different responses to evil and suffering: first, that God gave human beings free will to choose between good and evil; and second, that God allows human beings to decide for themselves which of the two paths to follow. Earlier, we have argued that Abraham Lincoln was fiercely against the idea of human free will, much as John Calvin was in his *Christian Institutes*, as well as Martin Luther and other Reformers; but during the Civil War, Lincoln often raised the issue of why a good God would allow so much evil and suffering to occur to humans, as well as to other creatures, on the Earth.

60. Lincoln, second inaugural address, March 4, 1865.

61. Ibid.

62. Ibid.

63. Lincon–Douglas debate in Quincy, October 13, 1858.

Nevertheless, in the final analysis, then, Abraham Lincoln employed the divine plan theory, the free will defense, the test perspective, the moral qualities view, the view that God allows evil rather than causes evil, collective retributive justice theory, and the response of his great compassion and charity in terms of the tragedy of others, with respect to the issues of theodicy and the problem of evil. We have labeled this latter view the "practical approach" to the issues of theodicy and the problem of evil.

We also have seen in this seventh chapter of this essay on Mr. Lincoln's religion that the sixteenth president seemed to have been decidedly against the idea of human free will, and in favor of the theory of ethical egoism— that all human beings primarily act from their own self-interests.

In summary, then, Abraham Lincoln employed the following philosophical and theological responses to the issues of theodicy and the problem of evil:

1. The moral qualities view,

2. The Test Perspective,

3. Against the free will defense,

4. Collective retributive justice theory,

5. Compassion and charity, or the practical approach,

6. And, finally, the divine plan perspective.

For Mr. Lincoln, the most significant of these approaches is theory number 6—that God has a divine plan in which all evil and suffering will be seen as part of a greater good, or what the president called "good ends," or "God's good purposes."[64] We shall turn now to a final chapter on the major conclusions we have made in this essay.

---

64. Lincoln, second inaugural address, March 4, 1865.

CHAPTER *8*

Some Conclusions on Lincoln's Faith

The real Lincoln is elsewhere. He is to be found, for those able to
read old prose, in his own writings. According to Lincoln's law
partner William Herndon, "He was the most continuous and severest
thinker in America."

—GORE VIDAL, "First Notes on Abraham Lincoln"

When you read the reminiscences of Lincoln's friends and you
hear them describe him in their terms, he's always the most
depressed person they have ever seen. It is always this radical
gloom that they were shocked by.

—JOSHUA WOLF SHENK, *Lincoln's Melancholy*

Fondly do we hope—fervently do we pray—that this mighty
scourge of war might speedily pass away. Yet, if God wills that it
might continue, until the wealth all piled up by the bond-man's
two hundred and fifty years of unrequited toil shall be sunk . . . as
it was said three thousand years ago, so still it must be said, "The
judgments of the Lord are true and righteous altogether."

—ABRAHAM LINCOLN, Second Inaugural Address

THE MAIN AIM OF this eighth, and closing, chapter of this work on President Abraham Lincoln's religion is to sketch out as clearly as possible the highlights, or major conclusions, we have made in this essay, on the various topics we have presented and discussed.

Therefore, in this eighth and final chapter of this study, we will describe and discuss and, therefore by extension, review the major conclusions we have made in the other seven chapters of this essay. We began with the role of religion in Mr. Lincoln's early life, and we have ended with the place of religious belief at the end of his life, when he was president, from 1861 until 1865, in which time, as we have suggested, the sixteenth president experienced a religious conversion of sorts. This was, perhaps, a return, if you will, to the frontier Separate Baptist faith of his youth.

In the opening chapter of this study, we have explored the religious background of the early life of Abraham Lincoln. In that chapter we spoke of the sect of Lincoln's parents, called the Separate Baptists, and discussed the group's central beliefs, and the scriptural support, or proof texts, of those points of view. Among the beliefs of the Separate Baptists we described and discussed in chapter 1 of this essay were their points of view on Scripture; the dual nature of Jesus; the Trinity, the ministry, or the priesthood of all believers, and how ministers were to be trained and paid; conversion and regeneration; resurrection of the body; predestination; the Sabbath; ordinances, or the term the Separate Baptists employed for what some would call "sacraments"; the Holy Spirit; baptism by immersion; the physical return of Jesus in the second coming; and many other central Christian and Calvinist beliefs.

As we have said earlier, it is not clear, however, just how reverent the young Abraham Lincoln was when it came to his parent's Separate Baptist faith; nevertheless, we have sketched out in chapter 1 of this essay the major beliefs of that sect, at the turn of the eigtheenth century to the nineteenth century, in Kentucky, Indiana, and in Illinois, where Mr. Lincoln spent his childhood and adolescent years.

Regarding this early period of Mr. Lincoln's life, we have made four separate conclusions about his early religious beliefs. First, he attended his parents' Separate Baptist church as a child, in Kentucky, Indiana, and Illinois; second, he often read the three-volume family Bible that his father, Thomas Lincoln, had purchased in 1819, a version of the Geneva Bible, beginning when Abe was ten years old; third, he used to lecture from tree stumps, repeating the homilies he had heard in church or from travelling preachers on the frontier in the early nineteenth century; and finally, his early life was filled with the tragedies of several deaths in his family—his mother, brother Thomas, and sister Sally—before the age of twenty-two, not to mention the death of Mr. Lincoln's first love, Ann Rutledge, at age twenty-two, in New Salem, in 1835, when the president was still in his early twenties as well.

We also have suggested that in this early period of the life of Mr. Lincoln he seems to have been turned off by his parents' ecstatic and sweaty version of Calvinism, with its altar calls, conversion experiences, and movements by the Spirit. The Separate Baptist movement in the late eigtheenth and early nineteenth centuries held to the importance of conversion and regeneration, much like the religion of the American slave communities.

We also have shown in the first chapter of this work that the Second Great Awakening church known as the Separate Baptists were not all that different from the "born again" Christians of the late twentieth and early twenty-first centuries in America, with their shared beliefs of biblical literalism, their declarations that Jesus is Lord and Savior, and their emphases on conversion and being "born again" in the Spirit, as outlined in third chapter of the Gospel of John.

In the second chapter of this study, we have described what we have called Mr. Lincoln's period of skepticism, which began in his twenties, when he left his father's home to venture out into the world on his own, and continued well into his forties, and in which he appears to have rejected a number of the central claims of the traditional Christian churches. Among these rejected beliefs were the divinity of Jesus, original sin, creation out of nothing, or what Lincoln called "special creation," the value and the validity of the divine revelation of Scripture, the atonement, the forgiveness of sins, and belief in eternal damnation.

Additionally, we have suggested that Mr. Lincoln, even early on, rejected the idea of human free will, primarily because of his belief in the "law of necessity," or fatalism, which contradicted any idea, in Lincoln's mind, of free choice.

There is also some evidence, as we have shown, that Lincoln was decidedly against the idea of eternal damnation, purely on moral grounds, and that his belief that slavery is morally wrong was held by the Separate Baptist faith of his parents. Thus, he held these two positions on Slavery and necessity from very early on in his life.

Lincoln also appears to have replaced these beliefs with a scientific form of naturalism and what he called the "law of necessity." By this Mr. Lincoln meant, as we have shown, that he assented to a form of determinism, or what John Calvin had called "double predestination."[1] By "scientific naturalism" we mean something akin to what we would call the "laws of nature," or a "scientific worldview."

---

1. See Calvin, *Institutes of the Christian Religion*, 3.22.10.

In the first chapter of this work, we also have maintained there are two central beliefs of the Separate Baptists that appeared to have had lasting effects on the life of Lincoln. These were the sect's rejection of the practice of slavery, and what the sixteenth president referred to as the "law of necessity," as we have indicated in chapter 1, which is a reformulation of John Calvin's view of double predestination, a form of fatalism or determinism, or what the Greeks called *moirai*.

Mr. Lincoln's two inaugural addresses and their religious content were the subject matter of the third chapter of this study. In that chapter, we have shown that between 1862 and 1865 Mr. Lincoln appears to have given up his scientific naturalism and replaced it with a firm faith in the all-good, all-powerful, and all-knowing God of Christianity. Indeed, in chapter 4 of this essay, we have outlined the particulars of that religious conversion at the end of Lincoln's life. In fact, we have given a number of strong arguments in this essay that Mr. Lincoln returned to the Christian faith of his childhood during the Civil War, at the end of his life, and after the death of his sons, Eddie in 1850, and Willie in February of 1862.

Chapters 5, 6, and 7 of this work have been more overtly philosophical and theological. Chapter 5 was dedicated to Mr. Lincoln's views of the Bible. There we have maintained that the sixteenth president regularly quoted from the Holy Scriptures, often using the Bible when circumstances seemed to demand it. There is no indication, however, that Mr. Lincoln was aware of the historical-critical or form critical methods of interpreting the Bible that were burgeoning, and quite popular among biblical scholars in the nineteenth century, like Julius Wellhausen, for example.

We also have introduced and discussed a number of Bibles that played roles in the religious life of Abraham Lincoln, from the version of the Geneva Bible in his childhood home, in Kentucky and Illinois, from 1819 on; to the Bible given him by the Speed family in 1841; to the Bible that came to be known as the "Lincoln Bible," which was originally borrowed for Lincoln's first oath of office in 1861, and now is owned by the Library of Congress; and, finally, to the King James Version of the Bible given to Mr. Lincoln by African-American ministers from Baltimore, during Mr. Lincoln's presidency, in 1864. This latter text, as we have mentioned, is owned by the Library of Fiske University, a traditional African-American University in Nashville, Tennessee.

Ethics and Mr. Lincoln's views on morality, as well as moral theory, were the context of chapter 6 of this study on Lincoln's religion. In that chapter, we have demonstrated that the sixteenth president employed four major ethical theories in his mature life. These were: Aristotle's virtue theory, Kant's deontological theory, Bentham and Mill's utilitarianism, or teleological theory, and Ayn Rand's ethical egoism, or self-interestedness.

Mr. Lincoln appears to have applied whatever theory he deemed applicable in any given situation, sometimes applying more than a single theory at the same time; but there is no direct evidence that Mr. Lincoln knew about any of these four major theories of the nature of the moral good, yet he could have learned about them in his reading, particularly in Springfield.

In chapter 7 of this essay on Mr. Lincoln's religion, we have explored the sixteenth president's views on the issues of theodicy and the problem of evil. In that chapter, we have argued that Mr. Lincoln employed a number of traditional responses to those issues. Among those responses were the test view, the moral qualities perspective, the free will defense, the notion that God permits evil but does not cause it, and a collective form of retributive justice, or *lex talionis*, which Lincoln applied in regard to the sins or "offenses" of the practice of slavery in the Civil War—both North and South.

We also have maintained that the overarching perspective that Mr. Lincoln took in regard to the issues of theodicy and the problem of evil was what we have called the divine plan theory. Additionally, we have shown that Mr. Lincoln was staunchly against the notion of the free will defense in regard to evil and suffering, principally because of his doctrine of necessity, and his opposition to the idea of eternal damnation, mostly on moral grounds.

Additionally, we have suggested in this essay that in President Abraham Lincoln's early life he was what we have called a "Hardshell" Separate Baptist in Kentucky, Illinois, and Indiana. That term, as we have indicated, meant that the Separate Baptists were "hard" on the many "shalls" of the New Testament, such as at Matthew 1:21, for example, which says in the King James Version, "And she shall bring forth a son, and she shall call his name Jesus. For he shall save his people from their sins." Thus, the name went from "Hard Shall" Baptists to "Hardshell" Baptists, and that name regularly was used by believers on the Western frontier in the beginning of the nineteenth century, in America.

This was followed by a period of skepticism during his years in New Salem and Springfield, Illinois. We also have shown that, beginning with the death of Eddie Lincoln in 1850, when Mary Todd Lincoln joined Dr. James A. Smith's church, Mr. Lincoln turned to Presbyterianism, as well, and that that faith was strengthened by the death of his son Willie and the horrible suffering of the Civil War period, in the early 1860s.

In the preceding pages of the first seven chapters of this essay, we have suggested that the religious beliefs of Abraham Lincoln went through either a two-stage or a three-stage development. One point of view, as we have indicated, that was championed by Lincoln's third law partner, William H. Herndon, who has suggested that the sixteenth president went from his parents' Separate Baptist faith to a religious skepticism, beginning in his early twenties, that never abated for the remainder of Lincoln's life.

The other perspective—the one we have taken and shall continue to take in this eighth and final chapter of this essay—is that Mr. Lincoln experienced, at the end of his life, a form of religious conversion, beginning around the time of the death of his two sons, Eddie in 1850, and Willie in 1862, and continuing throughout the remainder of his life.

There can be little doubt that the young Abraham Lincoln held to a number of the religious beliefs of the Separate Baptists of the beginning of the nineteenth century in America. As we have argued earlier, of those beliefs two seem to have had a more lasting effect.

The first was the conviction of Thomas Lincoln, as well as the Separate Baptists in general, that the practice of slavery is morally wrong by its very nature. Mr. Lincoln was raised to understand slavery in just these terms, and he appears to have understood the phenomenon of slavery in just those terms for the remainder of the life of the man. Indeed, in letters as late as 1864 and 1865, Mr. Lincoln firmly continued his vociferous views against the practice of slavery and human captivity.

One prime example is a letter from the sixteenth president to Albert G. Hodges, dated April 4, 1864. In this correspondence, Mr. Lincoln speaks of his aversion to slavery, as well as his view that "I claim not to have controlled events, but I confess plainly that events have controlled me," an obvious reference to Mr. Lincoln's "theory of necessity." He also closed the letter with a theological comment. Lincoln wrote, "We of the North, as well as you of the South, shall pay dearly for our complicity in that wrong [slavery]. Impartial history will find therein new causes to attest and revere the justice and goodness of God."[2]

Mr. Lincoln firmly believed that the suffering of the Civil War was to be understood as a kind of collective retributive justice for the sins and what he called the "offenses" of the war between the states. In Lincoln's view, both sides got what was coming to them. Ultimately, however, in his view the justice and goodness of God—or divine plan theory—would prevail.

The other religious belief of Thomas Lincoln and the Separate Baptists that appears to have had a lasting effect on Abraham Lincoln was the belief in what he labeled the "law of necessity." By this term Mr. Lincoln seems to have meant, as we have shown in several places in this essay, that he was a firm believer in a religious form of determinism or fatalism, in which all

---

2. Lincoln, letter to Albert G. Hodges, April 4, 1864.

that happens occurs simply by the will of God, or what the Greeks called *moirai*, or fate.

In Calvinistic language, this is a belief in the principle of predestination, or double predestination. This is why Mr. Lincoln frequently described himself as a leaf floating on the ocean, or what he meant when he wrote, "I have not controlled events, events have controlled me."[3]

There is very little additional evidence of Abraham Lincoln's other early religious beliefs. We don't know, for example, if he adhered to total immersion in baptism, to the physical return of Jesus in the second coming, or to the many other religious precepts of the Separate Baptist church we have outlined in chapter 1 of this work. In fact, the evidence we have of the sixteenth president about his early life is that he loved to read, including the Bible, and that he sometimes mimicked the sermons he heard from Separate Baptist preachers or traveling Christian ministers or preachers on the frontier.

Sometimes Mr. Lincoln appears to have believed that those foundational values of America are objectively held by all members of the nation. If values like equality and freedom are objectively held, this appears to contradict what the president indicated to Mr. Ingersoll about what he thought about ethics and morality, as we have seen in the chapter on ethics and moral theory in this study, chapter 4, particularly whether or not there is an objective standard for morality.

Nevertheless, what Mr. Lincoln appears to have replaced these central Christian beliefs with during his period of skepticism was a combination of scientific naturalism and his law of necessity or determinism. Mr. Lincoln believed "There are no accidents."[4] All that occurs, for him, are the accumulated effects of what he would call the "laws of nature," or a scientific worldview.

As we have indicated earlier, Mr. Herndon believed these rejections of fundamental and central Christian beliefs continued all the way to the end of his life. Mr. Herndon, in his biography of Lincoln, spoke of the president being part of a group of "freethinkers" during his time in Springfield.[5] Although Mr. Lincoln directly mentions the Divine in a number of places in his first inaugural address, it is quite possible that these mentions of God are still in the context of the president's religious skepticism.

In his first inaugural address, Mr. Lincoln imagined providence, the power of sustaining and guiding human destiny, as a remote and mechanistic

---

3. Ibid.
4. Ibid.
5. Herndon, *Life of Lincoln,* 35–36.

force, a hidden or distant God. "Man is simply a tool, a mere cog in the wheel, a part, a small part, of this vast iron machine, that strikes and cuts, grinds and mashes, all things, including man, that resist it."[6]

Thus, here Mr. Lincoln seems to be assenting to a belief consistent with scientific naturalism, or a scientific worldview. By the time of his second inaugural in 1865, however, we believe his rejection of Christianity no longer held sway. During his presidency, providence began to take on a new understanding in the mind of Mr. Lincoln. God was now more mysterious, more personal, and more active in human history, and much more hidden and silent.

When his son Willie died of typhoid fever in February of 1862, religion seems to have taken a more central role in the life of the president and of the nation. The eulogy delivered at Willie's funeral by the Rev. Phineas Gurley may well have been the piece of straw that broke the back of Mr. Lincoln's skepticism. In his homily, Gurley observed, "What we need in this hour of trial, and what we should seek by earnest prayer, is that things will turn out well."[7]

In this passage, we have argued that Abraham Lincoln employed both the test view as well as the divine plan perspective. The words "hour of trial," are in regard to the former, and "things will turn out well" is a nod in the direction of the latter theory, with respect to the issues of theodicy and the problem of evil.

The Rev. Phineas Dunsmore Gurley (1816–1868) was the pastor of New York Avenue First Presbyterian Church in Washington, DC. He was also, for a time, chaplain for the United States Senate. Mr. Lincoln once observed about the Rev. Gurley, "I like that he does not preach Politics, I get enough of that during the week."[8]

Something from this sermon of the Rev. Gurley's at the funeral of Willie Lincoln resonated in the heart of Mr. Lincoln, so much so that he asked the Rev. Gurley for a copy of the sermon. Seven months later, in September of 1862, Mr. Lincoln sat at his desk in the White House and composed what has come to be called his "Meditation on the Divine Will." This fragment was discovered by one of Mr. Lincoln's secretaries, John Hay, in the president's desk, immediately after Mr. Lincoln's death.

John Milton Hay (1838–1905), in addition to being Lincoln's secretary, was also an 1858 graduate of Brown University, after which he read law in his uncle's office, in Springfield, not far from Lincoln's office. He was also the

---

6. Lincoln, first inaugural address, March 4, 1861.

7. Gurley, funeral sermon for William Lincoln, Washington, DC, February 24, 1862.

8. Lincoln, quoted in Press, *How the Republicans Stole Religion*, 68.

secretary of state under President William McKinley, as well as Theodore Roosevelt. This fragment of "Meditation on the Divine Will" begins with these words: "The Will of God prevails. In great contests each party acts in accordance with the Will of God. Both may be, and one must be wrong. God cannot be for and against the same thing at the same time."[9]

Again, the language of Lincoln that "the Will of God prevails" is a words that a believer in divine plan theory might employ. In this passage, Mr. Lincoln applies the law of contradiction to the question of slavery—both sides cannot be morally right at the same time. Later, in the same work, Mr. Lincoln adds:

> In the present Civil War it is quite possible that God's purpose is something different from the purposes of either party—and yet the human instrumentalities, working as they do, are of the best adaptation to effect His purpose. I am almost ready to say that this is probably true—that God wills this contest , and wills that it shall not yet end.[10]

This passage, as well, with its mention of "God's purposes," is again an indication of Mr. Lincoln's belief in, and his dedication to, the divine plan theory. Mr. Lincoln also indicated that God willed the war, and now he wishes it to continue. The fragment, which Lincoln's secretary, John Hay, found in his desk after the president's death, closes this way:

> By His mere great power, on the minds of the now contestants, He could have either saved or destroyed the Union without a human contest. Yet the contest began. And having begun, He could give the final victory to either side any day. Yet the contest proceeds.[11]

The sixteenth president begins by mentioning God's omnipotence and his ability to save or destroy the Union. Then, Mr. Lincoln indicates that either side may win the war. In this fragment, Mr. Lincoln also appears to be searching for signs of the will of God on the question of emancipation. He had resisted freeing the slaves, until now convinced it was better not to do so. Nevertheless, the president mentions that "the Will of God prevails" and "God's purposes" in the fragment that Mr. Hay labeled "Meditation on the Divine Will."

These are obvious references to Mr. Lincoln's belief that God has a divine plan, by which all will work out for the best, "in the best of all possible

9. Ibid.

10. Ibid.

11. Ibid.

worlds," as Leibniz would say, or "Whatever is, is right," as Alexander Pope would say, or for God's "good ends," in the language of Mr. Lincoln.[12]

Historian Michael Nelson sums up the importance of the fragment in question when he writes:

> Clearer evidence would be hard to find in demonstrating not only that Lincoln's religious views had changed over the years, but also how they had changed. In his 1846 election Handbill, Lincoln had written that the human mind is governed by some power, over which the mind has no control. Sometime between then and 1862, he had identified to his own satisfaction its source—no longer 'some power,' but rather his "mere quiet power.' Lincoln no longer believed in a mere abstract force, but in Divine Agency, a Being with an independent Will and the Power to implement it.[13]

Mr. Nelson speaks of the theological shift in Mr. Lincoln, from his 1846 response to the charge of infidelity, to his 1862 commitment to divine plan theory. It is important to remember, however, that the fragment was not intended for public display or publication, but rather it was a reflection of Mr. Lincoln's private thoughts. Samuel Calhoun and Lucas Morel, in their essay "Abraham Lincoln's Religion," fully agree. They comment about the "Meditation," "It was not written to be seen of men in the awful sincerity of a perfectly honest soul trying to bring itself into closer communion with its maker."[14]

It is of some interest that in the same month Mr. Lincoln wrote the "Meditation on the Divine Will" he also issued his preliminary "Emancipation Proclamation," which stated that those states or parts of states still in rebellion as of January 1, 1863, would be declared free. Just one hundred days later, with the rebellion abated, Mr. Lincoln issued the final "Emancipation Proclamation," which declared, "That all persons held as slaves, within the rebellious areas, are, and henceforth shall be free."[15] This proclamation freed the slaves of the states in rebellion, but it did nothing for captives in the border states. They would not receive their freedom until the passing of the Thirteenth Amendment soon after, in April of 1864.

We also have shown in this work that Mr. Lincoln had seen two of his generals, Hunter and Fremont, as insubordinate in regard to the issue of

---

12. Ibid.

13. Nelson, quoted in Basler, *Collected works of Abraham Lincoln*, 403–4.

14. Calhoun and Morel, "Abraham Lincoln's Religion."

15. Lincoln, Presidential Proclamation 93 (preliminary to the "Emancipation Proclamation"), September 22, 1862.

emancipation. Indeed, both generals, in their separate territories, declared Black men to be free long before the "Emancipation Proclamation," only to be rescinded by the president, after he heard of the decisions of these generals.

By 1863, Mr. Lincoln had begun to search for signs, signals from God that his plan was in the works and would end, in his view, when God's purposes had been fulfilled. The same month as his "Meditation," September of 1862, Mr. Lincoln also gathered his cabinet together to tell them that if Union forces drove the Southern rebels from Antietam Creek, in rural Maryland, it would be the sign for which Mr. Lincoln had so patiently waited.[16] Secretary of the Navy Gideon Welles recorded the president as saying, at the cabinet meeting, "God has decided this question in favor of the Slaves. He was satisfied that he was right, and was confirmed and strengthened in his action by the vow and by its results."[17]

Mr. Welles indicates that Mr. Lincoln was confident that he was on the side of the moral right in the war. Clearly, the sixteenth president was referring to emancipation with the words "in favor of the slaves." By the end of the war, of course, all African-Americans would be free by virtue of the Thirteenth Amendment to the U.S. Constitution, passed into law on April 8, 1864.

For Mr. Lincoln, then, the Battle of Antietam was another turning point in his life, as well as the life of the nation; but Mr. Lincoln's priorities were now quite different. No longer was the main concern the preservation of the Union. Instead, his major goal now seemed to be "in favor of the slaves." Indeed, on New Year's Day of 1863, Mr. Lincoln signed the "Emancipation Proclamation," freeing all slaves in the Confederacy.[18] This was soon followed by the Thirteenth Amendment, which freed all slaves in America.

Indeed, with the passing of the Thirteenth Amendment to the Constitution, which was passed by the Senate on April 8, 1864, and by the House on December 6, 1865, both slavery and involuntary servitude were abolished in the United States completely and irrevocably.

By 1864, some close to Mr. Lincoln, like Judge David Davis and one of his secretaries, John Hay, urged the president to rescind the proclamation, in which case they believed that the South could be persuaded to return to the Union. Mr. Lincoln refused. Were he to do so, he is reported to have told

16. Lincoln, "Meditations on the Divine Will."

17. Welles, *Civil War Diaries*, 448.

18. Lincoln, Presidential Proclamation 95 ("Emancipation Proclamation"), January 1, 1863.

one visitor, "I should be damned in time and in eternity."[19] Mr. Lincoln, perhaps, seems here to be worried about his own salvation—something rare for
the president, for he was nearly always, as we have shown, a self-deprecating
man, one more concerned with the interests of others than his own.

A series of other events in the summer and autumn of 1862 also pro-
pelled Mr. Lincoln into a new religious direction. Slavery was disintegrating
in various parts of the South. The U.S. Congress had abolished slavery in
the District of Columbia. They also authorized Mr. Lincoln to enroll Blacks
in the army, as well as free to the slaves of pro-Confederate owners in areas
under military control, or martial law. Thus, Mr. Lincoln signed into law all
of these measures in the summer of 1862.

In total, by the end of the Civil War, 179,000 Black troops had served
in the Union army. 20,000 more men were in the Union's navy. 110,000
died for the Union over the course of the conflict, and another 30,000 were
infected with disease.[20] This, of course, is to say nothing of the wounded and
the maimed during the war. At Gettysburg alone, the battle left 7,058 dead,
33,269 wounded, and 10,790 missing in action.

We also have maintained earlier in this work that after the Battle of
Antietam Mr. Lincoln appears to have begun to change the goal of the war.
Before that time, his goal was the preservation of the Union; but after the
Battle at Antietam Creek in rural Maryland, near Sharpsburg, he began to
understand the Union's goal as the freeing of slaves, in both Southern and
border states.

When the sixteenth president took his second presidential oath on
March 4, 1865, in Washington, DC, the war was not yet over but the end
was near. Ulysses S. Grant, who was now the army's commander, had been
successful at Vicksburg and elsewhere. Mr. Lincoln did not gloat, nor did
he use heated words against the South. Instead, he drew on his deep knowledge of Scripture and the wisdom he had gained in his political life to offer
a profound theological reflection on the meaning of the suffering of the
American Civil War. Garry Wills called the speech "Mr. Lincoln's Theodicy,"
in his book on the Gettysburg address.[21]

Mr. Lincoln, at his second inaugural address, observed that day:

> Neither party expected for war, the magnitude, or the duration,
> which already has been attained . . . Both read the same Bible
> and pray to the same God, and each invokes His aid against

19. Quoted in Hay, *Abraham Lincoln*, 197.

20. These figures come from the Civil War Trust. See http://civilwar.org/learn/
articles/civil-war-statistics.

21. Wills, *Lincoln at Gettysburg*, 149.

the other . . . The prayers of both could not be answered. That of neither has been answered fully. The Almighty has His own purposes.[22]

Using his fine ability at comparing and contrasting, Mr. Lincoln points out here that the two sides of the war read the same Bible, pray to the same God, and invoke that God as an aid against the other side. He also refers to the divine plan theory in the language about "God's purposes," or "good ends," with respect to the issues of theodicy and the problem of evil.

Mr. Lincoln's second inaugural address was his final speech to the American public. In it, the sixteenth president endowed the American Civil War with sacred and holy meanings. In a real way, he also created an American scripture and articulated an American civil religion that he had begun in his Gettysburg address, in the fall of 1863, and continued in his second inaugural address, in 1865, a little more than a month before his assassination.

Indeed, forty-one days after his second inaugural address, Lincoln himself became a tragic casualty of the Civil War, just a day before Easter Sunday. Indeed, Lincoln was shot on Good Friday, and died the following day. Mourned and grieved, it was inevitable that he would be compared to Jesus. In the end, Mr. Lincoln's final words about religion were his dedication to the fact that God had "his purposes, perhaps unknown to humans." In the final analysis, as we have indicated, the sixteenth president appears to have been dedicated to the idea of the divine plan theory in regards to evil and suffering.

Along the way in this study, we also have made a number of observations about Mr. Lincoln's other religious beliefs. Among these other topics of this work were Lincoln's views on the Bible, his understanding of ethics, what he had to say about the issues of theodicy and the problem of evil, the uses of religion in his inaugural addresses, and how the two sides of the Civil War, as well as the slaves, all employed religion as a tool in the conflict.

All of these other religious beliefs of Mr. Lincoln, however, were subservient to his dedication to the divine plan point of view, as outlined in his "Meditation on the Divine Will" and in his second inaugural address. It is our view that Mr. Lincoln died a Christian, returning, in the final analysis, to the rugged Christian upbringing he had on what was then the Western frontier of America.

In regard to Mr. Lincoln's views on ethics and morality, in chapter 4 of this essay, we have maintained that the sixteenth president employed all four of the traditional moral theories in regard to the nature of the moral

22. Lincoln, second inaugural address, March 4, 1865.

good to be found in the history of Western philosophy. These views are Aristotle's theory of moral virtues, Kant's deontological perspective, Bentham and Mill's utilitarianism, or teleological theory, and Ayn Rand's theory of ethical egoism. This latter view, as we have seen, was Mr. Lincoln's belief that all human beings, by their very natures, are essentially selfish and self-interested and that, inherently, they should always act that way. *This is a most peculiar conclusion.*

Additionally, we have maintained in the chapter of this study on Lincoln's ethics and morality that our sixteenth president was dedicated to a collection of core moral values that were the foundation of all of his comments on ethics and morality. This core consisted of the ideas of freedom, equality, honesty, and the right to profit from one's labor. This latter point, as we have shown, was garnered from Lincoln's understanding of a passage in the book of Genesis, at 3:19, which tells us in the King James Version, "In the sweat of thy face shalt thy eat bread, til thou return unto the ground."

In fact, in Genesis 3:19 Mr. Lincoln found an argument against slavery, in that all men have the right to the benefit of their labor, and in slavery this right was denied to the captives, for their owners were the primary benefactors of their labor.

We also have maintained that Mr. Lincoln employed Genesis 1:27–31—with its emphases that humans were created in the image of God, as well as made "very good," as opposed to the remainder of creation, which was simply "good"—as another argument against the practice of slavery in the world.

Among President Lincoln's most important leadership qualities, we have introduced five that were most significant in Lincoln's life. These were his ability to keep his vision, or goals, always in mind, even if he changed a goal or vision later on, as he did; his uncanny ability to manage his emotions; his skill as a great communicator; his outstanding capacity to keep the needs and feelings of others in view; and his dedication to and expression of his tendency toward humility and self-deprecation.

We also have pointed out in the chapter of this essay dedicated to Mr. Lincoln's ethics, chapter 4, that the sixteenth president, in the midst of the Civil War, understood himself as a man who was responsible for the survival of democracy throughout the world. For Lincoln, as we have shown, the United States was the supreme example of democracy to be emulated by other nations, particularly in Europe.

Indeed, Mr. Lincoln thought that the life of democracy itself was at stake in the battle between the states. Mr. Lincoln also suggested that the debates with Stephen Douglas were little more than "good versus evil."[23]

23. Lincoln–Douglas debate in Alton, October 15, 1858.

Clearly, the sixteenth president believed he was on the side of the good, while Judge Douglas, Lincoln thought, represented evil, in regard to the extension of slavery into the Western Territories. But we also pointed out that although Judge Douglas had evil ideas, that did not mean that Mr. Lincoln thought he was an evil person.

Additionally, we have shown that many of Mr. Lincoln's most important pronouncements about ethics and morality came in the context of the 1858 debates with Stephen Douglas, and that the disagreement over the expansion of slavery into the Western Territories was fundamentally a moral debate for the sixteenth president. We indicated that Mr. Lincoln often associated moral principles with the ethics of Jesus in the Gospels, like the Golden Rule at Matthew 7:12; with the Ten Commandments, in chapters 25 of Exodus and chapter 10 of Deuteronomy; and with the documents of the founding fathers of this nation, such as the Declaration of Independence and the U.S. Constitution, among other documents, with their emphases on freedom and equality.

When it came to Abraham Lincoln's views on the Bible, in chapter 5, we have arrived in this work on four major conclusions. First, Lincoln knew the Scriptures intimately and quoted them regularly throughout his adult life. Second, Lincoln employed both his family's Geneva Bible and the King James Version of Holy Scripture. Third, most of the allusions to the Bible in his speeches and written works come in eight works: his Peoria address (1854); his "House Divided Speech" (1858); his Chicago address (1858); his Lewistown address (1858); his "Words Fitly Spoken Speech" (1857); the Gettysburg address (1863); and Lincoln's two inaugural addresses (1861 and 1865).[24]

A fourth conclusion we have made about Mr. Lincoln's employment of Scripture is that he sometimes employed other sources independent of the Bible, for scriptural or religious purposes. His uses of William Shakespeare (1564–1616) and John Wycliffe (1330–1384) are two fine examples where he borrows directly from them to make a biblical or metaphysical point. We pointed out that a number of Bibles had a significant place in Mr. Lincoln's life, including the family Geneva Bible purchased by Thomas Lincoln; the Bible he borrowed for his first presidential oath from the clerk of the U.S. Supreme Court, Thomas Carroll Clark, which came to be called the "Lincoln Bible; the King James Bible given to the sixteenth president as a present from the Speed family in Kentucky, in 1841; and another King James Bible given to President Lincoln by a group of African-American ministers from Baltimore, during the Civil War, in 1864.

24. See the bibliography for the citations of these works.

We also have shown that at times Mr. Lincoln appears to have made up on the spot what appeared to be biblical quotations, when, in fact, they were spurious and uttered for utilitarian or other immediate, or pragmatic, purposes. On several occasions, the sixteenth president selected an apt biblical passage, or simply invented one on the spot, in an impromptu manner.

We also have indicated several passages in this work where Mr. Lincoln is quoted verbatim, when in fact there is very little evidence that he actually said or wrote those words. Mr. Lincoln is frequently, and erroneously, misquoted, as much as any important thinker in the nineteenth century.

Additionally, we also have shown in this study that the Old Testament book most quoted by Mr. Lincoln was the Psalms, and that he was very fond of the Twenty-Third Psalm, which he knew by heart, as well as Psalms 56, 90, 137, and 147, among others. Mr. Lincoln quoted directly from Genesis, Exodus, First and Second Kings, First and Second Samuel, the Psalms, the book of Daniel, the book of Job, Ecclesiastes, the prophet Micah, and many other Old Testament works.

Mr. Lincoln's favorite New Testament book, as we have shown, was Revelation, particularly during the Civil War era, for the book's references to the end times, and other cataclysmic events and tribulations in the book, served as biblical parallels to the destruction in the Civil War period.

Mr. Lincoln employed Revelation and the four Gospels much more often than he used the letters of Saint Paul and the Catholic Epistles. He quoted directly from Matthew, Mark, Luke, John, Revelation, as well as other New Testament texts; but Lincoln, like Mr. Jefferson, appears to have eschewed the epistles of Saint Paul.[25] In fact, several Enlightenment thinkers, including Voltaire, Jefferson, Rousseau, and many others, believed that Saint Paul had corrupted the central message of love in Jesus's mission, chiefly by the invention of early Christian doctrines like original sin.

We also have indicated that the most often discussed themes in Lincoln's two inaugural addresses were: slavery, the legal status of the South, the use of force, secession, the protection of slavery where it existed, the extension of slavery into the Western Territories, and federal offices in the South, such as the postal service.

We also have shown in this essay that God, the Bible, and responses to the issues of theodicy and the problem of evil show up more often in the two inaugurals than any other theological questions; and these theological issues occur more often in the second inaugural than any other text of Mr.

---

25. For both Jefferson and Lincoln, the letters of Paul are hardly quoted by the two presidents.

Lincoln's corpus of work, with the possible exception of the 1862 fragment called "Meditation on the Divine Will."

Along the way, we also have maintained that both the North and the South had several uses of religion in the War Between the States, as did the slaves themselves. Both sides saw that "God was on their side" in the war, and both the North and the South saw themselves as a "New Jerusalem," if for slightly different reasons. For the North, it was simply a moral matter. For the South, on the other hand, slavery was thought to be required by Holy Scripture.

We also have pointed out an irony in regard to biblical views of slavery. The Old Testament, at Exodus 21:2–11, suggests that after a period of six years of service as a slave, a master ought to set the captive free. If this would have been actually practiced in the American South, of course, few slaves would have remained on most farms and plantations in the South.

We also have spoken of a third perspective on slavery and the Civil War—one often neglected by historians. That is, what slaves themselves thought of the sins and "offenses" of the Civil War and of slavery. As we have shown, the slaves, too, saw themselves as a "chosen people," much like the Israelites escaping slavery in Egypt in the ancient world. Mr. Lincoln was often called the "Moses of America" by American Blacks in the late 1860s, after his assassination, as well as by abolitionists both before and after the war; or Lincoln was seen as a "new Joshua" who led the Israelites after the death of Moses.

Indeed, American slaves saw that the biblical text was staunchly on the side of emancipation, while both the North and South used the same Bible for their own purposes. They also believed that God had salvation in store for those who could endure the hardships of American captivity. The believers in the North and the South were not the only religious people in America in the days of slavery. Many slaves clearly were religious, as well, and had their own Black preachers. Interestingly enough, even the slaves themselves believed that God was on their side.

In 1901, W. E. B. Du Bois, in his classic essay "Faith of the Fathers," suggested that slave religion in America could be characterized by three aspects. These were: preachers, music, and what he called "frenzy or shouting."[26] Subsequent scholars of the phenomenon point out that he might well have added a fourth characteristic, the conversion experience, or being "born again."

---

26. Du Bois's essay "The Faith of the Fathers" is in his collection called *Essays Collection.*

In fact, the experience of conversion was an essential element in the religious life of the slave in America. For them, the only path to salvation was in the "lonesome valley" wherein the "seekers" underwent a conversion, an experience that was treasured as one of the peak moments in the slave's life, or that of his family.

The slave's conversion was frequently preceded by a period where the slave had anxiety over his salvation. This period may have lasted for days, or even weeks. Slave Josiah Henson, for example, at the age of eighteen, was struck by these words from a sermon: "Jesus Christ, the Son of God, tasted death for every man; for the high, for the low, for the rich, for the poor, the bond, the free, the negro in his chains, the man in gold and diamonds."[27]

Mr. Henson points out that when it comes to the atonement, the rich man has no better status than the slave. He went on in his autobiography to say, "I stood and heard it. It touched my heart and I cried out, 'I wonder if Jesus died for me.'"[28] It appears that Mr. Lincoln did the same thing at the end of his life, and he answered that question in the affirmative.

George Liele (1750–1820), an African-American and emancipated slave who became the founding preacher of First Bryan Baptist Church in Savannah, Georgia, also wrote of his conversion experience. He said, "I was convinced that I was not on the way to Heaven, but on the way to Hell," a reference to his period of anxiety over religion.[29] The Rev. Liele continued:

> This state I labored in for five or six months . . . I was brought to believe that my life hung by a slender thread . . . And I found no way where I could escape damnation to Hell, but only through the merits of my dying Lord, Jesus Christ.[30]

The religious experiences and conversions of Americans were not all that different from the frenzy and movement of the Spirit in Lincoln's parents that we have described in chapter 1 of this essay. Conversion and regeneration were very much a part of the religious lives of the Separate Baptists in early nineteenth-century America, as well as the lives of American slaves; and not that very different from contemporary American "born again" Christians.

Additionally, along the way in this essay we have shown that President Lincoln was fully dedicated to a number of moral values garnered from the founding fathers. Chief among these were freedom, equality, fairness, and

27. Henson, *Life of Josiah Henson.*

28. Ibid., 53–54.

29. Shannon, *George Liele's Life and Legacy,* 119.

30. Ibid.

the right to gain from one's labor. After receiving a letter from John Johnston, one of his stepbrothers, in which the brother asks for a loan of eighty
dollars, Mr. Lincoln expresses his thoughts on idleness and hard work. Mr.
Lincoln wrote back to his stepbrother about the priority of men's right to the
benefits of their own labor:

> At the various times when I have helped you a little, you have
> said to me, "We can get along very well now," but in a very short
> time I find you in the same difficulty. Now this can only happen
> by some defect in your conduct. What that defect is, I think I
> know. You are not lazy, and still you are an idler. I doubt whether
> since I saw you last, you have done a good whole day's work, in
> any one day.[31]

Mr. Lincoln expresses his disappointment with his stepbrother, and he also
extols the value of hard work. Indeed, Mr. Lincoln, in his speeches, his published writings, and in his letters, regularly spoke of the value of hard work,
and the accompanying right that a man should be allowed to benefit from
the proceeds of his own Labor. Mr. Lincoln evangelized for these two values,
freedom and the right to profit from one's labor, and he also exemplified
those two values; they also were the foundation of his opposition to the
practice of slavery, as we mentioned earlier in regard to passages in the book
of Genesis, in chapters 1 and 3.

In fact, Mr. Lincoln regularly turned to the words of Genesis 3:19
as support that all men have the right to the proceeds of their own labor,
another further argument against slavery. Lincoln also employed Genesis
1:27–31, with the creating of man in the image and likeness of God as
another argument against slavery, and that the remainder of creation was
made "good," while humans were made "very good," as another indication
that humans are sacred and have a special place in God's scheme—even
slaves.

We also have maintained in this study on Lincoln's religion that, in
regard to the issues of problem of evil and theodicy, the sixteenth president
employed retributive justice theory, in regard to the sin of slavery. He used
both the moral qualities view and the test view, in connection with the questions of evil and suffering, as well as the idea that God permits evil but does
not cause it; but we also have suggested that the primary understanding of
these theological questions of Mr. Lincoln was to be found in what we have
called the divine plan theory, whereby all the evil and suffering of the war
was to be understood solely in the context of what Mr. Lincoln referred to
as God's "grand ends" or "good purposes."

31. Lincoln, letter to John David Johnston, January 2, 1851.

Mr. Lincoln's extraordinary speaking and writing skills also have been extensively discussed in this essay. We have pointed out the sixteenth president's uses of several literary techniques, such as alliteration, repetition, his penchant for metaphors, his ability to utter memorable words, as well as his employing of the passive voice, his penchant for comparing and contrasting, and his use of other literary sources besides the Bible—such as William Shakespeare and John Wycliffe, for examples—that contributed to his deep religious and spiritual life.

In fact, while on the legal circuit in the 1840s, Mr. Lincoln insisted on reading all opinions out loud. He thought this was a useful tool in judging the quality of legal opinions and prose in general, and he did the same thing before his speeches in the White House, as well as other venues.

Along the way, we also have maintained that President Abraham Lincoln changed his vision during his administration. Originally, it was simply to preserve the integrity of the Union; but later in his administration, and during the war, his new vision became the eradication of slavery and giving to African-Americans all the rights and obligations that all White Americans possessed, and that are guaranteed by the U.S. Constitution to all its citizens.

We also have shown in this essay that in the late 1840s and early 1850s lawyers and judges, Mr. Lincoln among them, would travel the circuit from small town to small town, trying local cases. These small towns, as we have shown, were often too sparsely populated to have their own full-time legal officials, thus the birth of the circuit, and the origins of the American term "circuit court." Many reports from Mr. Lincoln's days of circuit-riding have suggested that after the legal proceedings were finished for the day, Mr. Lincoln is said to have often traded yarns with the town's people, and he shared in their hospitality and friendship, as well.

Each of Mr. Lincoln's trips on the circuit covered approximately four hundred to five hundred miles and would keep him from home for nine or ten weeks, with stops for court sessions in seven or eight circuit towns. Among Mr. Lincoln's circuit companions were Henry Clay Whitney (1831–1905) and Judge David Davis (1815–1886). Mr. Davis, of course, later served on the U.S. Supreme Court under Abraham Lincoln.[32] Henry C. Whitney also published a two-volume biography of Mr. Lincoln. The first volume is called *Lincoln, the Citizen*; the second volume is *Lincoln, the President*.

As we have shown earlier in this essay, the Maryland-born Judge Davis and Mr. Lincoln traveled together on the circuit and developed a deep friendship. During Lincoln's 1860 presidential campaign, Davis served as

32. See Wilson, *David Davis*.

his campaign manager. Later, the former was appointed by the latter to the United States Supreme Court.[33]

In sum, we have shown that the major conclusions concerning Abraham Lincoln's religion are the following. He was raised in the Calvinist Separate Baptist church, and he read the Scriptures, even to his stepsiblings, early and often in his life. In early adulthood, beginning in his twenties, he went through a period of religious skepticism that culminated in the time after the deaths of his sons Eddie and Willie. Although he rejected metaphysics in his early adult life, he appears to have gone through a kind of religious conversion at the end of his life, beginning with the death of his sons Eddie and Willie, in 1850 and 1862, respectively. Finally, Mr. Lincoln appears to have been dedicated to the idea of the divine plan theory, when it came to the sixteenth president's understanding of the issues of theodicy and the problem of evil, particularly in relation to the evil and suffering in the Civil War.

At Oak Ridge Cemetery in Springfield, Illinois, on May 4, 1865, Methodist bishop Matthew Simpson delivered a eulogy when Mr. Lincoln's body, along with that of his son Willie—Lincoln's favorite and the most like his father—were moved by train to be interred in Springfield. The Rev. Simpson admitted in his eulogy that he could not speak "definitively" about the faith of Mr. Lincoln, but Simpson, nevertheless, observed that Mr. Lincoln had "believed in Christ."[34] The sixteenth president's brother-in-law, Ninian Edwards, later agreed;[35] and in 1873 the Rev. James A. Smith, the pastor of Springfield's First Presbyterian Church, also assented to the Christian faith of President Abraham Lincoln.[36]

Ninian Edwards (1809–1888) was the husband of Mary Todd Lincoln's sister. He served for many years as the "Superintendent of Public Instruction," a fancy name for the head of public schools in Springfield. The Rev. Dr. James A. Smith (1789–1871) was a Scottish-born Presbyterian clergyman. He was ordained in 1829 and pastored the First Presbyterian Church of Springfield from 1844 until 1856, when the Lincoln family attended services there.

Both Mr. Edwards and the Rev. Smith were convinced that the sixteenth president of the United States was dedicated to Jesus Christ.[37] Mrs.

33. See Shannon, *George Liele's Life and Legacy*, 100–121.

34. Quoted in Wood, *Peerless Orator*, 113.

35. Edwards, *History of Illinois*. The final chapter of the book deals with Mr. Lincoln.

36. Mr. Lincoln first heard the Rev. Dr. Smith preach when he was sixteen years old, when the minister preached at a revival meeting in Rockford, Indiana. Later, the two became close friends in Springfield.

37. Edwards, *Materials Towards a History*, 229.

Lincoln joined Smith's Presbyterian church just after the death of her son Eddie, in 1850—the beginning, we believe, of Mr. Lincoln's return to the Christian faith.

We also have maintained that following the deaths of Eddie and Willie, Mary Todd Lincoln began employing the services of mediums, both in the White House and in Georgetown, as well. We even have shown that Mr. Lincoln attended at least one séance in Georgetown, and perhaps other sittings in the White House, as well. Indeed, we even have supplied the names of several American mediums associated with Mrs. Lincoln.

As we have shown, for Mr. Lincoln, all the evils and sufferings of the Civil War eventually would be seen as part of a divine plan by which everything works out for the good. Mr. Lincoln specifically refers to this as God's "good ends."[38] This view is also perfectly consistent with universal salvation—something Mr. Lincoln favored—and against the idea of eternal damnation—something he was staunchly against, as we have said many times in this work on Mr. Lincoln's faith, principally on moral grounds.

The sixteenth president could not understand how a perfectly good God could prescribe eternal damnation to any being, human, angelic, or otherwise. We also have shown that Mr. Lincoln was decidedly against the idea of the free will defense, chiefly because of his dedication to the "law of necessity," or his fatalism or determinism—what the Greeks called *moirai*, or fate.

Additionally, we have maintained in this essay that President Abraham Lincoln, at different times and places, appears to have assented to the following Christian explanations to the issues of theodicy and the problem of evil: the free will defense; the moral qualities view; the test perspective; collective retributive justice theory; the view that God permits evil but does not cause it; the practical approach to suffering, with its emphases on compassion and charity; and, above all, Mr. Lincoln appears to have been a firm believer in the divine plan theory.

In addition, we also have suggested that the sixteenth president's perspective in terms of reconstruction and reconciliation after the war was that Americans on both sides should behave much like the figure of Jesus in the Gospels—to wit, that we should respond to others in the face of suffering with both compassion and charity, much like Jesus behaved toward the poor and the disabled in the Gospels.

Near the end of the Civil War, in the continued throes of evil and destruction brought by that war, Mr. Lincoln paused to sum up his views of human nature and humanity's relationship to God. Mr. Lincoln remarked,

38. Lincoln, second inaugural address, March 4, 1865.

"God loves us the way we are, but too much to leave us that way. I have held many things in my hands, and I have lost them all; but whatever I have placed in God's hands, that I still possess."[39]

In this letter, Mr. Lincoln expressed his disappointment in human nature and its capacity for great violence; but he then turned to the losses of his mother, his brother Thomas, his sister Sarah in childbirth, his first love, Ann Rutledge, at age twenty-two, the deaths of his sons Eddie and Willie, in 1850 and 1862, respectively, as well as the destruction of nearly 700,000 men in the Civil War during his watch; and through all this, his final word is about the divine plan and being placed in the hands of God, despite the evils and sufferings of the Civil War.

In the course of this work, we also have shown that President Abraham Lincoln served as a volunteer in the Illinois militia during the Black Hawk War, from April of 1832 until July of that same year. Although he never saw combat, he was elected captain of his company. Lincoln's service appears to have had a lasting impression on him and he related tales about it later in life with modesty, as well as a bit of humor. Writing in the third person, in his "autobiography" of 1860, he observes about his military service, "Abraham joined a volunteer company, and to his own surprise, he was elected Captain of it. He says he has not since had any success in life which gave him so much satisfaction."[40]

It is significant that the men of his company overwhelmingly elected him to be the head of the unit. Even early on, in the early 1830s, Mr. Lincoln already was displaying his many leadership qualities. But, unlike many of his fellow soldiers, Mr. Lincoln managed to avoid the first major cholera epidemic of the Great Lakes. To compensate for his service, the U.S. government awarded Lincoln with a tract of land in Iowa. In later campaigns for political office, Lincoln claimed that his military service entailed "A good many bloody struggles with mosquitoes."[41]

We also have shown that while Mr. Lincoln was president, he frequently expressed consternation at his generals. In fact, he fired half a dozen of them, General McClellen twice. Most of this consternation, as we have shown, was related to military strategy and planning.

Additionally, in the course of this study we have shown that Mr. Lincoln's frustration and depression during the war deepened as the Union's military defeats continued from 1861 until 1863. The Union army, of course, as well as the navy, had the clear advantage in terms of numbers

39. Quoted in Marschell, "Not Praying that God Is on Our Side."
40. Lincoln, *Autobiography*, 131.
41. Ibid.

and firepower, but the North failed to assemble the military leader necessary to mount an effective campaign. Indeed, the sixteenth presi replaced generals and changed the command structure several times in the later stages of the war, as we have shown several times in this work—before Mr. Lincoln finally settled on General Ulysses S. Grant to take command of the army.

General Grant had gained Mr. Lincoln's trust and respect after winning crucial victories at Vicksburg, Mississippi, and elsewhere in the Western Territories. In General Grant the sixteenth president finally found a general that could muster the full strength of the Union's forces against the army of the Confederacy. Mr. Lincoln had not formed trusting relationships with many of his generals earlier in the war. One key as to why this was so was the case of General William T. Sherman, who only visited the White House one time, while Lincoln was president and sherman was in command.

General Sherman, among others, was convinced, early on, that Mr. Lincoln was naïve about the ways of war. Like General George Meade, Sherman was a graduate of West Point, but he too was never very effective in the field. It was only by March of 1864 that Lincoln began to feel comfortable with his top commanders, and especially with General Grant.

In the course of this essay on Mr. Lincoln's religion, we also have shown that the sixteenth president was not without his flaws. He clearly did not act decisively enough on the slavery issue. At times he could be brisk with his subordinates, both generals and politicians alike. Lincoln at times made contradictory statements, such as on the nature of Blacks folks. He said they are free, "but not free in every respect."[42] The question of whether Mr. Lincoln did or did not assent to the idea of an objective standard for morality is another example of his tendency to be contrary. Mr. Lincoln also expressed contradictory views on the colonization of African-Americans back to Africa, as we shall see below.

We also have shown that Mr. Lincoln may have had a genetic predisposition toward depression, on both his mother's and his father's sides of the family, as Dr. Joshua Wolf Shenk, in his book *Lincoln's Melancholy*, has suggested. Indeed, many of Lincoln's closest friends spoke of him as gloomy and detached throughout most of his adult life.

Additionally, we also have suggested in this study that the sixteenth president of the United States, Abraham Lincoln, most likely suffered from a form of clinical depression. Indeed, in 1836 he had a nervous breakdown and was in bed for six months. We might add, however, that the source of this view about the nervous breakdown was Mr. Herndon and his biography

42. Guelzo, "Abraham Lincoln and the Doctrine of Necessity," 59.

of the sixteenth president. Mr. Herndon reports that Mr. Lincoln took to his bed for six months in 1836, ate only sporadic meals, lost several pounds, and was, according to his third law partner, William Henry Herndon, "suicidal in that period."[43]

President Lincoln also was not without his flaws. He made a number of bad decisions, and he frequently admitted them later on. One good example was his avoiding the city of Baltimore on his way to his first inaugural in 1861 because he heard a rumor that he might be assassinated there. Later, he lectured in Baltimore at the Sanitary Fair there, among other reasons to atone for his earlier slight of the city. Another contradiction is that Mr. Lincoln favored the colonization of African-Americans but later changed his mind about the matter.

Nevertheless, Mr. Lincoln ran for public office a total of twelve times, and he was defeated in eight of them. In addition, Lincoln twice failed in businesses, once going bankrupt, when he was a partner in a general store, in New Salem.[44] Lincoln was also ineffective as postmaster in New Salem in the 1830s.[45] Mr. Lincoln was one of two U.S. presidents who had served as postmaster, the other being Harry S. Truman.

Abraham Lincoln arose from humble backwoods origins to become, perhaps, the greatest president of the United States. In his efforts to preserve the Union during the Civil War, he assumed more power than any preceding president. Although necessity almost made him a dictator, he was always both a Democrat and a Republican. He was a superb politician, and attempted to persuade with reasoned speech and calm words. Lincoln has had a lasting influence on American political institutions; most importantly, he acted decisively in a time of national crisis.

One of the main reasons that President Lincoln loved to ride on the legal circuit is that he came into contact with simple country people not all that different from his family and the neighbors he met in his time growing up in Kentucky, Indiana, and Illinois.

Mr. Lincoln came far in his personal faith journey. As a young boy in Indiana, he would stand upon a tree stump and mimic the emotional sermons he heard in his parents' Separate Baptist churches on Sundays, or he may have heard them from evangelists traveling on the circuit. As a young

43. Shenk, *Lincoln's Melancholy.*

44. Mr. Lincoln was appointed as postmaster in New Salem on May 7, 1833. He retained the position until the post office moved to Petersburg, on May 30, 1836. One tale among locals about how Mr. Lincoln originally got the job at the post office is that the previous postmaster, Samuel Hill, spent more time drinking whiskey with the male customers than selling stamps and doing post office work.

45. Herndon, *Life of Lincoln*, 41.

man in his twenties in New Salem, he read many critics of Christianity, like David Hume, Thomas Paine, and Francois Volney, and he became a skeptic and a fatalist, at the same time.

By the 1850s and 1860s, Mr. Lincoln went through a kind of religious experience in which he began to see the evil and suffering of the Civil War as part of a larger divine plan, by which all ill would work toward God's good ends, or what he sometimes called "Providence's good purposes."

Rarely in the literature of Abraham Lincoln do writers use the word "grace," even though it is doubly appropriate for Mr. Lincoln. Ulysses S. Grant suggested that the only answer as to why he was not injured in the battles of the Civil War was the grace of God. Clearly, it was only with the grace of God that Mr. Lincoln so expertly managed the nation through the Civil War—and he accomplished it with style, calm, and, of course, uncommon grace. Mr. Lincoln was the captain of the ship in bringing about a change of orders. He spoke of this in his Gettysburg address when he said in November of 1863:

> That this nation, under God, shall have a new birth of Freedom—and the government of the people, by the people, for the people, shall not perish from the Earth.[46]

In fact, Abraham Lincoln embodied the words of Alfred Tennyson(1809–1892) when he wrote:

> The old order changeth yielding place to a new. And God fulfills himself in many Ways Lest a good custom should corrupt the world. Comfort thyself: what comfort is In Me I have lived my life and that which I have done May he within himself make Pure But thou If thou shouldst never see my face again Pray for my soul. More things Are Wrought by prayer than this world dreams of.[47]

We would say—and Mr. Lincoln surely would say—"Amen to that!"

46. Lincoln, Gettysburg address, November 19, 1863.
47. Tennyson, "Passing of Arthur."

Biblical and Foreign Words and Expressions

Hebrew

Cuphah   "Whirlwind"   166

Hevel   "Vanity"   112

Jehovah   "God"   183

Yetzer ha ra   "Evil imagination"   77

Yetzer tov   "Good imagination"   77

Latin

Ageratina altissima   Species name for white snakeroot   6

Deo vindici   "Our God triumphs"   187

Lex talionis   "Law of retribution"   24

Classical Greek

Despote   "Master"   190

Arabic

French

Bibliography

"African-American Ministers Giving Bible to Mr. Lincoln." *Baltimore Sun*, September 7, 1864.

Alexander, Edward Porter. *Military Memoirs of a Confederate*. Createspace, 2014.

"Ann Rutledge." Abraham Lincoln Research Site. http://rogerjnorton.com/Lincoln34.html.

Armenti, Peter. "Lincoln as Poet." Presidents as Poets. Library of Congress. https://www.loc.gov/rr/program/bib/prespoetry/al.html.

Bailey, Laurel. "Dr. Anna and the Fight for the Milksick." *Illinois History*, April 1996.

Barbee, David R. "President Lincoln and Dr. Gurley." *Abraham Lincoln Quarterly* 5/1 (March 1948).

Barton, William E. *The Soul of Abraham Lincoln*. San Bernadino, CA: Ulan, 2012.

Basler, Roy R., ed. *The Collected Works of Abraham Lincoln*. 9 vols. New Brunswick, NJ: Rutgers University Press, 1953–55.

Bauckham, Richard. "Universalism: An Historical Survey." *Themelios*, September 1978, 47–64.

Bayle, Pierre. *Great Contests of Faith and Reason*. London: Forgotten Books, 2012.

Belze, Herman. "Abraham Lincoln and the Natural Law Tradition." Witherspoon Institute, 2011. http://www.nlnrac.org/american/lincoln.

Benedict, David. *General History of the Baptist Denomination*. London: Forgotten Books, 2017.

"Black Civil War Soldiers." History Channel online, 2010. http://www.history.com/topics/american-civil-war/black-civil-war-soldiers.

"Black Ministers Give Lincoln Bible." *New York Times*, September 11, 1864.

Bray, Robert., "What Lincoln Read." *Journal of the Abraham Lincoln Association*. Summer 2007.

Brooks, Noah. *Washington in Lincoln's Time*. London: Forgotten Books, 2017.

Burt, John. "Collective Guilt in Lincoln's Second Inaugural Address." *American Political Thought* 4/3 (2015) 467–88.

———. *Lincoln's Tragic Pragmatism*. Cambridge, MA: Harvard University Press, 2013.

Calhoun, Samuel, and Lucas Morel. "Abraham Lincoln's Religion." *Journal of the Abraham Lincoln Association* 33/1 (2012) 38–74.

Camus, Albert. *The Plague*. Translated by Stuart Gilbert. New York: Vintage, 1991.

Carpenter, Francis B. "On Describing Lincoln." *New York Tribune*, February 6, 1864.

——. *Six Months at the White House wtih Abraham Lincoln*. Washington, DC: White House Historical Association, 2008.

Carson, Thomas L. *Lincoln's Ethics*. Cambridge: Cambridge University Press, 2015.

Carter, Stephen I. "Mr. Lincoln's Top Hat." *Smithsonian Magazine*, November 2013.

Carwardine, Richard. *Lincoln: A Life of Purpose and Power*. London: Vintage, 2007.

Chittenden, Lucius. *Recollections of President Lincoln and His Administration*. Kindle ebook ed. New York: Harper, 1996.

Colburn, Nettie. *Was Abraham Lincoln a Spiritualist?* Washington, DC: Library of Congress, 1891.

Cozzens, Peter. "Shenandoah Valley Campaign of 1862." *Encyclopedia Virginia*. Viginia Foundation for the Humanities, November 29, 2012. https://www.encyclopediavirginia.org/Shenandoah_Valley_Campaign_of_1862.

Crooks, George. *The Life of Bishop Matthew Simpson*. New York: Harper, 1890.

Dallimore, Arnold. *George Whitfield's Enlightenment*. Wheaton, IL: Crossway, 2010.

Dearinger, Lowell A. "Dr. Anna and the Milksick." *Outdoor Illinois*, March 1967.

"The Death of Willie Lincoln." Abraham Lincoln Online. http://www.abrahamlincolnonline.org/lincoln/education/williedeath.htm.

Dekle, George R. *Prairie Defender: The Murder Trials of Abraham Lincoln*. Carbondale: Southern Illinois University Press, 2017.

Dickens, Charles. *Barnaby Rudge*. London: Penguin, 2003.

Donald, David Herbert. *Lincoln*. New York: Simon and Schuster, 1995.

Douglas, Ann. "Father and Son in 'Billy Budd.'" In *Melville's Short Novels*, edited by Dan McCall. New York: Norton, 2017.

Douglass, Frederick. *The Life and Times of Frederick Douglass*. Richmond: Wilder, 2008.

Du Bois, W. E. B. "The Crisis." In *The Souls of Black Folk*. New York: Dover, 1994.

——. "The Faith of the Fathers." In *Essays Collection*. CreateSpace, 2017.

Duncan, David Herbert. *Lincoln*. New York: Simon and Schuster, 1996.

Duncan, Kunigunde, and D. F. Nikols. *Mentor Graham: The Man Who Taught Lincoln*. Edinburgh: Kessinger, 2007.

Edwards, Morgan. *Materials Towards a History of the Baptists*. Athens, GA: Heritage Papers, 1984.

Epstein, Daniel M. *The Lincolns: Portrait of a Marriage*. New York: Ballantine, 2009.

Flowers, Frank A. *Edwin McMasters Stanton*. London: Kessinger, 2007.

Foner, Eric. *The Fiery Trial: Abraham Lincoln and American Slavery*. New York: Norton, 2010.

Fornieri, Joseph. *Abraham Lincoln's Political Faith*. Chicago: Northern Illinois University Press, 2005.

Garrison, William Lloyd. "The Great Crisis." *Liberator* 2/52 (December 29, 1832).

Goen, C. C. *Revivalism and Separatism in New England, 1740–1800: Strict Congregationalists and Separate Baptists in the Great Awakening*. Middleton, CT: Wesleyan University Press, 1987.

Goldman, David P. Neither America, nor Civil, nor a Religion." Review of Walter McDougall's *The Tragedy of American Foreign Policy: How America's Civil Religion Betrayed the National Interest*. *Claremont Review of Books* 27/2 (Spring 2017) 64–67.

Guelzo, Allen. "Abraham Lincoln and the Doctrine of Necessity." *Journal of the Abraham Lincoln Association* 18/1 (1997) 57–81.

——. *Redeemer President*. Grand Rapids: Eerdmans, 2002.

Gurley, Phineas. *The Assassination of Abraham Lincoln.* London: Forgotten B 2017.

Hawn, C. Michael. "The Battle Hymn of the Republic." *Discipleship Ministries,* July 2009.

Hay, John. *Abraham Lincoln: A History.* Vol. 1. New York: Cosimo, 2009.

Henson, Josiah. *The Life of Josiah Henson.* New York: Dover, 2015.

Herndon, William Henry. *Abraham Lincoln: The True Story of a Great Life.* 2 vols. New York: Appleton, 1892, 1896.

———. *Herndon on Lincoln.* Edited by Douglas L. Wilson and Rodney O. Davis. Chicago: University of Illinois Press, 2016.

———. *A Life of Lincoln.* Charleston, SC: Nabu, 2011.

Heuser, Herman J. "Lincoln and the Holy Land." *American Scholarly Review* 60/4 (1919) 353–59.

Holzer, Harold. "A Curious Death." *Wall Street Journal,* February 13, 2016.

———. "The Sound of Lincoln's Silence." *New York Times,* November 23, 2010.

Horrock, Thomas A. *Lincoln's Campaign Biographies.* Carbondale: Southern Illinois University Press, 2012.

Hsavlik, Robert J. "Abraham Lincoln and the Rev. James Smith." *Journal of the Illinois State Historical Society* 92/3 (1852).

Hume, David. *Dialogues Concerning Natural Religion.* New York: Hackett, 1998.

Ingersoll, Robert G. *Lecture on Lincoln.* New York: Farrell, 1909.

Johnson, William J. *Abraham Lincoln the Christian.* Kindle ebook ed. Forgotten Books, 2014.

Kant, Immanuel. *Lectures on Ethics.* Translated by Louis Infield. Indianapolis: Hackett, 1980.

Kazin, Alfred. "The Almighty Has His Own Purposes." Chapter 6 in *God and the American Writer.* New York: Vintage, 1997.

Keckley, Elizabeth. *Behind the Scenes, or, Thirty Years a Slave and Four Years in the White House.* Hillsborough, NC: Eno, 2016.

Keiper, Caitrin. "A Very Peculiar God: Reading Lincoln's Second Inaugural Address." https://www.whatsoproudlywehail.org/curriculum/the-american-calendar/a-very-peculiar-god-reading-lincolns-second-inaugural-address.

Lamb, Brian. Interview of Allen Guelzo. *Booknotes,* C-Span, April 2000.

Lamon, Ward Hill. *The Life of Abraham Lincoln as President.* Springfield: Mont Clair, 2011.

Lang, Stephen. *The Christian Historical Devotional.* New York: T. Nelson, 2012.

Leibniz, G. W. *Discourse on Method.* New York: Hackett, 1991.

Leidner, Gordon. *Lincoln on God and Country.* Washington, DC: Crown, 2000.

———. "Lincoln's Faith in God." https://greatamericanhistory.net/lincolnsfaith.htm.

———. *Theodicy: Essays on the Goodness of God, the Freedom of Man, and the Origin of Evil.* Chicago: Open Court, 1998.

Lincoln, Abraham. *Autobiography.* New York: Tandy, 1905.

"Lincoln, Sherman and Grant Meet." History Channel online, 2009. http://www.history.com/this-day-in-history/lincoln-sherman-and-grant-meet.

"Lincoln's Faith." *Chicago Herald,* June 17, 1892.

Lotz, Denton. *Celebrating 400 Years of Baptist Life.* March 2003. http://centerforbaptiststudies.org/400years/400march2003.pdf.

Lumpkin, William. *Baptist Foundation in the South.* Eugene, OR: Wipf and Stock, 2006.

Macartney, Clarence E. N. *Lincoln and the Bible*. Nashville: Abingdon-Cookesbury, 1949.

Mackie, John Milton. *The Life of Godfrey William Von Leibniz:: On the Basis of the German Work of Dr. G. E. Guhrauer*. Boston: Gould, Kendall, and Lincoln, 1845.

Mansfield, Stephen. "Abraham Lincoln's Atheist Period." *Huffington Post*, January 16, 2013.

———. *Lincoln's Battle with God*. New York: T. Nelson, 2012.

McClarey, Donald. "March 4, 1865: The Greatest Inaugural Address." *American Catholic*, January 20, 2017. http://the-american-catholic.com/2017/01/20/march-4-1865-the-greatest-inaugural-address/. *nothing new*

McNulty, Edward. "Lincoln: Complex Man of Faith." https://www.readthespirit.com/explore/abraham-lincoln-religion-complex-man-of-faith/.

MacCartney, Clarence. *Lincoln and the Bible*. Dallas: Godspeed, 2014.

Marschell, Rick. "Not Praying that God Is on Our Side." Blog post, April 13, 2015. http://www.mondaymorningministry.com/blog/2015/04/12/not-praying-that-god-be-on-our-side/.

McPherson, James M. "How Lincoln Won the War with Metaphors." In *Abraham Lincoln*, by James M. McPherson, 93–112. Oxford: Oxford University Press, 2009.

———. "Lincoln as Commander in Chief." *Smithsonian*, January 2009.https://www.smithsonianmag.com/history/lincoln-as-commander-in-chief-131322819/.

Miers, Earl, ed. *Lincoln Day by Day: A Chronology, 1809–1865*. New York: Morganside, 2012.

Miller, William Lee. *Lincoln's Virtues*. New York: Vintage, 2003.

Milton, John. *Paradise Lost*. New York: Penguin, 2003.

Minor, Charles L. C. *The Real Lincoln*. Richmond, VA: Everett Waddey, 1901.

Minutes of the Nolynn Association of Separate Baptists. 1819–1884. http://www.separatebaptist.org/downloads/nolynn/NolynnMinutes1819-1884.pdf.

Morris, Jan. *Wellness Words of Wisdom* (blog), April 13, 2012. https://sophia.smith.edu/blog/wordsofwisdom/2012/04/13/when-i-do-good-i-feel-good-when-i-do-bad-i-feel-bad-and-that-is-my-religion-abraham-lincoln/.

Moss, Robert. "Lincoln's Dreams." *DreamGate* (blog), November 2012. http://www.beliefnet.com/columnists/dreamgates/2012/11/lincolns-dreams.html.

"Mr. Lincoln in Richmond." *Richmond Daily News*, January 19, 1864.

"Mr. Lincoln's Skepticism." *New York World*, June 28, 1875.

Nietzsche, Frederick. *Ecco Homo*. New York: Penguin, 1992.

———. *Twilight of the Idols*. Translated by Richard Polt. Indianapolis: Hackett, 1997.

Novak, Michael, and Jana Novak. *Washington's God: Religion, Liberty, and the Father of Our Country*. New York: Basic Books, 2007.

Nowlin, William. *Kentucky Baptist History*. Lexington: University Press of Kentucky, 1998.

Paine, Thomas. *The Age of Reason*. Philadelphia, 1794.

Peart, Norman A. *Separate No More: Understanding and Developing Racial Reconciliation in Your Church*. New York: Baker, 2000.

Peraino, Kevin. *Lincoln in the World*. New York: Broadway, 2012.

Peters, Madison C. *Abraham Lincoln's Religion*. New York: Leopold Classics Library, 1909.

Pope, Alexander. *An Essay on Man*. Princeton, NJ: Princeton University Press, 2016.

Prarie Fire: The Illinois Country before 1818. DeKalb, IL: Northern Illinois University Libraries, 2002. http://dig.lib.niu.edu/prairiefire/.

"Presentation of a Bible to the President." *New York Times*, September 11, 1864. http://www.nytimes.com/1864/09/11/archives/presentation-of-a-bible-to-the-president.html.

Press, Bill. *How the Republicans Stole Religion: Why the Religious Right Is Wrong about Faith and Politics and What We Can Do to Make It Right.* New York: Image, 2006.

"Quotations from Patriots." Cable News Network, July 4, 2017.

Rand, Ayn. *The Virtue of Selfishness.* New York: Signet, 1964.

Roberts, Paul Craig. "The Lincoln Myth: Ideological Cornerstone of the America Empire." Blog post, August 21, 2017. https://www.paulcraigroberts.org/2017/08/21/lincoln-myth-ideological-cornerstone-america-empire/.

Russell, Peter A. "Henry Wentworth Monk." *Dictionary of Canadian Biography*, vol. 12. Toronto: University of Toronto Press, 2003.

Sandburg, Carl. *Abraham Lincoln: The Prairie Years.* San Diego: Harvest, 1982.

"Says Record Shows Lincoln a Baptist." *New York Times*, October 31, 1921.

Schurz, Carl. "The Quincy Debate." *New York Tribune*, October 14, 1858.

Schwartz, Earl. "A Poor Hand to Quote Scripture." *Journal of the Abraham Lincoln Association* 23/2 (Summer 2002) 37–49.

Scott, Morgan. *History of the Separate Baptist Church: With a Narrative of Other Denominations.* Indianapolis: Hollenseck, 1901.

Scott, Robert N. *The War of Rebellion.* Ser. 1, vol. 19. *The Official Records of the Union and Confederate Armies and Navies.* U.S. War Department. Washington, DC: Government Printing Office, 1889.

Scripps, John, "Lincoln on Plutarch." *Chicago Tribune*, October 14, 1858.

Semple, Robert. "The Separate Baptists." In *Welsh Succession of the Primitive Baptists.* Cardif, 1800.

Separate Baptists in Christ. "Articles of Doctrine for All Associations." http://www.separatebaptist.org/index.php?page=ourbeliefs.

Shakespeare, William. *The Passionate Pilgrim.* London : T. Judson for W. Jaggard, 1599.

Shannon, David T., ed. *George Liele's Life and Legacy: An Unsung Hero.* Macon, GA: Mercer University Press, 2013.

Shavin, David. "Abraham Lincoln's Leibnizian Second Inaugural Address." *Executive Intelligence Review* 42/13 (March 27, 2015) 39–46.

Sheehan, Tim. "Overshadowed: The Value of Judith McGuire's *Diary of the Souther Refugee During the War.*" http://www.timthehistorynut.com/overshadoweddiaryofasouthernrefugee.html.

Shenk, Joshua Wolf. *Lincoln's Melancholy.* New York: Mariner, 2006.

Sightler, James. "The Separate Baptist Revival and Its Influence in the South." Sightler Publications, January 18, 2004. http://www.sightlerpublications.com/history/SeparateBaptistRevival.htm.

Smith, Gary Scott. "Abraham Lincoln and Slavery." *The Patriot Post*, February 13, 2013. https://patriotpost.us/commentary/16731-abraham-lincoln-and-slavery.

Smith, James A. *The Christian's Defence.* Edinburgh: Pickering and Inglis, 1839.

Snay, Mitchell. *The Gospel of Disunion: Religion and Separatism in the Antebellum South.* Cambridge: Cambridge University Press, 1993.

Sparks, John. *The Roots of Appalachian Christianity.* Lexington: University Press of Kentucky, 2001.

Stout, Henry. *Religion in the Civil War.* Oxford: Oxford University Press, 1998.

Tarbell, Ida. "A Progressive Look at Lincoln." *Journal of the Abraham Lincoln Association* 18/1 (1998) 37–56.

Tachack, James. *Lincoln's Moral Vision*. Jackson: University Press of Mississippi, 2004.

Tennyson, Alfred. "The Passing of Arthur." In *Tennyson Poems*, 141–50. London: Forgotten Books, 2017.

Trueblood, Elton. *Abraham Lincoln: Lessons in Spirituality*. San Francisco: Harper, 2012.

Tucker, Dan, ed. *Lincoln's Notebooks: Letters, Speeches, Journals, Notes, Poems, and Doodles*. New York: Black Dog and Leventhal, 2017.

Vidal, Gore. "First Notes on Abraham Lincoln." *Los Angeles Times*, February 8, 1981.

———. *Lincoln: A Novel*. New York: Vintage, 2000.

Viviano, Benedict T. "Eschatology and the Quest for the Historical Jesus." In *The Oxford Handbook of Eschatology*, edited by Jerry Walls, 73–90. New York: Oxford University Press, 2008.

Wall, James Kirk. "Was President Lincoln an Atheist?" *Chicago Tribune*, February 21, 2011.

War Department of the United States. *The War of the Rebellion : A Compilation of the Official Records of the Union and Confederate Armies*. Washington, DC, 1880–1901.

Warren, Louis Austin. *The Religious Background of the Lincoln Family*. New York: The Club, 1926.

Welles, Gideon. *Civil War Diaries*. Chicago: University of Illinois Press, 2014.

Wheeler, Samuel P. "The Mystery of Eddie Lincoln." *Journal of the Abraham Lincoln Association* 33/2 (2012) 39–46.

White, Ronald C. *The Eloquent President: A Portrait of Lincoln through His Words*. New York: Random House, 2006.

———. *Lincoln's Greatest Speech*. New York: Simon and Schuster, 2006.

Whitefield, George. *George Whitefield's Journals*. Edinburgh: Banner of Truth, 1986.

Whitney, Henry C. *Lincoln, the Citizen*. New York: Leopold Classics Library, 2016.

———. *Lincoln, the President*. London: Forgotten Books, 2015.

Wills, Garry. *Lincoln at Gettysburg*. New York: Simon and Schuster, 2006.

Wilson, Donald. *Lincoln's Sword*. New York: Vintage, 2007.

Wilson, Douglas. "William H. Herndon on Lincoln's Fatalism." *Journal of the Abraham Lincoln Association* 35/2 (2014) 1–18.

Wilson, James Grant. *David Davis*. New York: Appleton, 1900.

Winkle, Kenneth J. *Abraham and Mary Lincoln*. Carbondale: Southern Illinois University Press, 2011.

Wolf, William J. *The Almost Chosen People.* New York: Doubleday, 1959.

Wood, Ezra Morgan. *The Peerless Orator: The Rev. Matthew Simpson*. London: Forgotten Books, 2017.

Wycliffe, John. *The Wycliffe Bible*. Edited by Brett Burner. London: Lamp Post, 2009.

Addresses, Debates, and Public Documents

Blake, John Fulkner. "A Sermon on the Services and Death of Abraham Lincoln." Christ Church, Bridgeport, Connecticut, April 19, 1865. http://lincoln.digitalscholarship.emory.edu/blake.001/.

Gurley, Phineas. Funeral sermon for Willie Lincoln. Executive Mansion, Washington, DC, February 24, 1862. http://www.abrahamlincolnonline.org/lincoln/education/williedeath.htm.

Lincoln–Douglas debate in Ottawa, Illinois. August 21, 1858. https://www.nps.gov/liho/learn/historyculture/debate1.htm

———. Lincoln–Douglas debate in Quincy, Illinois. October 13, 1858. https://www.nps.gov/liho/learn/historyculture/debate6.htm.

———. Lincoln–Douglas debate in Alton, Illinois. October 15, 1858. In Tucker, 16 and 76–78; and online at https://www.nps.gov/liho/learn/historyculture/debate7.htm.

Lincoln, Abraham. Address at the Maryland Sanitary Fair. Baltimore, April 18, 1864. In Tucker, 194–95.

———. Address to the National Education Association. Quoted in the *Los Angeles Herald*, March 24, 1916.

———. Address to the New York Republican Association. March 21, 1864. In Basler, 7:259–60.

———. Address to the Young Men's Lyceum. Springfield, January 27, 1838. In Basler, 1:138.

———. Chicago address. 1857. In Tucker, 58.

———. Cincinnati address. February 19, 1860. In Basler, 5:58–59.

———. Cleveland address. February 15, 1861. Cleveland Historical Society, item 70.

———. Cooper Union address. New York, February 27, 1860. In Tucker, 83–87.

———. Eulogy for Henry Clay. July 6, 1752. In Basler, 6:319–20.

———. Executive Order 252. "Order of Retaliation." July 30, 1863. In Tucker, 72; and online at http://www.presidency.ucsb.edu/ws/index.php?pid=69908.

———. Farewell address. Springfield, Illinois, February 11, 1861. In Tucker, 97–98.

———. First inaugural address. March 4, 1861. In Tucker, 106–11; and online at http://www.presidency.ucsb.edu/ws/index.php?pid=25818.

———. Gettysburg address. November 19, 1863.

———. Handbill replying to charges of infidelity. July 31, 1846. http://teachingamericanhistory.org/library/document/handbill-replying-to-charges-of-infidelity/.

———. "House Divided Speech." Illinois Republican State Convention, Springfield, Illinois, June 16, 1858. In Tucker, 63–65.

———. Independence Hall address. Philadelphia, February 22, 1861. In Basler, 3:163.

———. Lewiston address. 1858. In Tucker, 66–68.

———. Peoria address. October 16, 1854. In Tucker, 50–52.

———. Presidential Proclamation 93. "Declaring the Objectives of the War Including Emancipation of Slaves in Rebellious States on January 1, 1863." September 22, 1862. In Basler, 3:352–65; and online at http://www.presidency.ucsb.edu/ws/index.php?pid=69782.

———. Presidential Proclamation 95 ("Emancipation Proclamation"). "Regarding the Status of Slaves in States Engaged in Rebellion Against the United States." January 1, 1863. In Tucker, 151–53; and online at http://www.presidency.ucsb.edu/ws/index.php?pid=69880.

———. Presidential Proclamation 97. "Appointing a Day of National Humiliation, Fasting, and Prayer." March 30, 1863. American Presidency Project, by Gerhard Peters and John T. Woolley. http://www.presidency.ucsb.edu/ws/index.php?pid=69891.

————. Presidential Proclamation 118 ("Thanksgiving Proclamation"). October 20, 1864. American Presidency Project, by Gerhard Peters and John T. Woolley. http://www.presidency.ucsb.edu/ws/index.php?pid=69998.

————. Reply to the delegates from the National Union League. June 9, 1864. In Basler, 7:383–84

————. Second inaugural address. March 4, 1865. In Tucker, 206–8; and online at http://www.presidency.ucsb.edu/ws/index.php?pid=25819.

————. Speech on the Dred Scott decision. June 26, 1857. In Basler, 1:740–41.

————. Speech to Congress on June 28, 1848. In Basler, 3:155.

————. "Word Fitly Spoken Speech." 1857. In Basler, 2:5.

Monroe, James. Second inaugural address. March 5, 1821.

Trump, Donald J. Inaugural address. January 21, 2017.

Personal Correspondence and Private Documents

Abbott, Francis E. Letter to William Herndon, March 27, 1870. Quoted in Douglas Wilson, 10.

Graham, William Mentor. Letter to William Herndon, July 15, 1865. In Basler, 8:186.

Herndon, William. Letter to Francis E. Abbott, February 18, 1870. Quoted in Douglas Wilson, 8.

Herndon, William. Letter to Francis E. Abbott, February 29, 1870. Quoted in Douglas Wilson, 9.

Lincoln, Abraham. Advice to Tad's teacher. February 5, 1862.

————. Fragment on the Constitution and Union. January 18, 1861.

————. Letter to Albert G. Hodges, April 4, 1864. In Tucker, 192–93.

————. Letter to Eliza Gurley, October 26, 1862. In Basler, 8:474.

————. Letter to Eliza Gurley, November 9, 1862. In Basler, 8:475.

————. Letter to Eliza Gurney, September 4, 1864. In Tucker, 199.

————. Letter to Henry L. Pierce, April 6, 1859. In Tucker, 78–79.

————. Letter to Horace Greeley, August 22, 1862. In Tucker, 139–40.

————. Letter to J. M. Peck, November 21, 1848. In Basler, 8:447.

————. Letter to John D. Johnston, November 4, 1851. In Tucker, 40.

————. Letter to Joshua F. Speed, August 24, 1855. In Tucker, 53–56.

————. Letter to Mary Speed. September 17, 1841. In Tucker, 74–75.

————. Letter to Richard Speer, October 23, 1860. In Tucker, 79.

————. Letter to Sojourner Truth, October 29, 1864. In Basler, 8:504.

————. Letter to Williamson Durley, October 3, 1845. In Tucker, 69–71.

————. "Meditations on the Divine Will." September 1862. In Tucker, 150–51.

Lincoln, Mary Todd. Letter to Emile Todd Helm, December 12, 1863. In Basler, 1:10.

Lynch, Mildred. Diary. 1860–1871. Viginia Historical Society, Mss. 5:1L9895:1.

McGuire, Judith. Diary of a Southern Refugee During the War. New York: E. J. Hale, 1867. QUOTED IN SHEEHAN.

Legal Cases of Abraham Lincoln

Fleming v. Crothers and Rogers ("Chicken Bone Case"). McLean County (Illinois) Circuit Court, 1856. See Dekle, 119–27; and Charles M. Hubbard, "Lincoln and the Chicken Bone Case" (*American History Magazine*, August 19, 1998; http://www.historynet.com/lincoln-and-the-chicken-bone-case-august-98-american-history-feature.htm); and "Lincoln, Medical Law, and Chicken Bones" (*Lincoln Legal Papers* 12, October–December 1989; http://www.papersofabrahamlincoln.org/Briefs/briefs12.htm).

Hurd v. Rock Island Railroad Company (*Effie Afton* case). U.S. District Court for Northern Illinois, 1857. See Michael A. Ross, "Hell Gate of Mississippi: The Effie Afton Trial and Abraham Lincoln's Role in It" (*Annals of Iowa* 68/3, Summer 2009).

Lewis v. Lewis. U.S. Supreme Court. 48 U.S. 776. 1849. See Dekle, 94–98.

People v. Armstrong. Sangamon County Circuit Court, 1858. Armstrong (1833–1889) was the defendant in a murder prosecution and was defended by Abraham Lincoln. The case was portrayed in the 1939 film *Young Mr. Lincoln*. See Dekle, 141–51; and "Death of William Armstrong" (*New York Times*, May 14, 1899).

People v. Trailor and Trailor. 1841. See Dekle, 35–48; and Laura Helmuth, "Abraham Lincoln, True Crime Writer" (*Smithsonian*, February 10, 2010; https://www.smithsonianmag.com/history/abraham-lincoln-true-crime-writer-7794088/).